I0837023

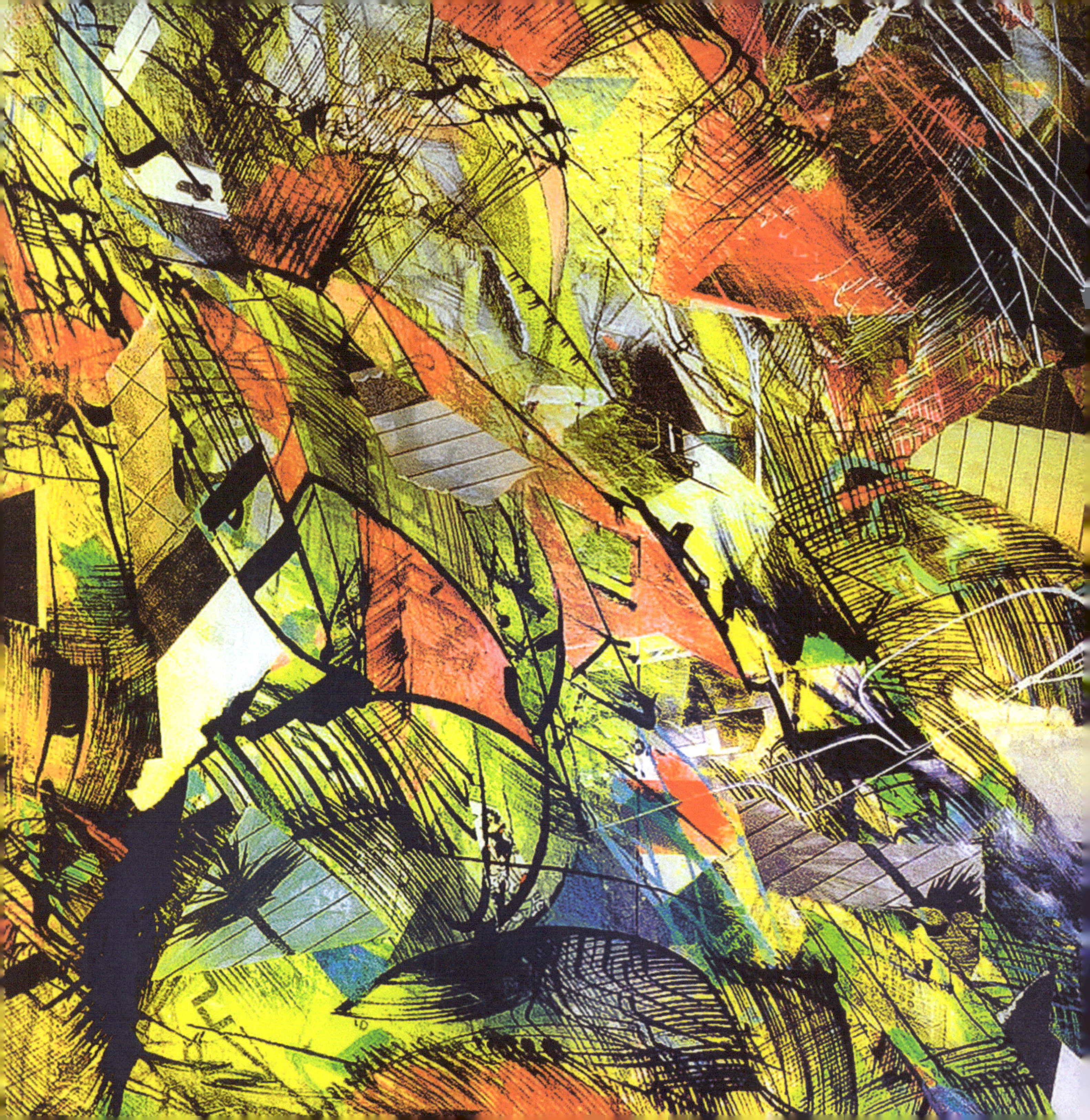

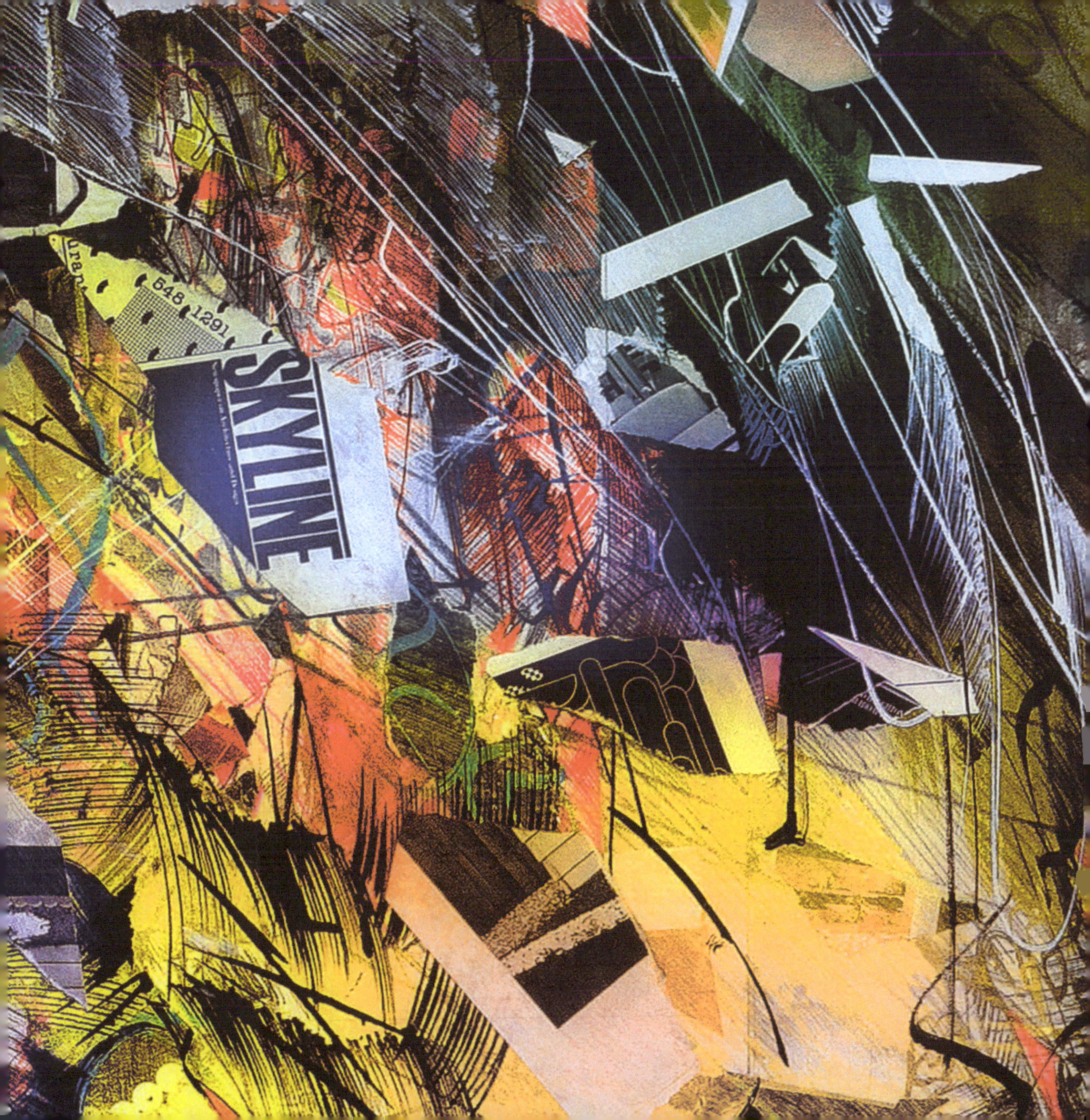
548 1291
SKYLINE

Detail, *The Eyes of All Wait*

Preceding and last page spreads: detail, *Flesh Turned to Atoms;* full image, p. 20

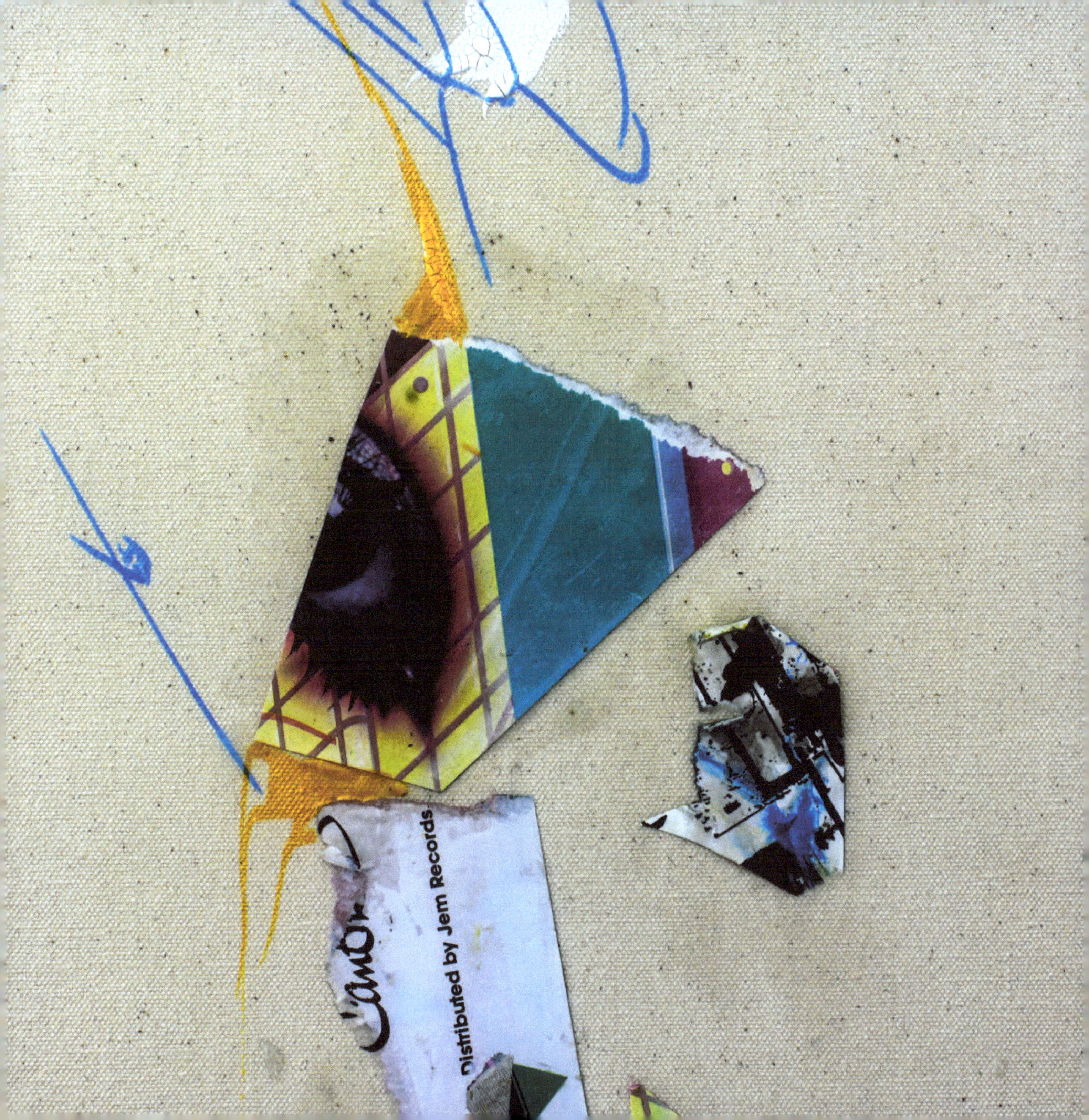
Distributed by Jem Records

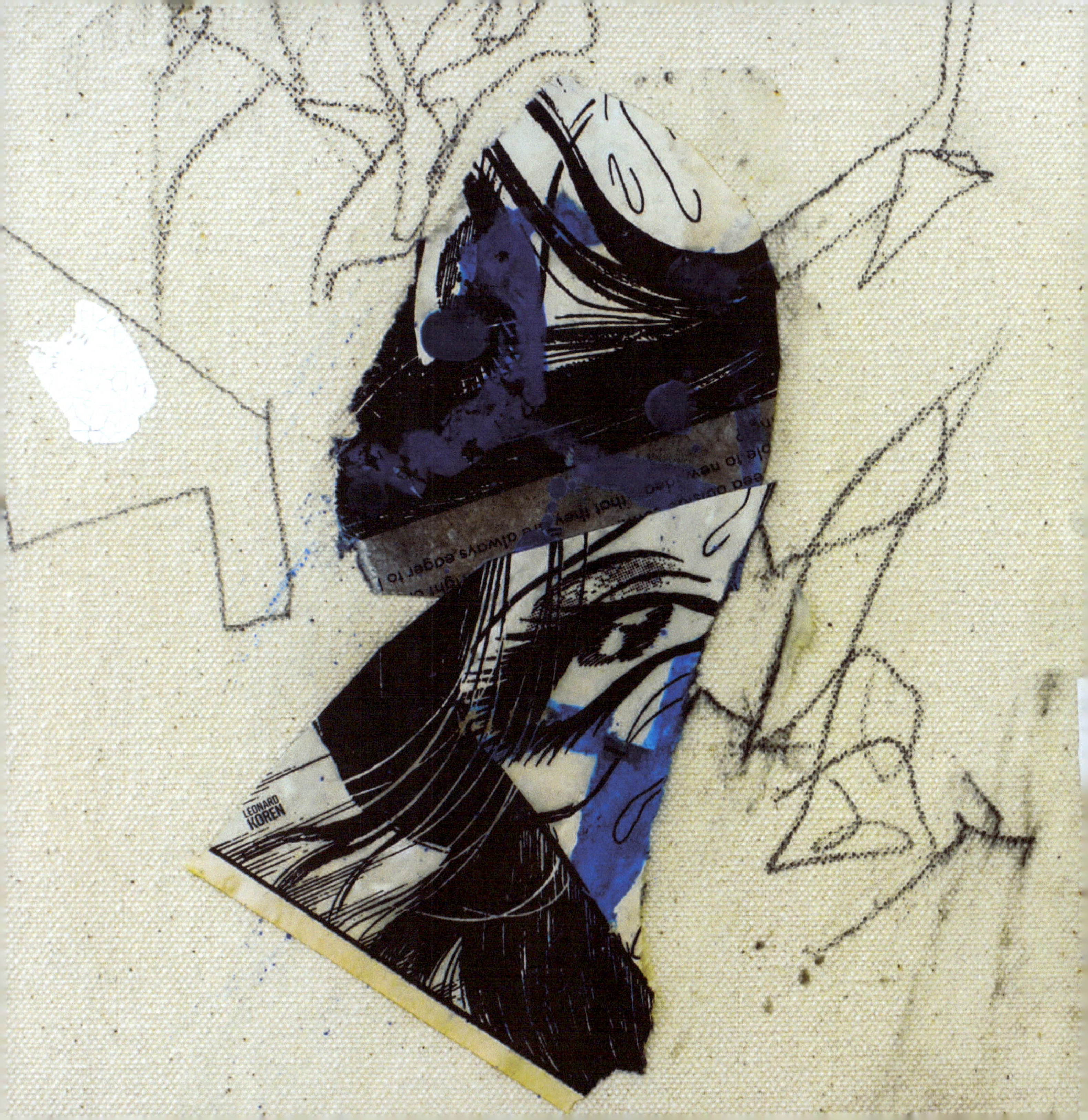
LEONARD
KOREN
that they are always eager to

EILEEN A. JOY, EDITOR

CHRISTINA MCPHEE
A COMMONPLACE BOOK

Detail, *The Eyes of All Wait*

Detail, *Aliens Rivulet*

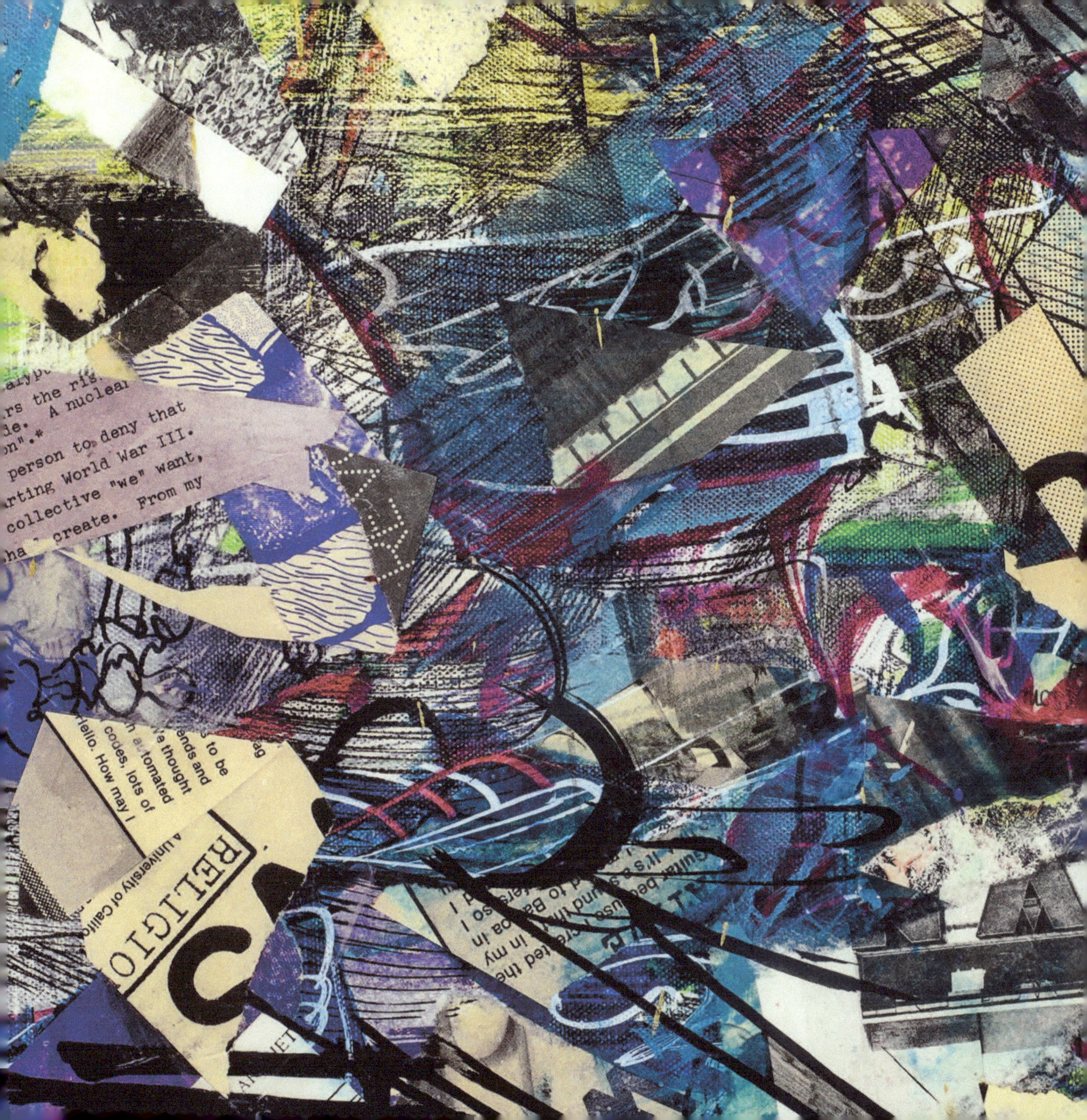
person to deny that
World War III.
collective "we" want,
create. From my
to be
codes, lots of
How may I

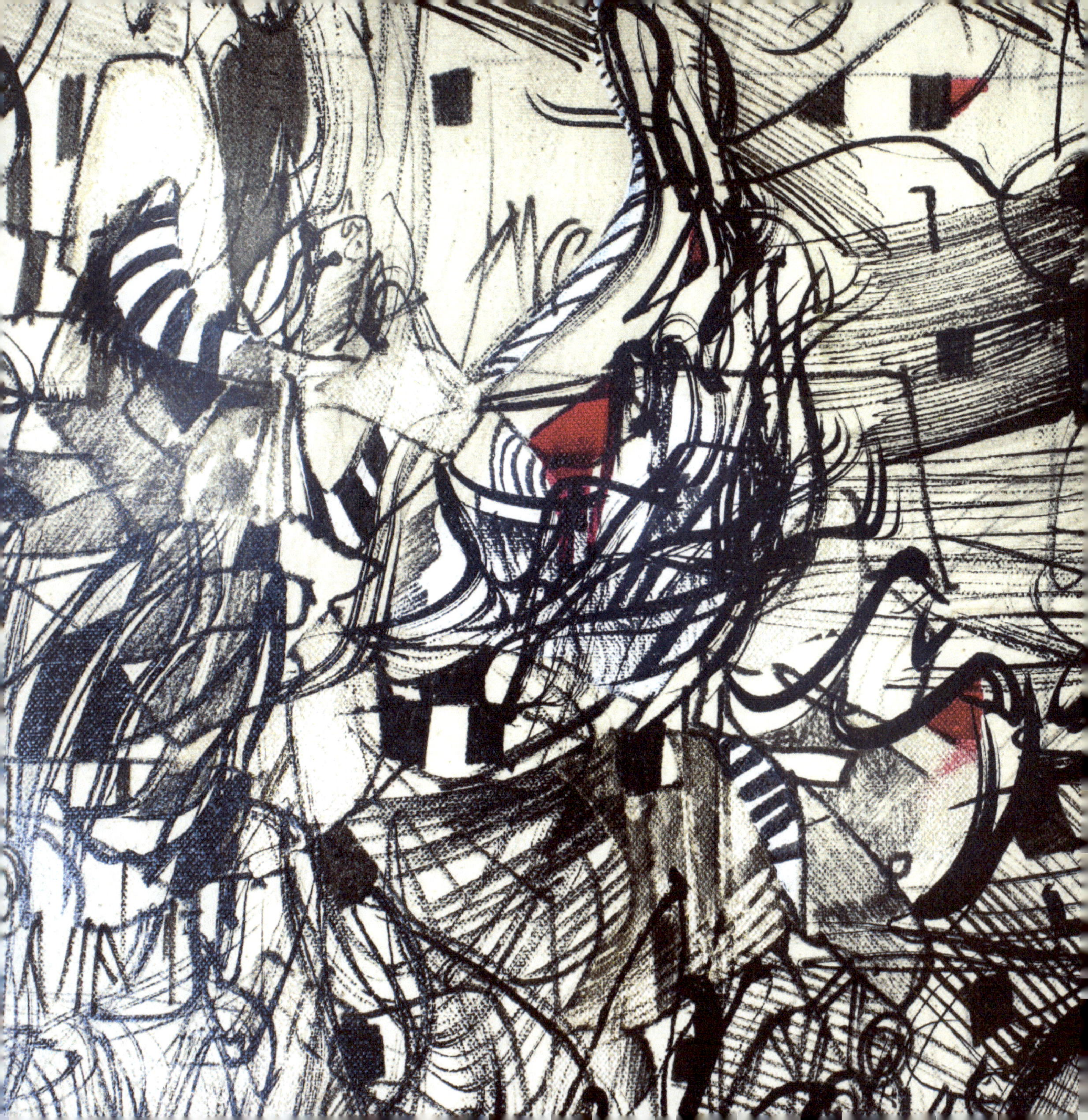

Detail, *Zebra Crossing*

Detail, *Obsidian Falls*

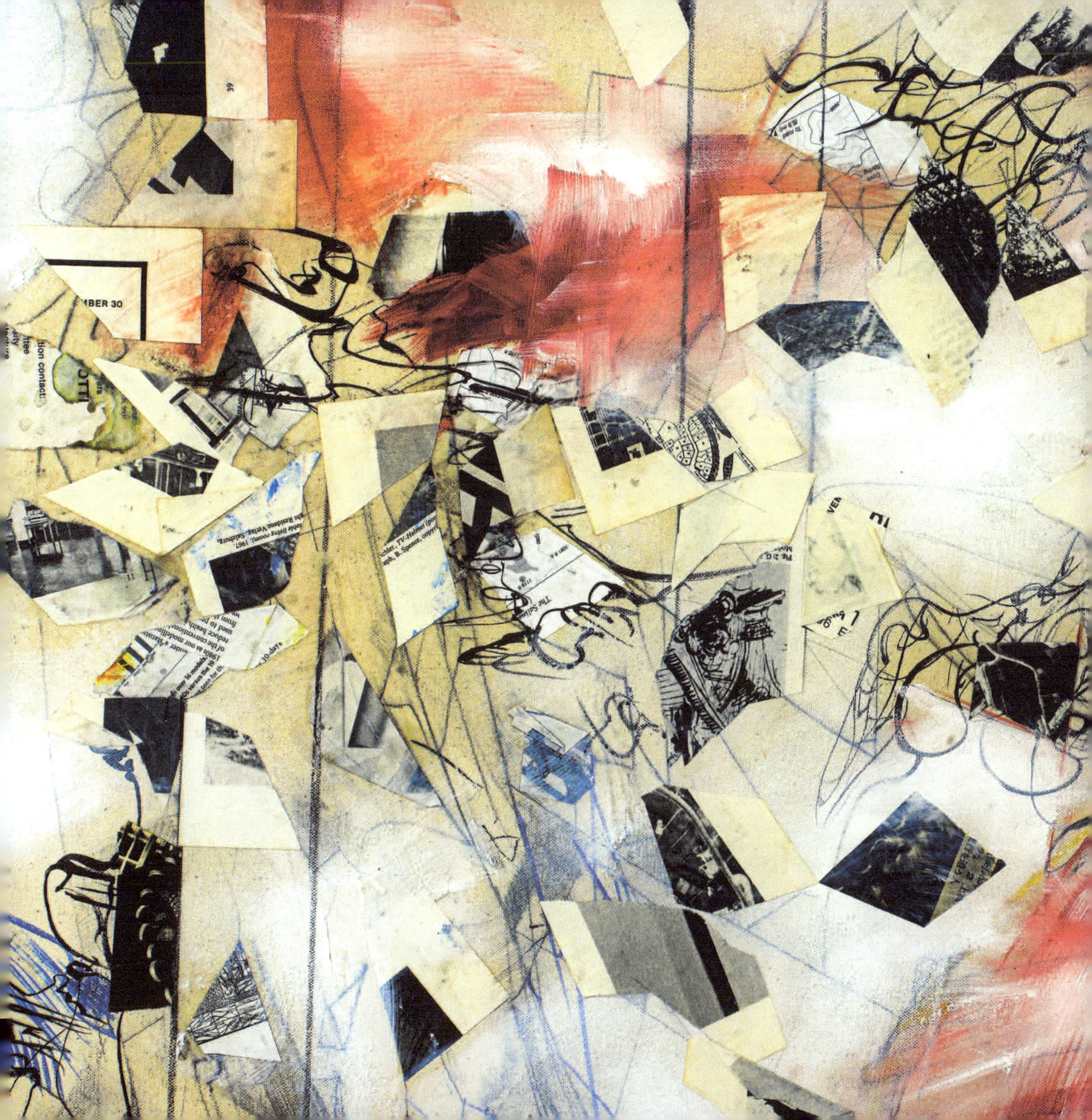

"Let us take down one of those old notebooks which we have all, at one time or another, had a passion for beginning. Most of the pages are blank, it is true; but at the beginning we shall find a certain number very beautifully covered with a strikingly legible hand-writing. Here we have written down the names of great writers in their order of merit; here we have copied out fine passages from the classics; here are lists of books to be read; and here, most interesting of all, lists of books that have actually been read, as the reader testifies with some youthful vanity by a dash of red ink."

Virginia Woolf, "Hours in a Library," 1916

Detail, *A Line of Flax in His Hand*

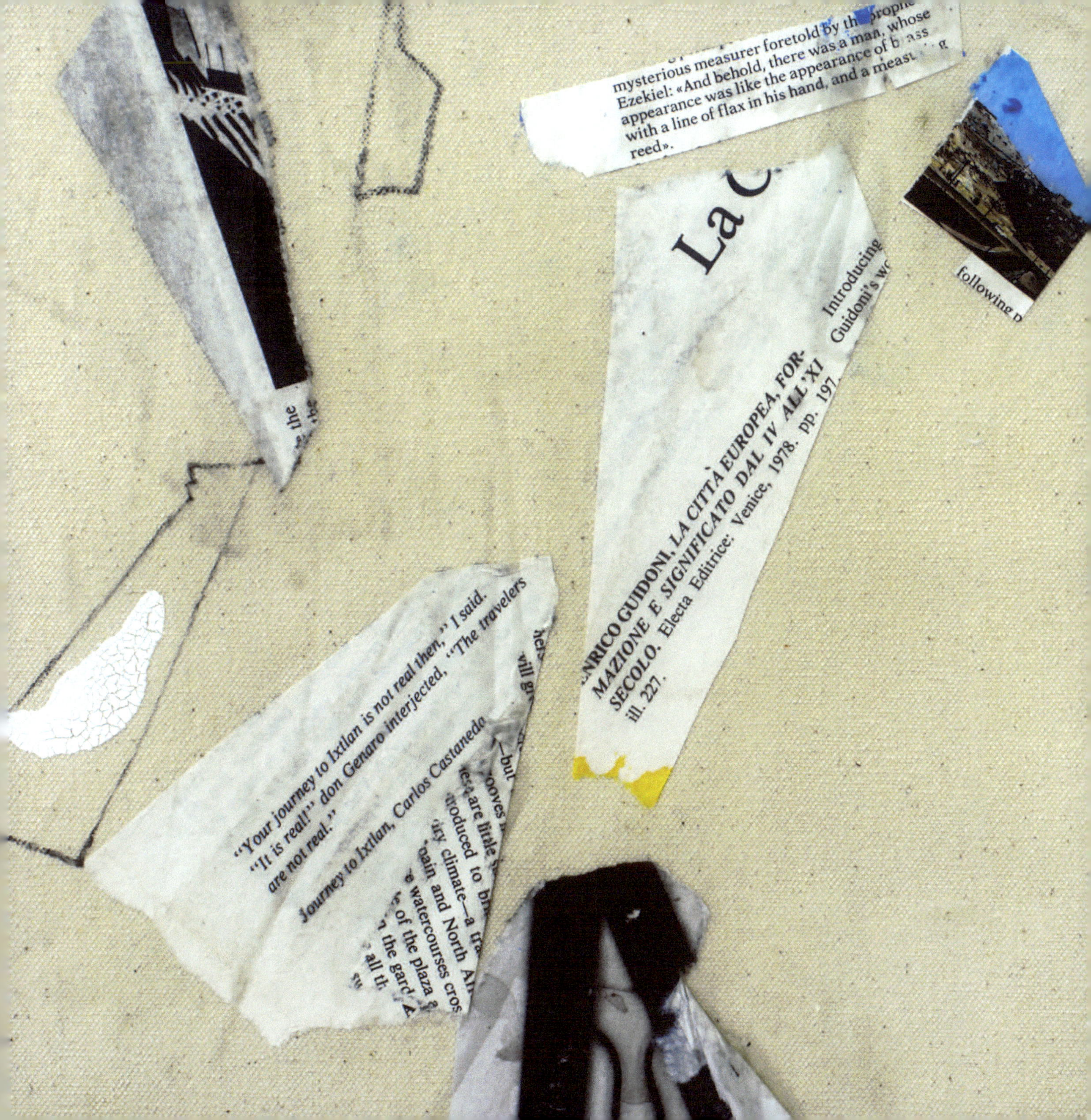

mysterious measurer foretold by the prophe
Ezekiel: «And behold, there was a man, whose
appearance was like the appearance of brass
with a line of flax in his hand, and a measu
reed».

La C

Introducing
Guidoni's wo

following p

ENRICO GUIDONI, *LA CITTÀ EUROPEA, FORMAZIONE E SIGNIFICATO DAL IV ALL'XI SECOLO*. Electa Editrice: Venice, 1978. pp. 197. ill. 227.

"Your journey to Ixtlan is not real then," I said.
"It is real!" don Genaro interjected. "The travelers are not real."

Journey to Ixtlan, Carlos Castaneda

Detail, *Pitfalls*

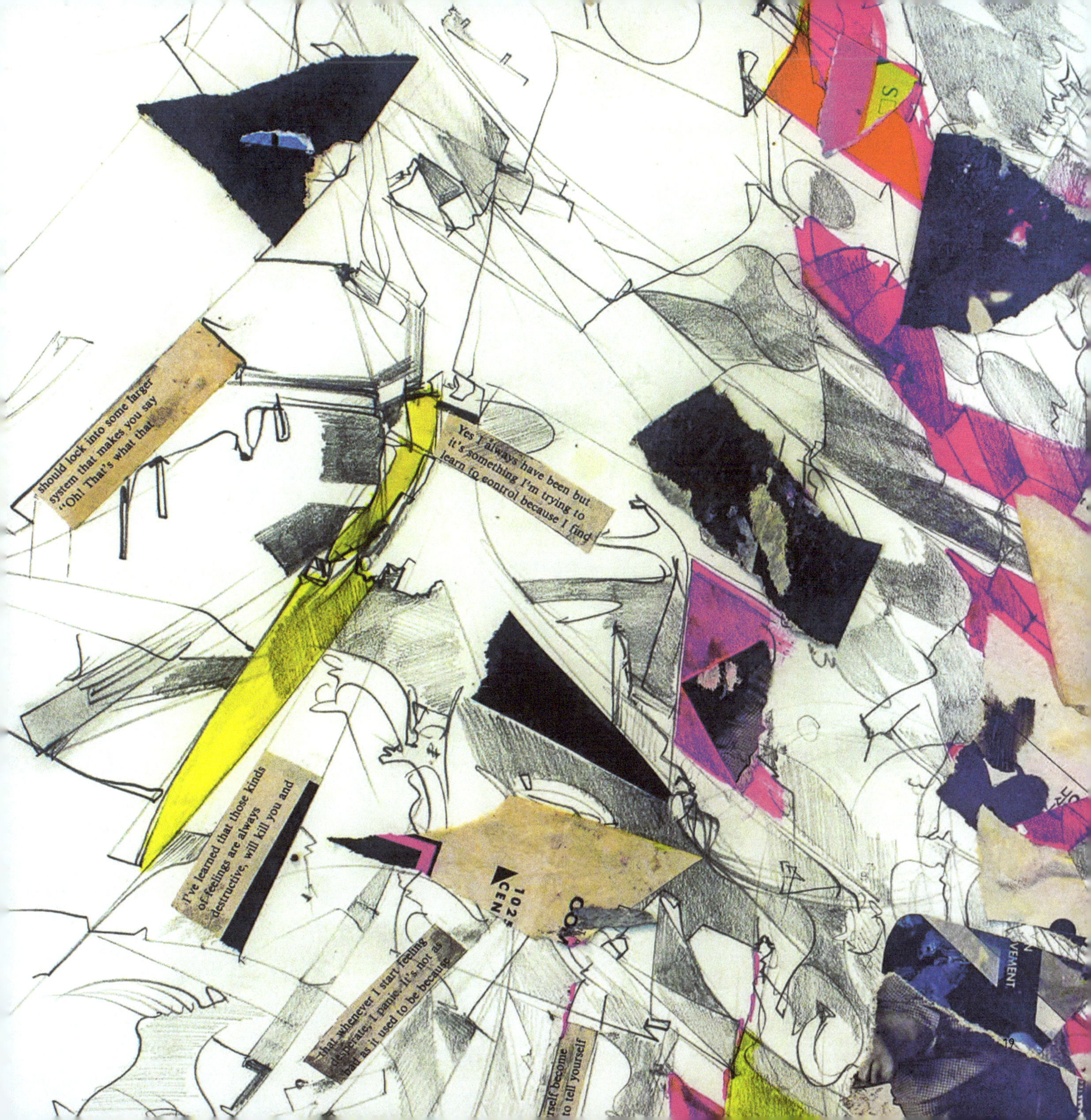

should lock into some larger
system that makes you say
"Oh! That's what that
Yes I always have been but
it's something I'm trying to
learn to control because I find
I've learned that those kinds
of feelings are always
destructive, will kill you and
that whenever I start feeling
desperate, I panic. It's not as
bad as it used to be because
rself become
to tell yourself

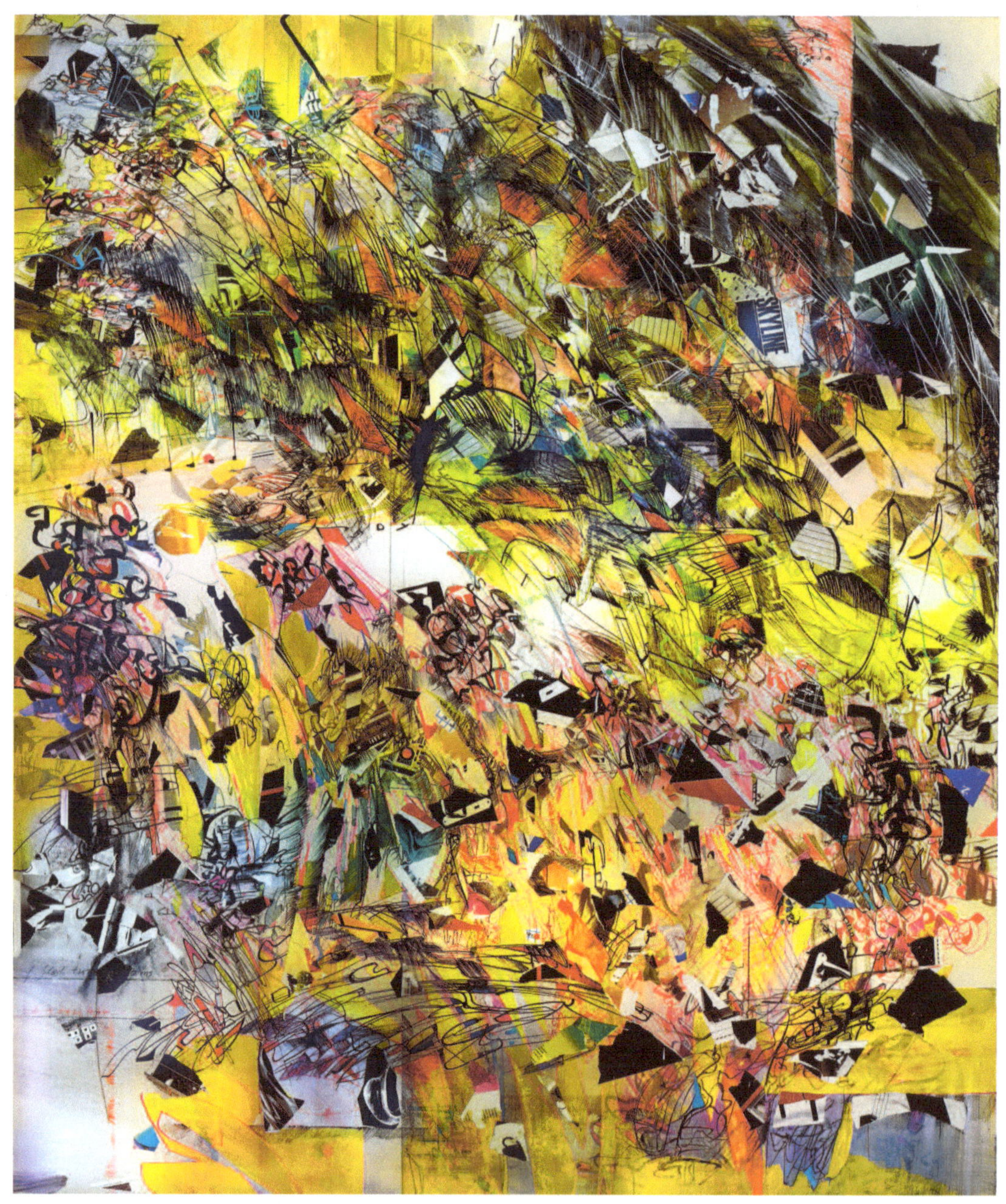

Flesh Turned to Atoms (after Virginia Woolf), 2017

Ink, oil and acrylic paint, paper collage from *Wet Magazine* and *Domus* (1980-82), on canvas, 165.7 x 137.6 x 6.3 cm / 65.25 x 54 x 2.5 in; detail, overleaf

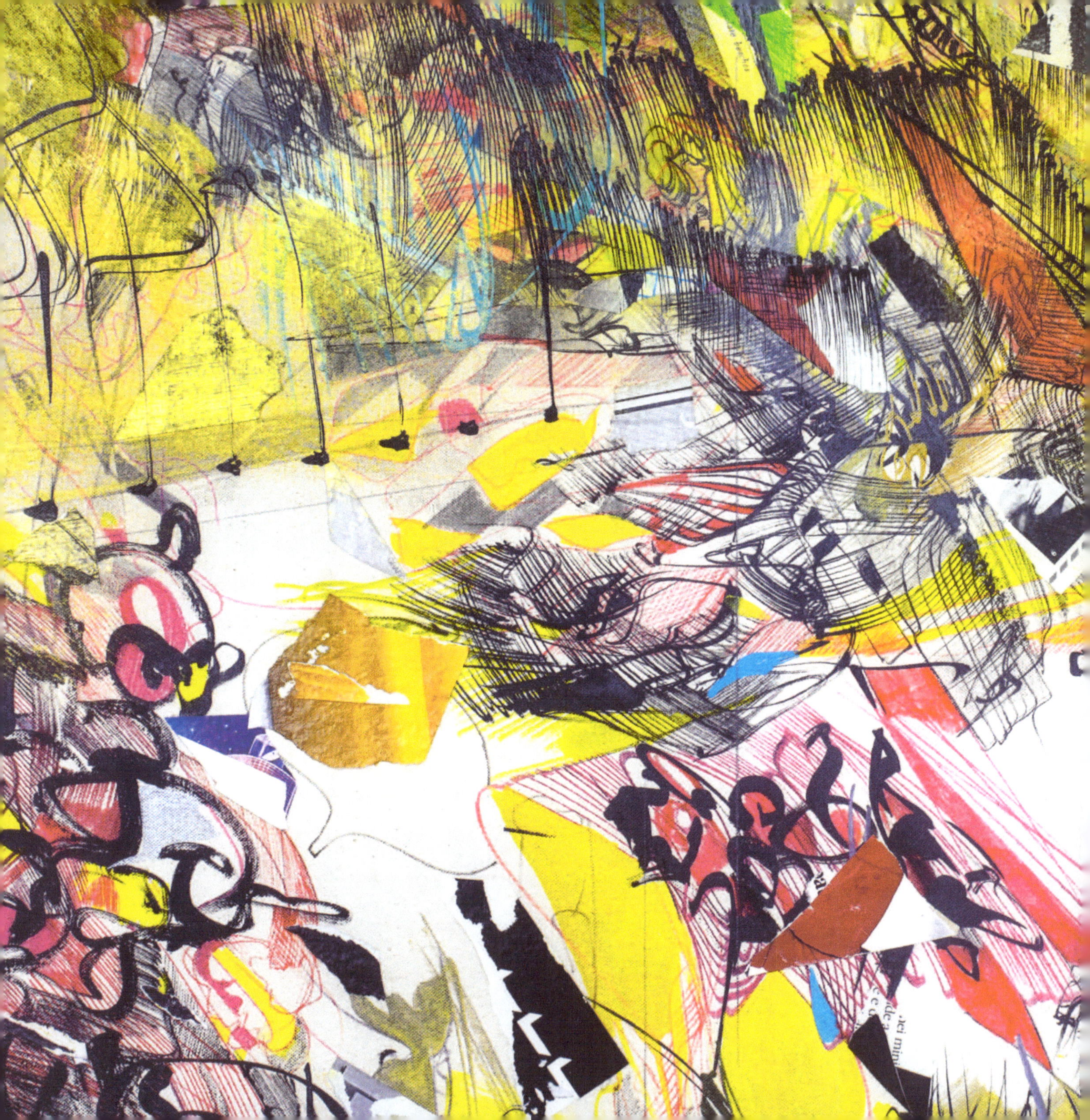

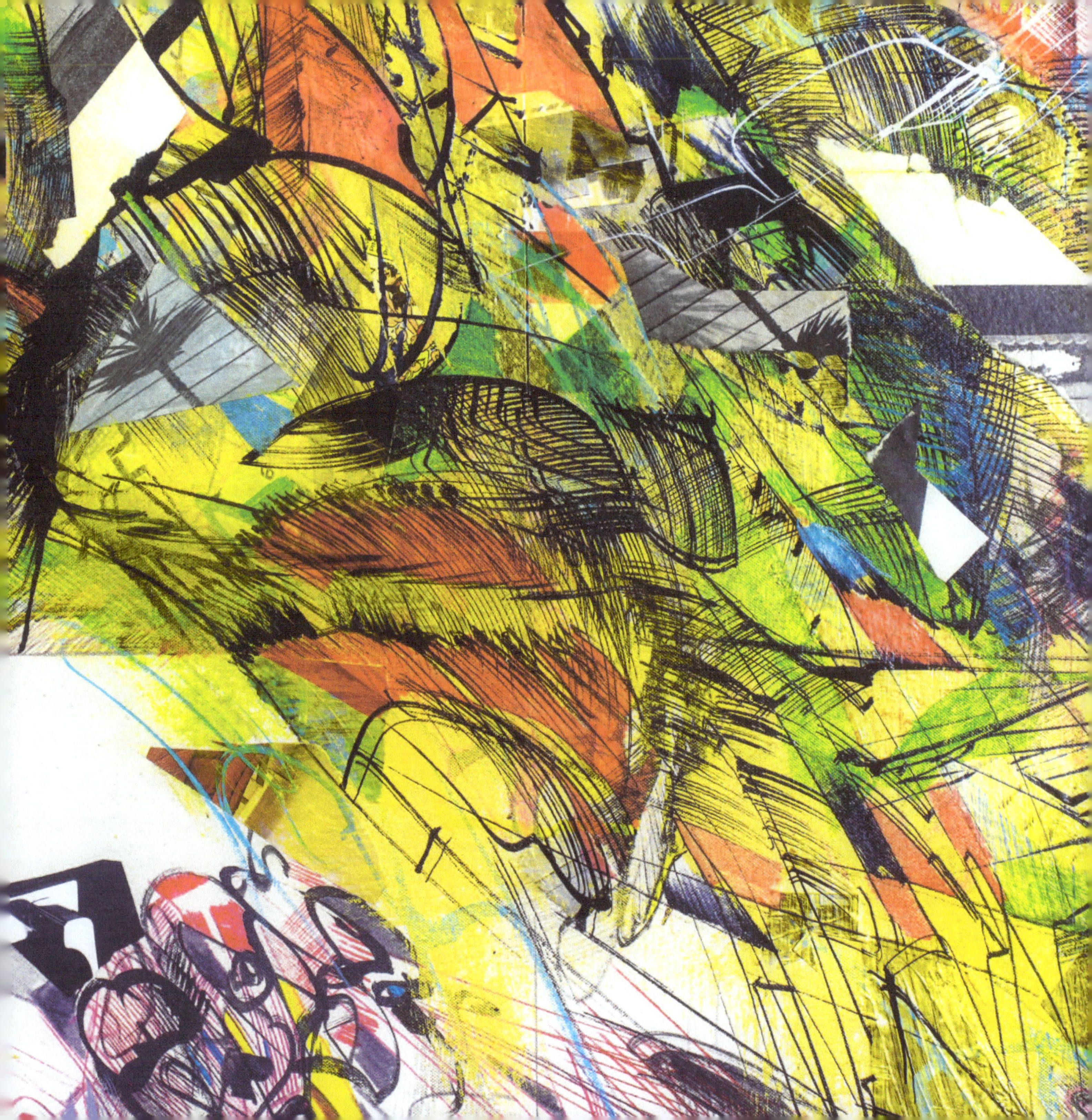

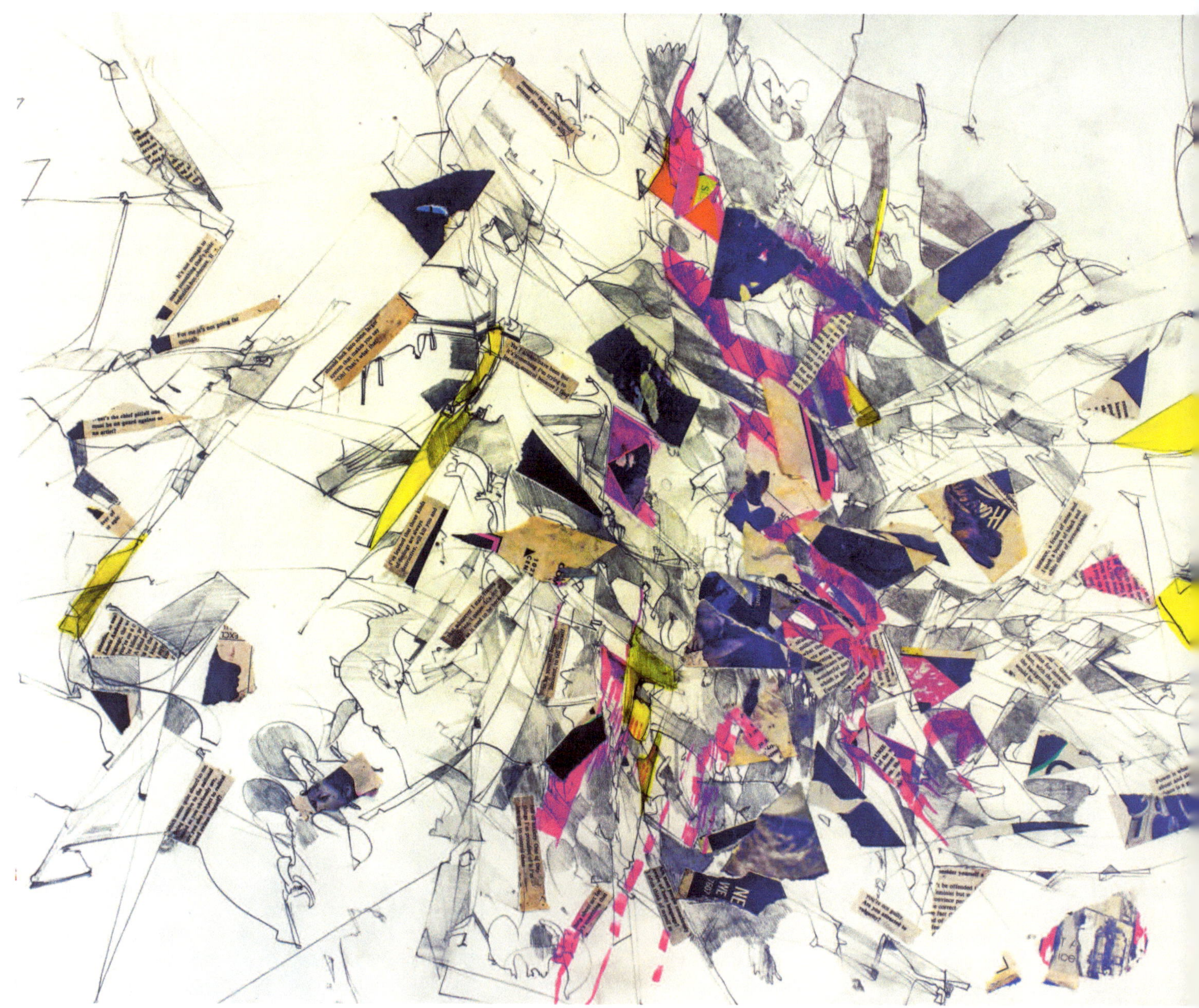

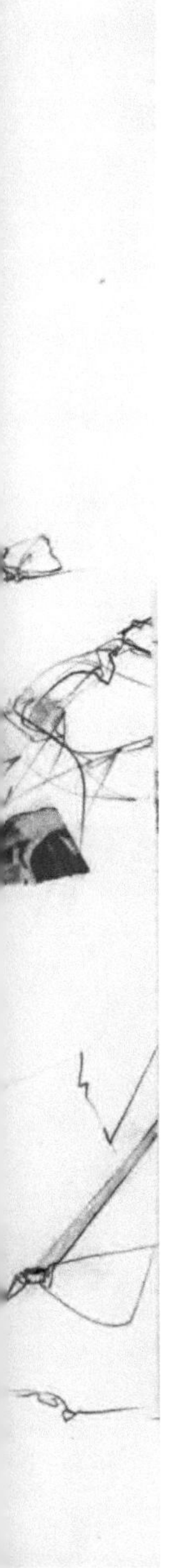

Pitfalls (After Laurie Anderson), 2017
Graphite, crayon, ink, and paper collage from *Wet* (1980), 55.8 x 76.2 cm / 22 x 30 in

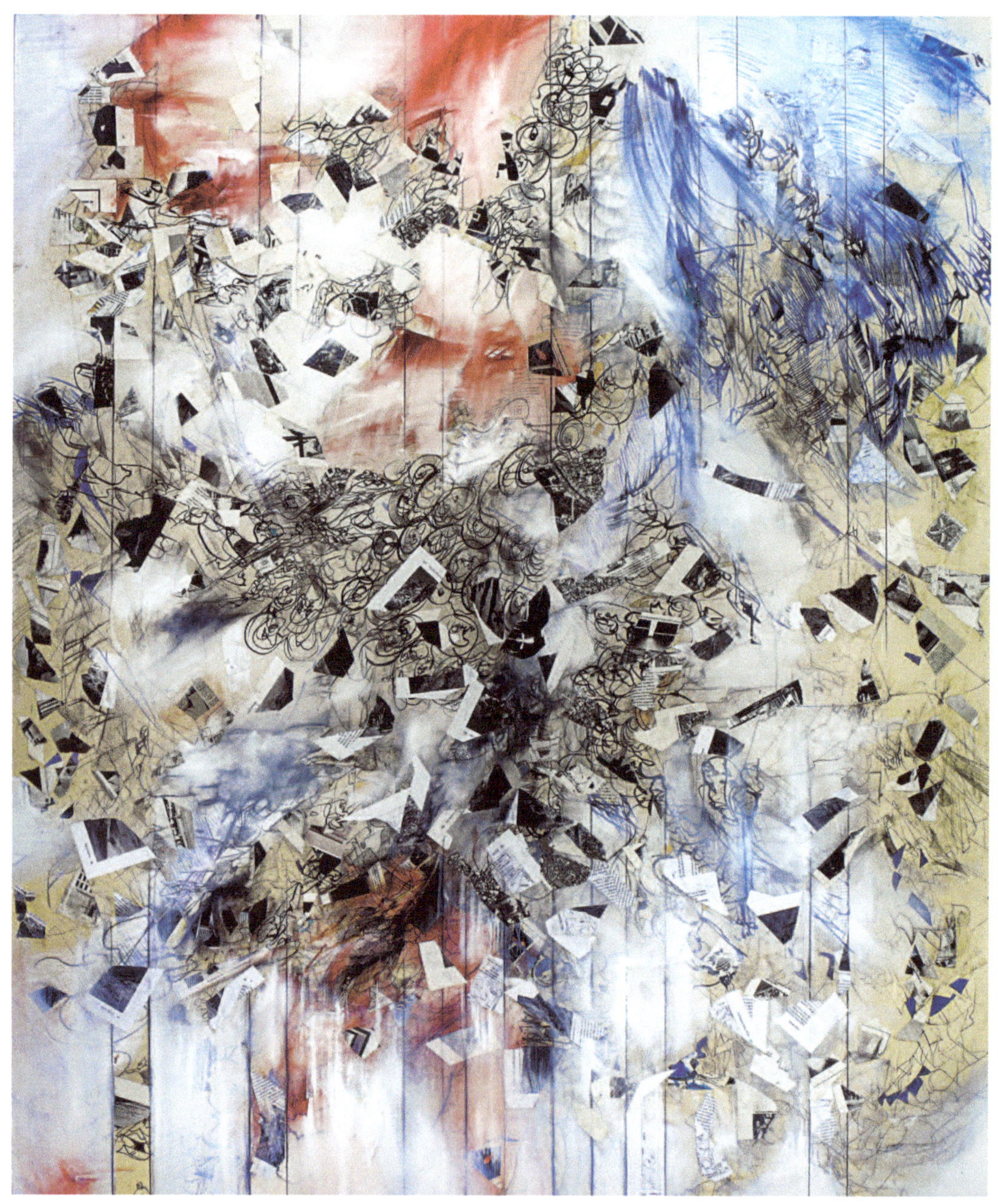

Obsidian Falls Mohave (Parable-Parabola), 2017
Ink, oil and acrylic paint, paper collage from *Archetype* (1979), on canvas, 165.7 x 137.6 x 6.3 cm / 65.25 x 54 x 2.5 in; detail, overleaf

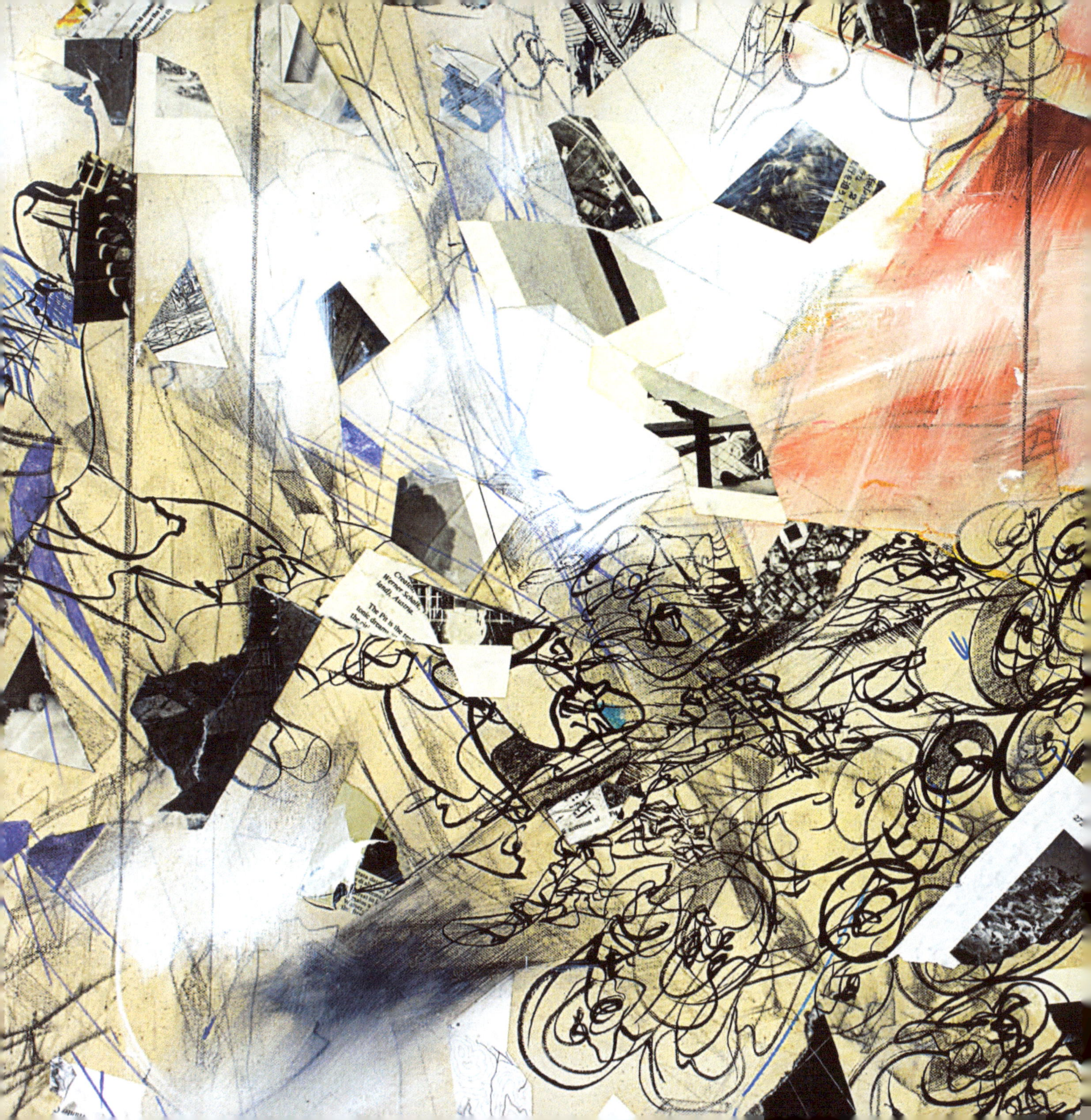

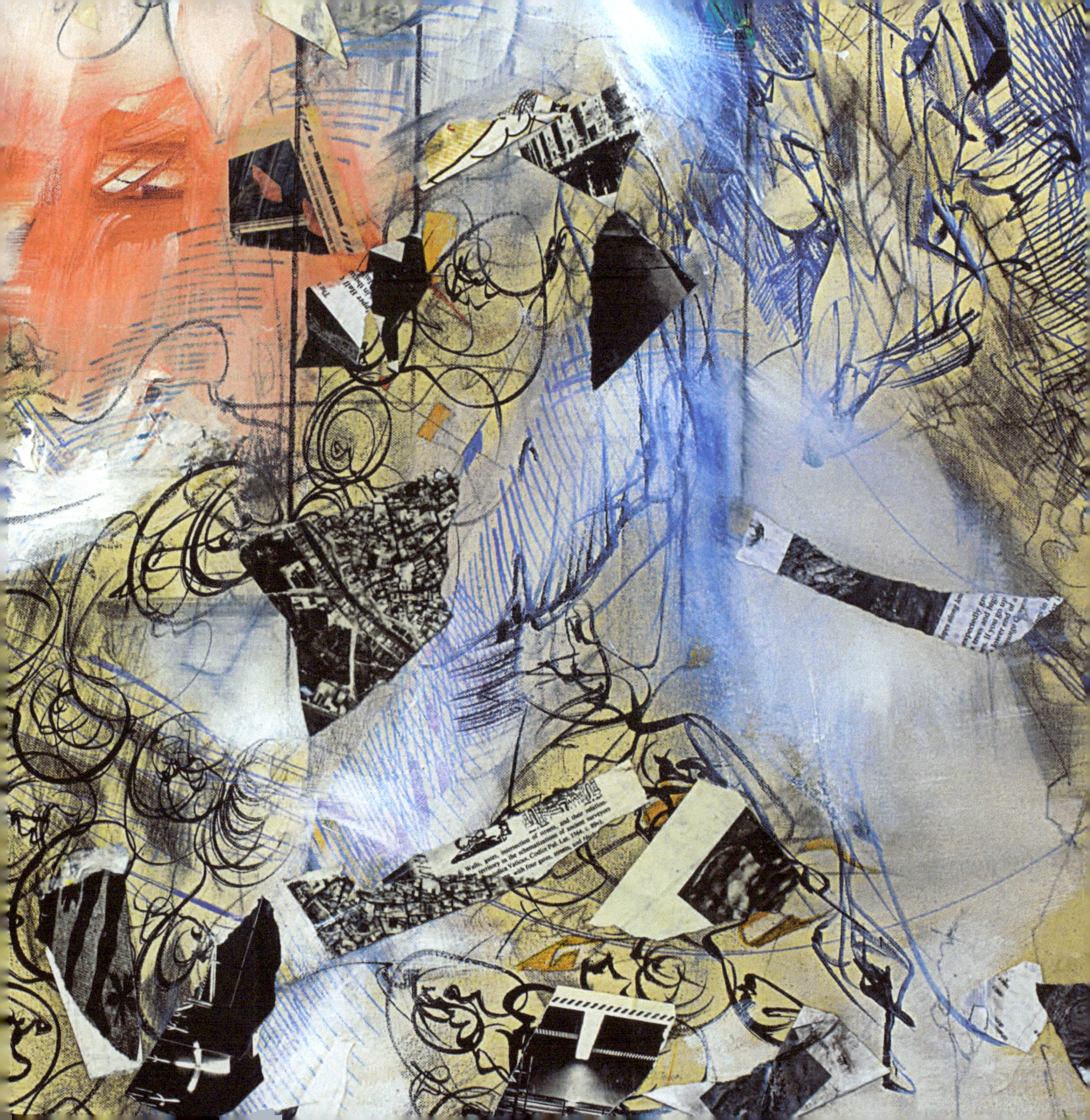

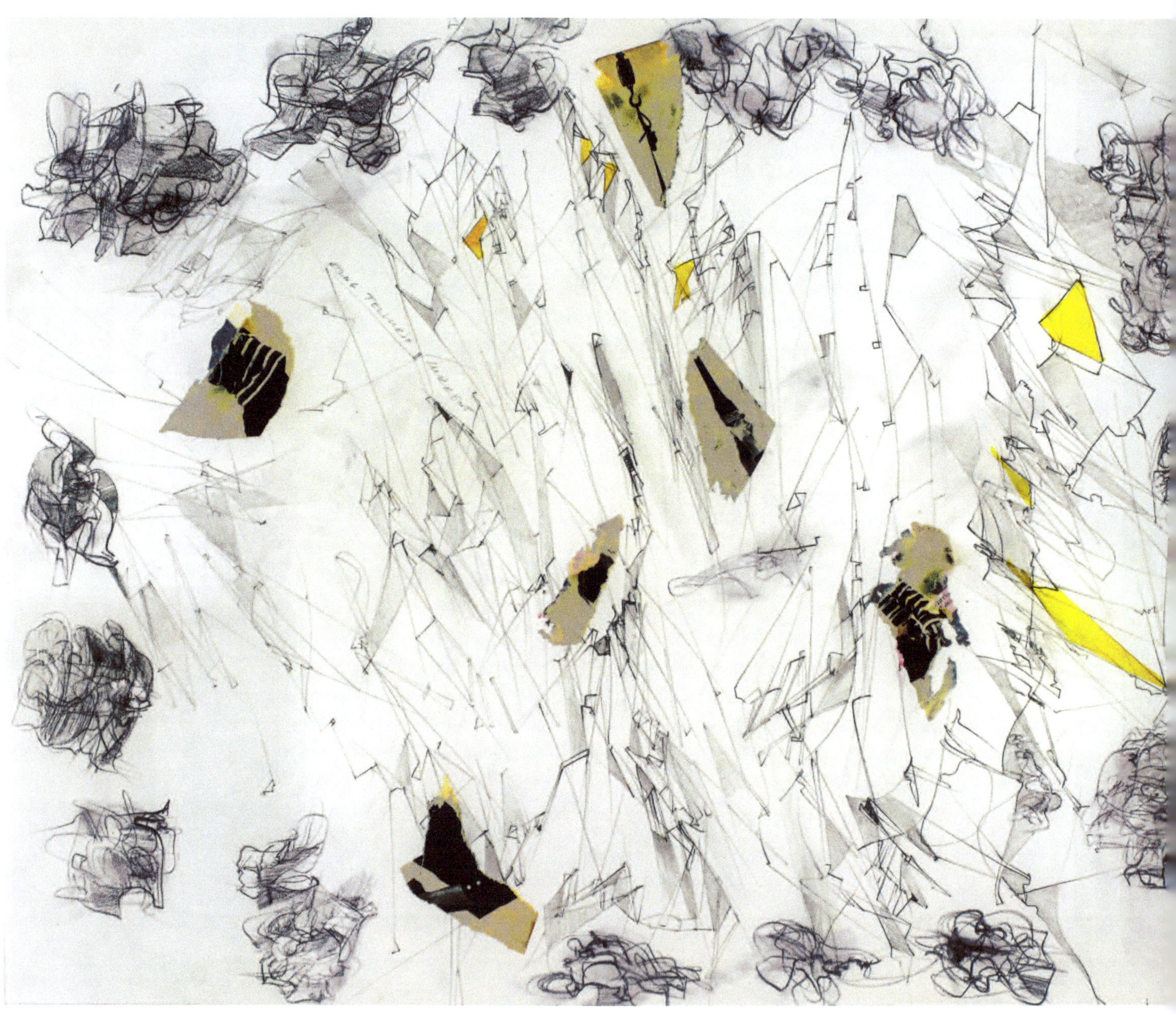

Riding Current (After Lidia Yuknavitch), 2017
Graphite, crayon, ink, and paper collage from *Life* (1954), 55.8 x 76.2 cm / 22 x 30 in

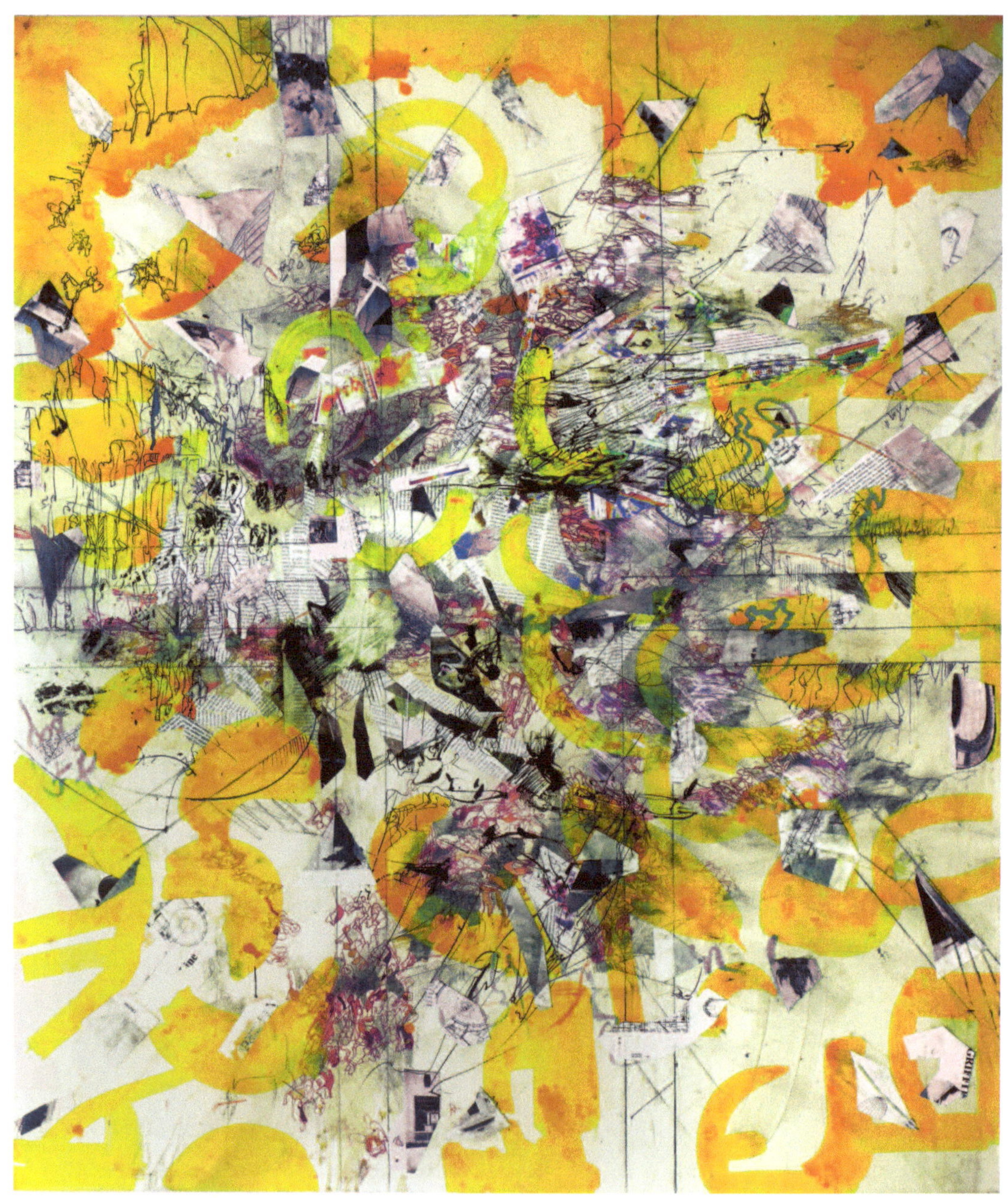

P-22 in Griffith Park, 2017
Ink, oil, paper collage from *Nature: Climate Change* (2013) and *Archetype* (1979), on canvas, 133.3 x 106.6 x 6.3 cm / 50.25 x 42 x 2.5 in; detail, overleaf

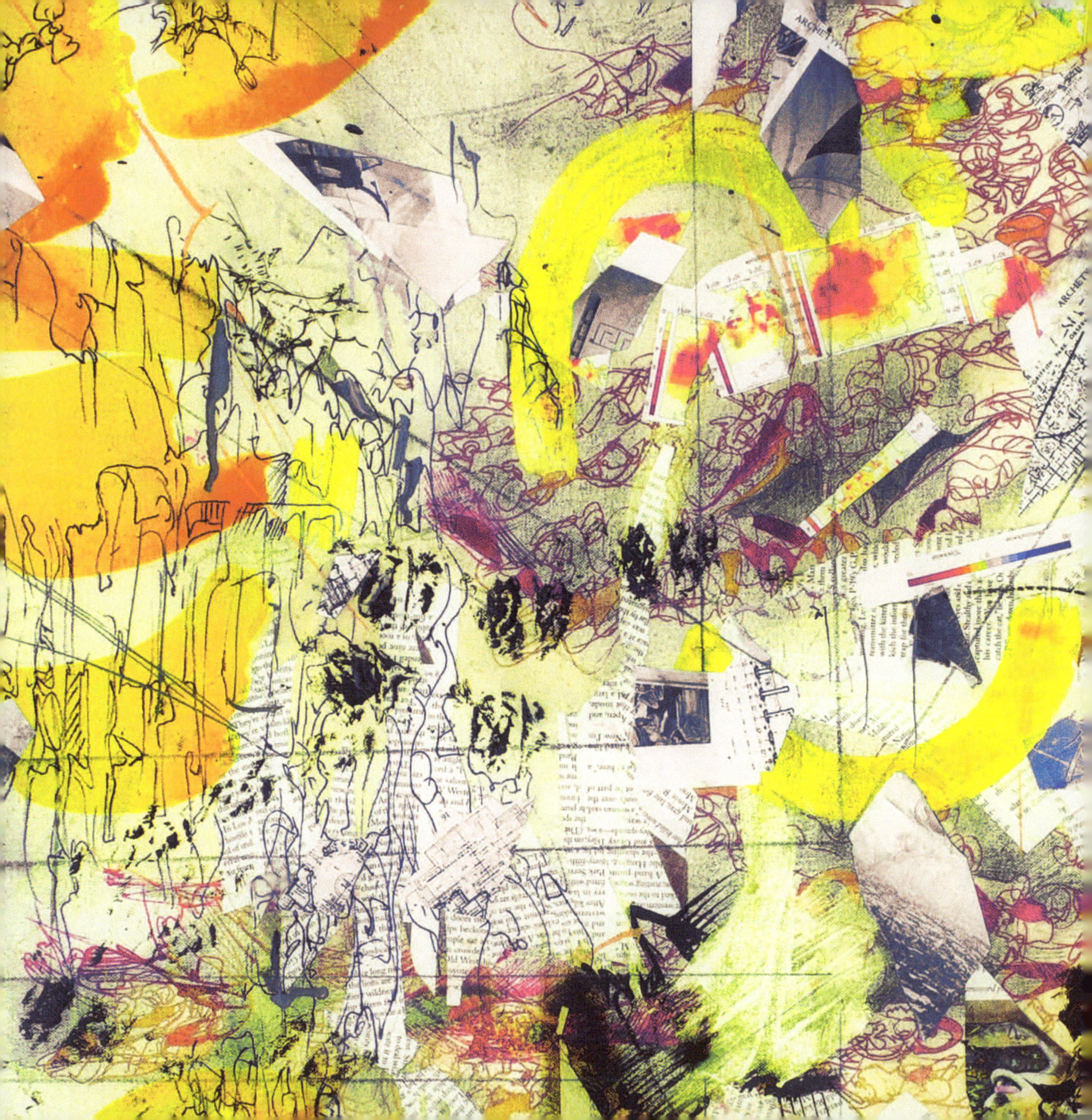

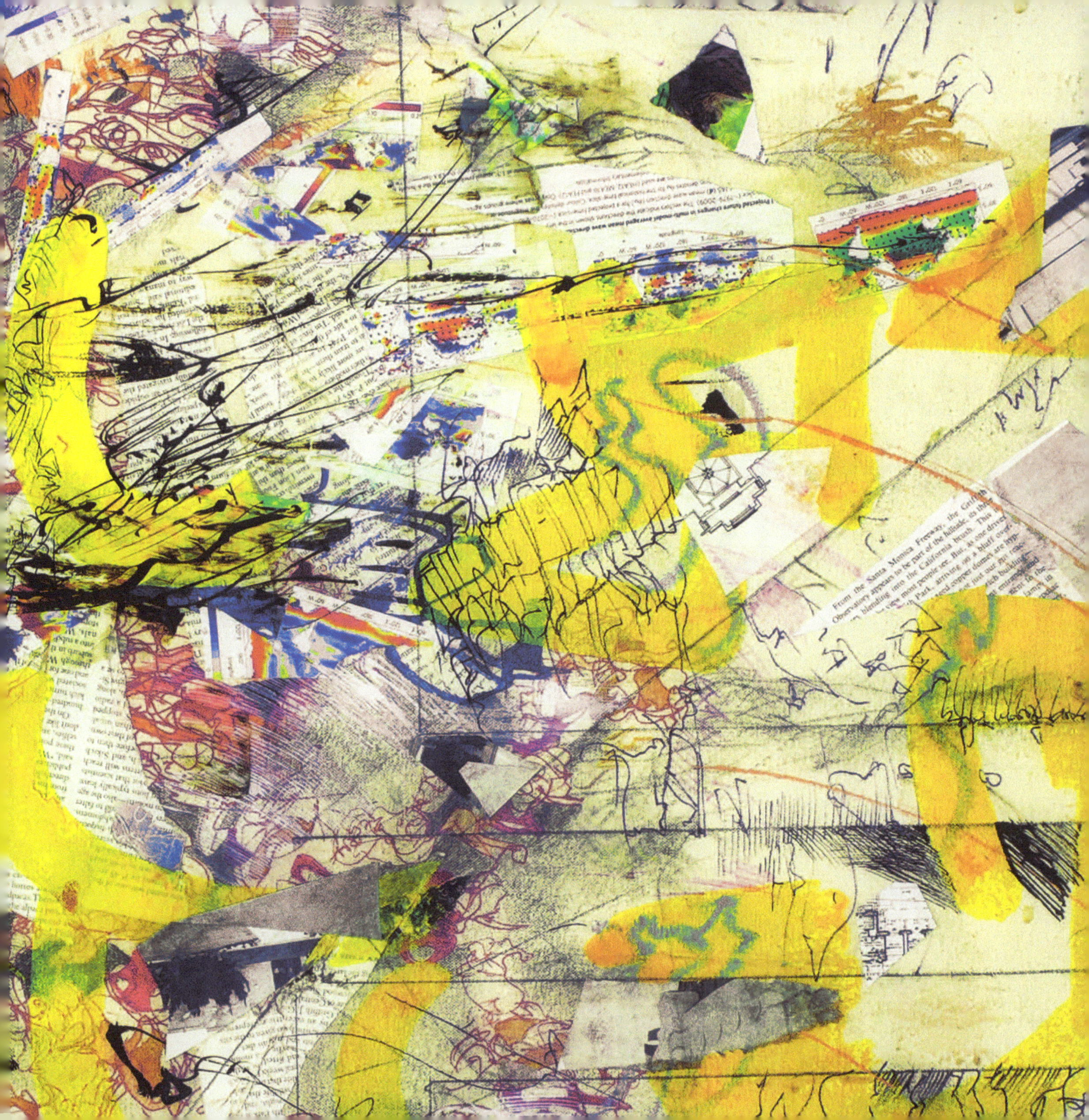

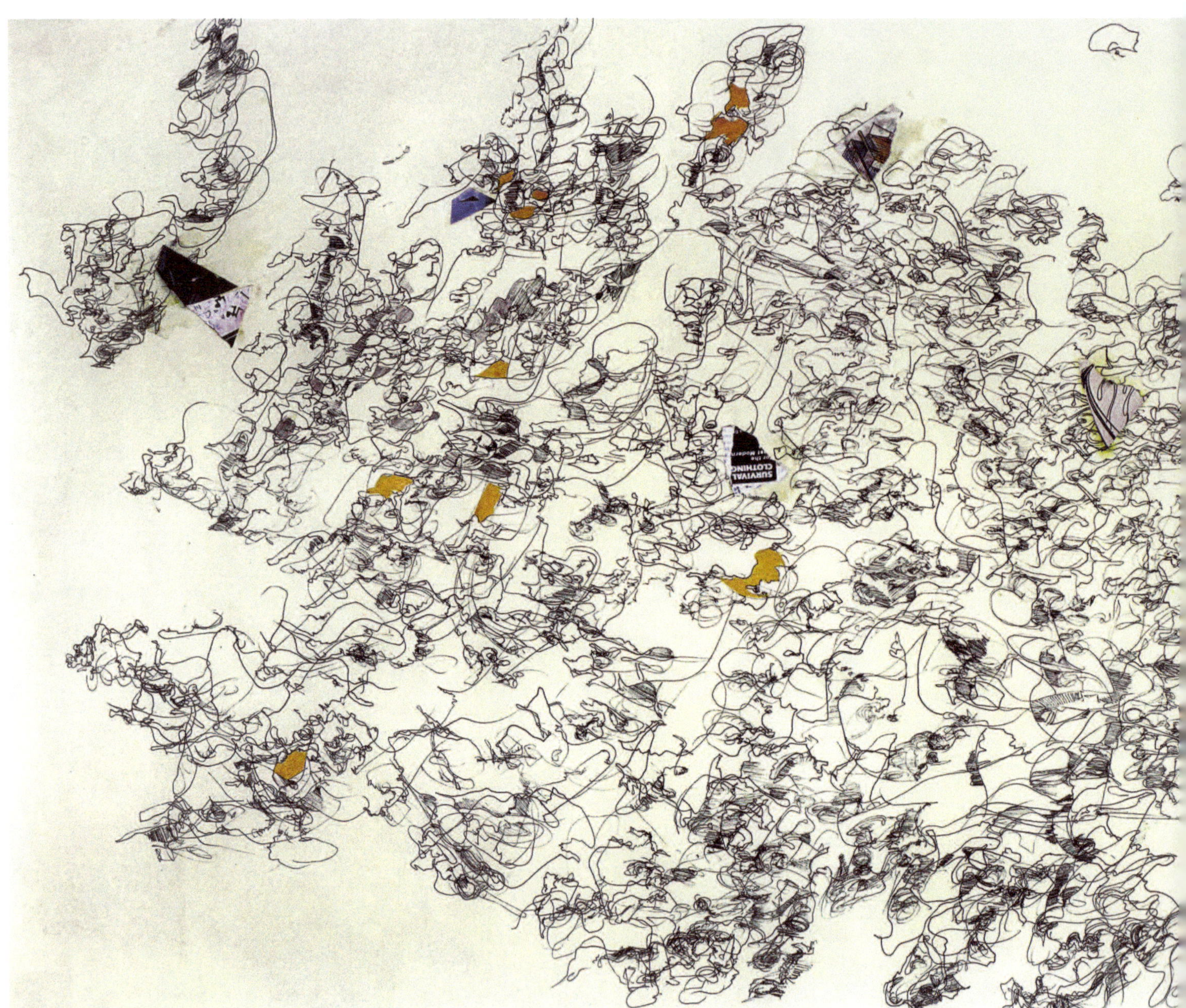
SURVIVAL
CLOTHING

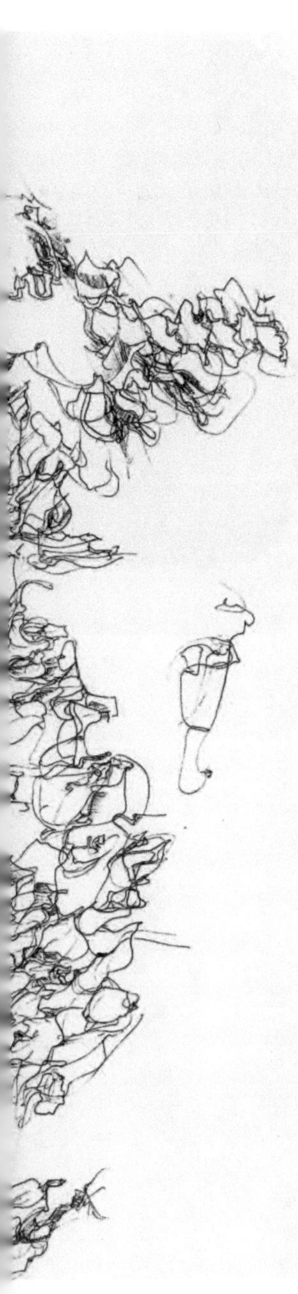

Survival Clothing, 2017
Ink, color pencil, paper collage from *Wet* (1980), and graphite on Takefu washi, 63.4 x 96.5 cm / 25 x 38 in

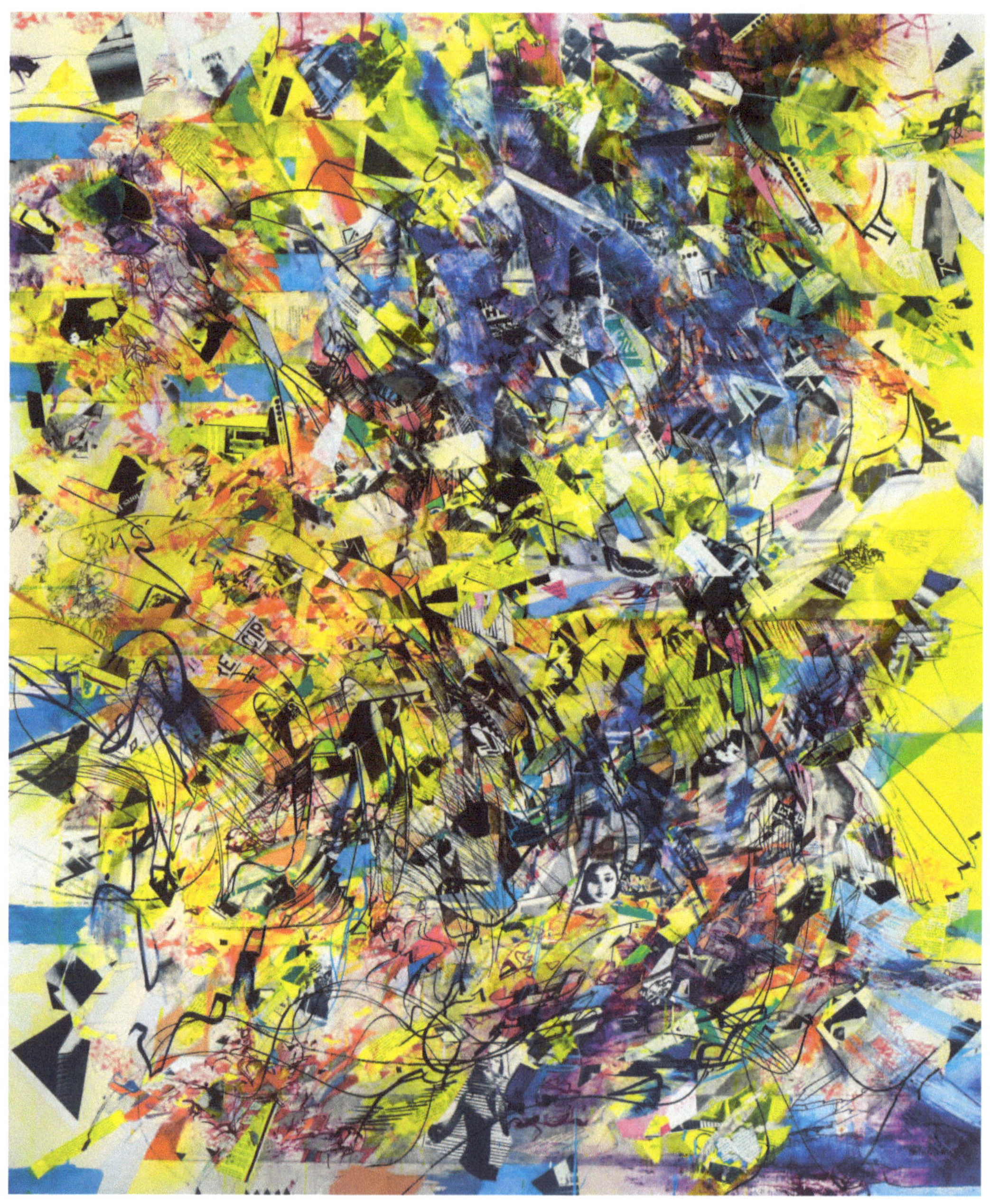

Flores House in Death Valley, 2017
Ink, oil, flashe, collage from *Wet, Nature: Climate Change (2013),* and *Archetype* on canvas, 165.7 x 137.6 x 6.3 cm / 65.25 x 54 x 2.5 in; detail, overleaf

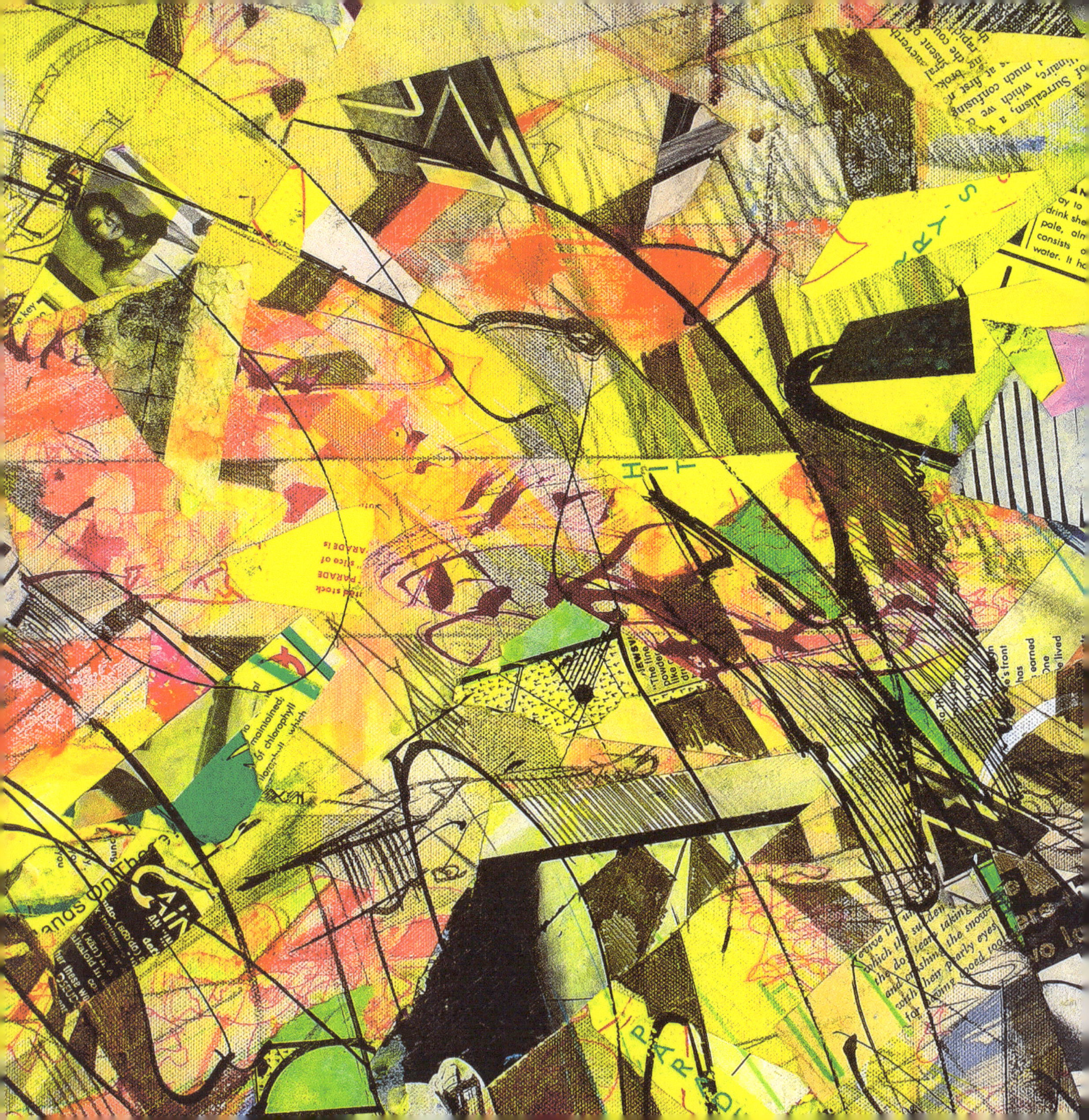

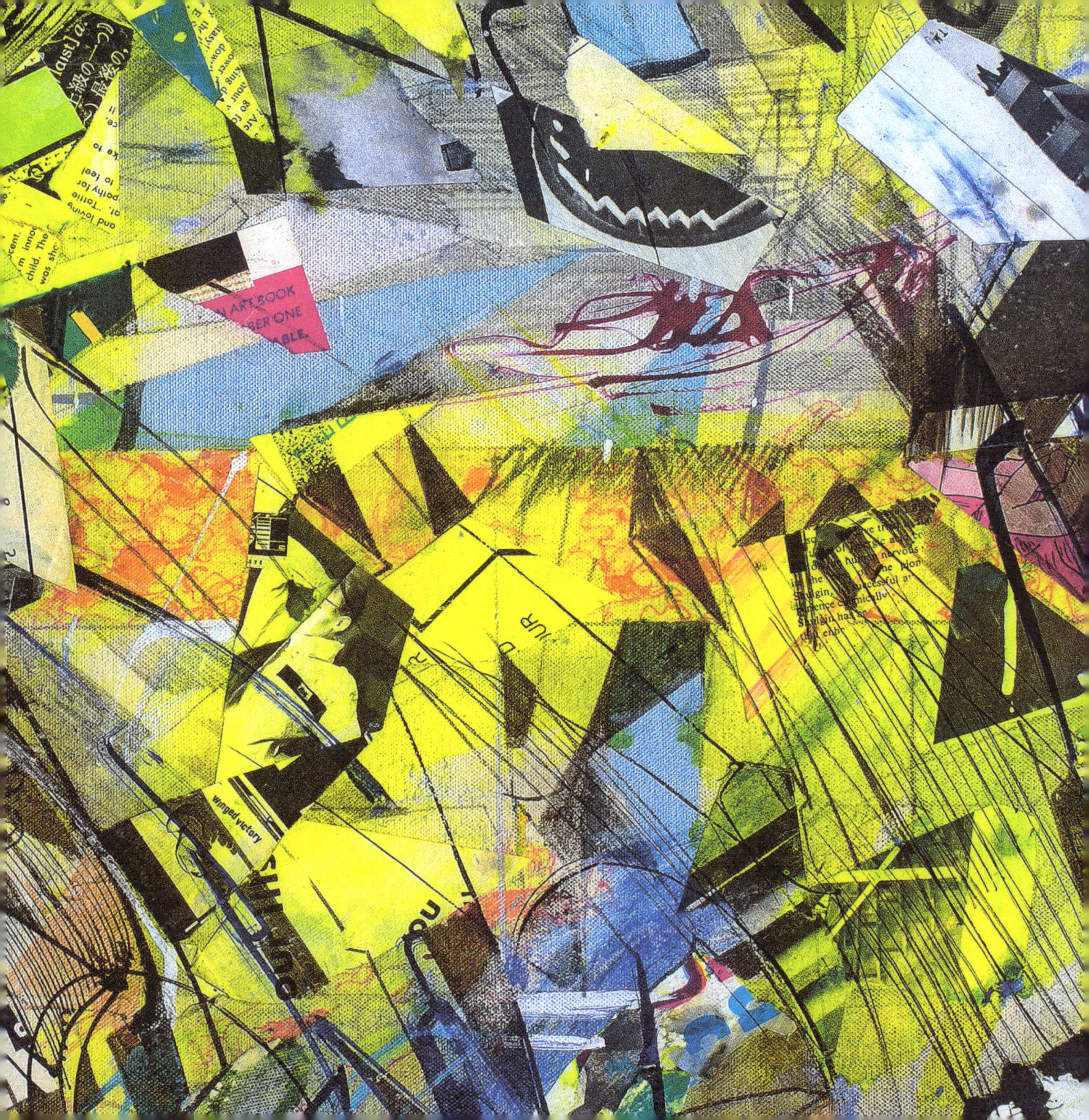

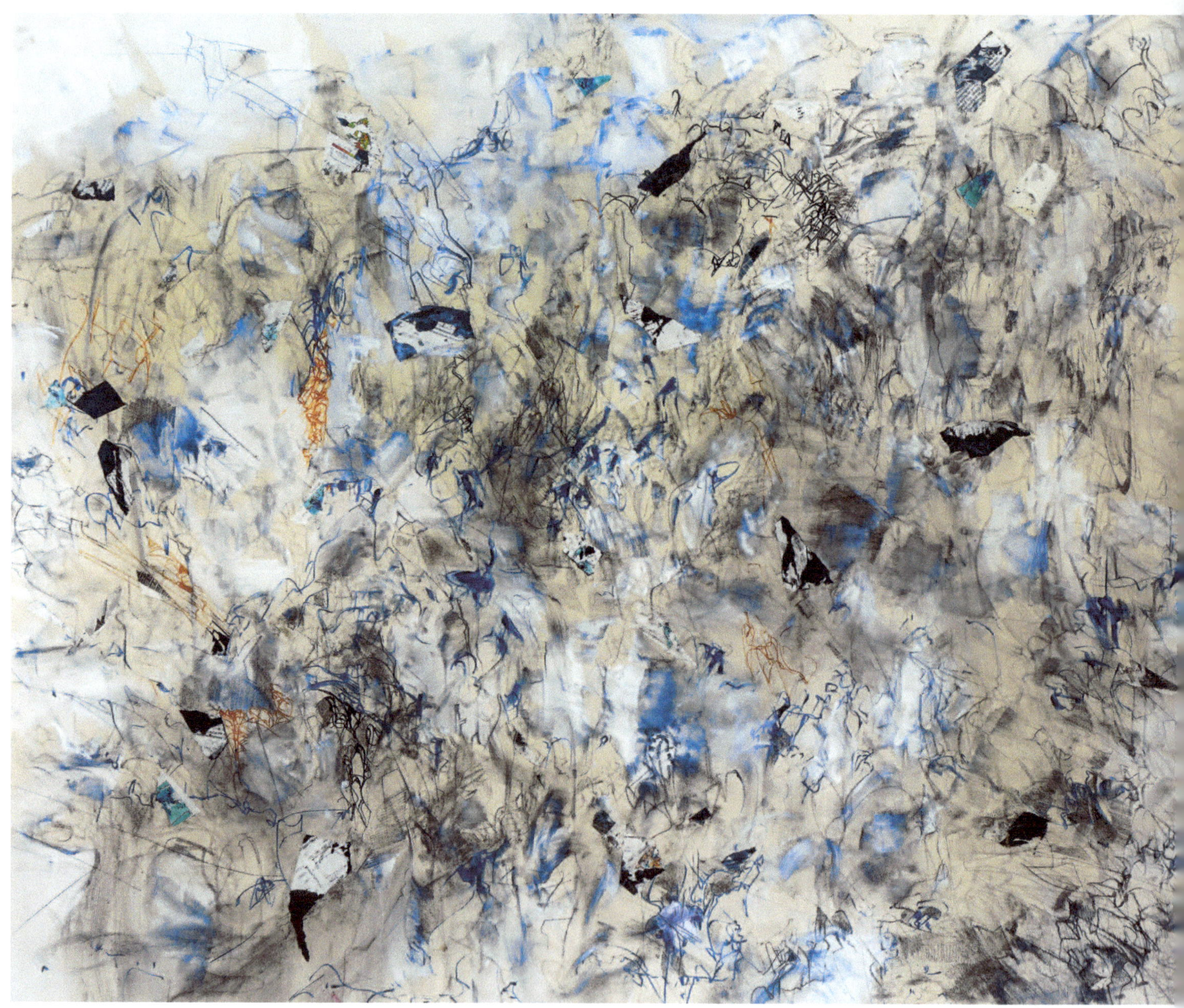

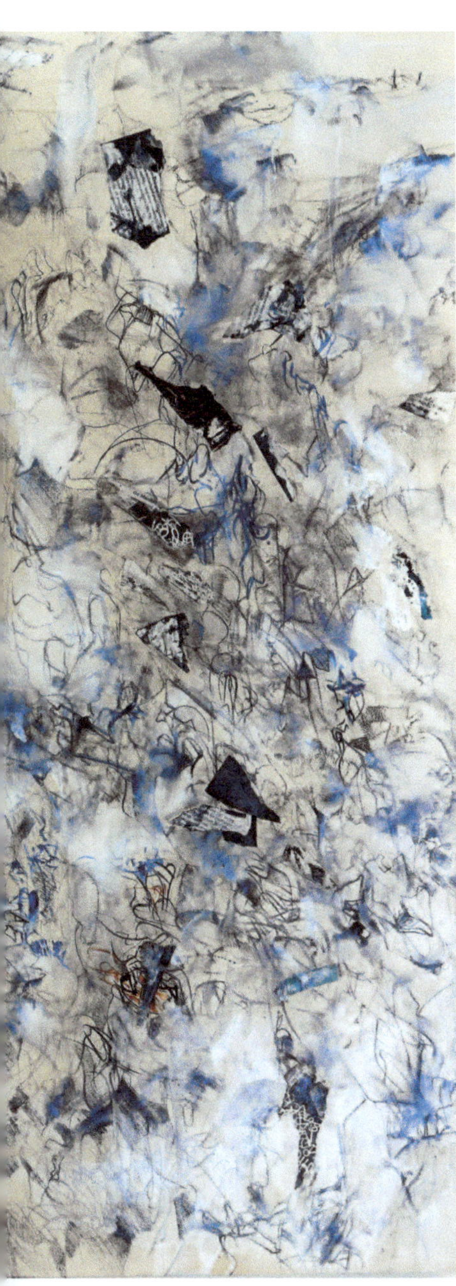

Summer Lake Hot Springs, 2017
Graphite, oil, ink, and paper collage from *Nature: Climate Change,* on muslin, 91.4 x 152.4 x 6.3 cm / 36 x 60 x 2.5 in

Detail, *Summer Lake Hot Springs*

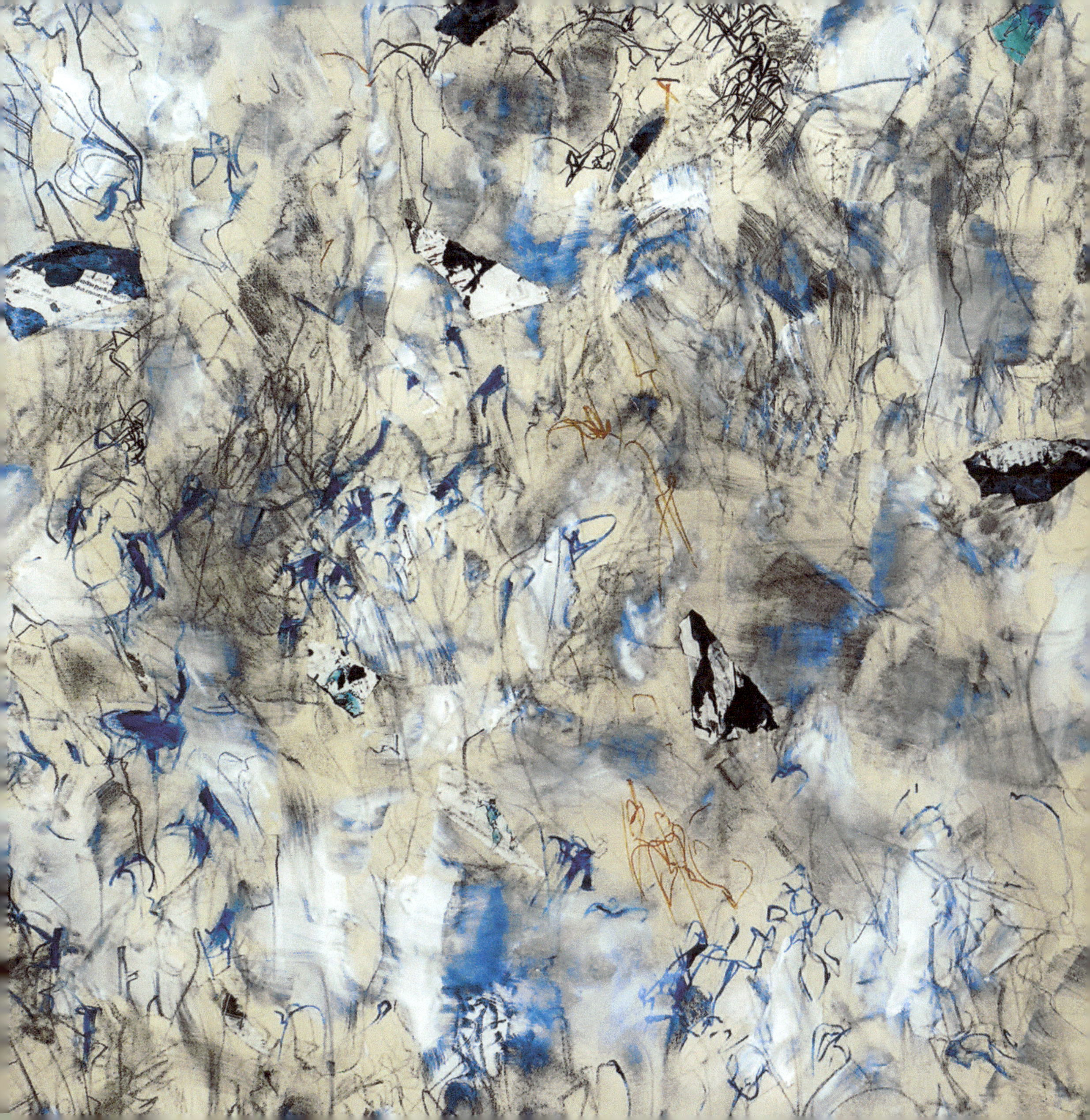

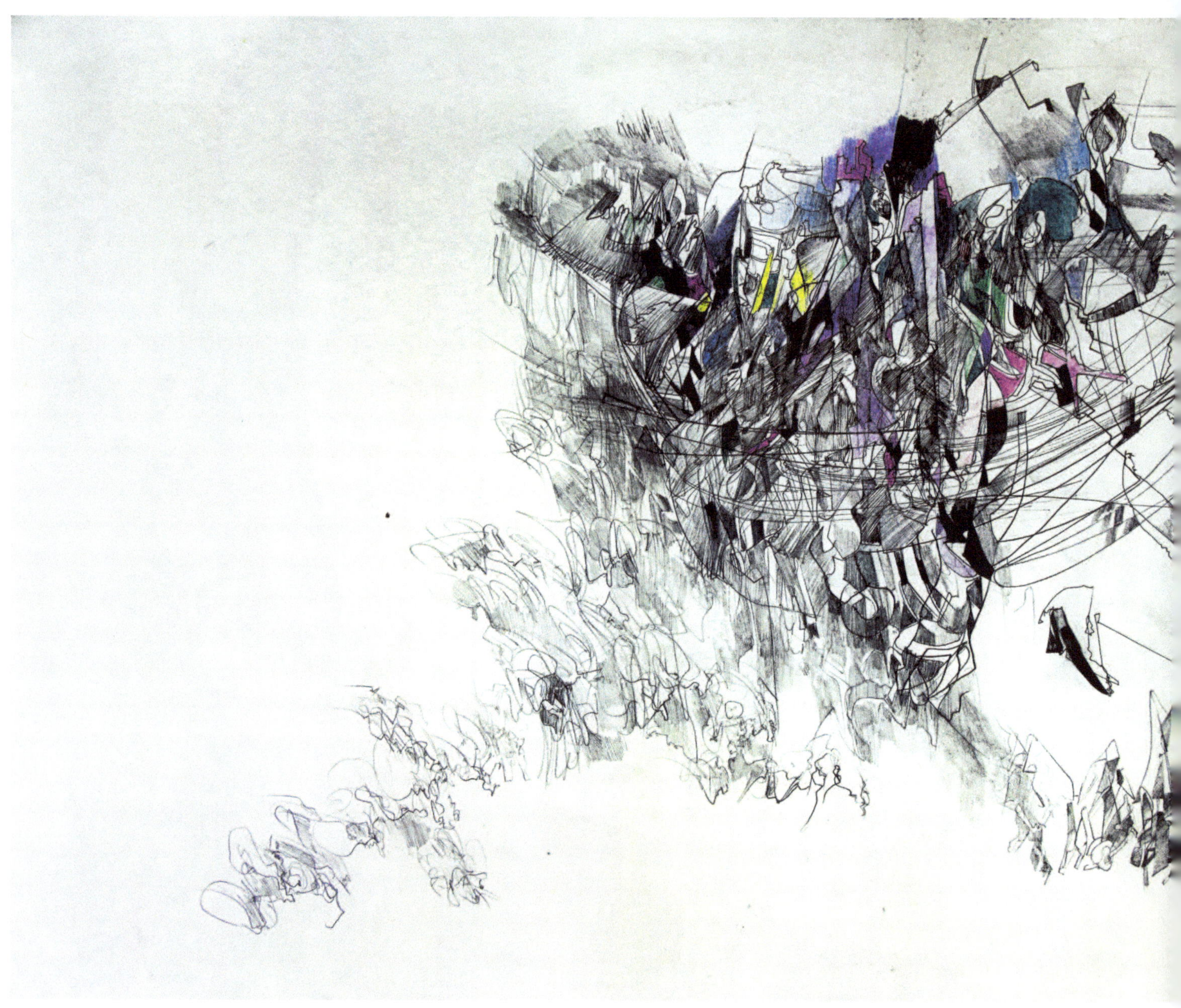

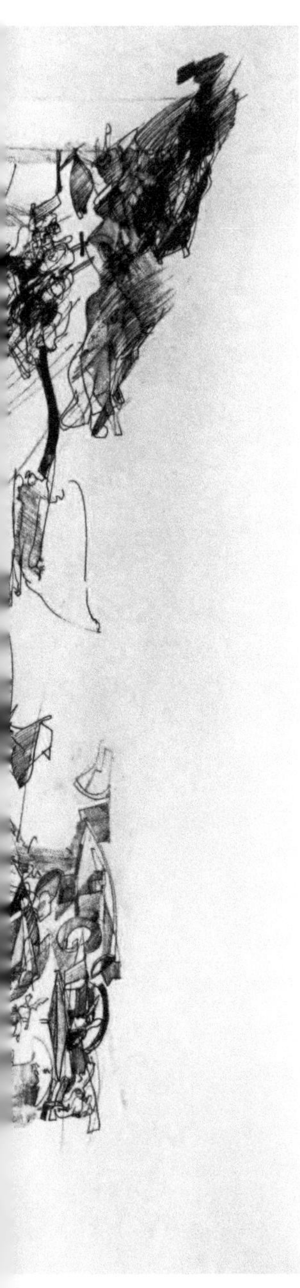

CONVERSATION
JUDITH RODENBECK WITH CHRISTINA MCPHEE

This conversation takes place within an ongoing exchange between Christina McPhee and Judith Rodenbeck around McPhee's drawing/shed practice and its relation to tectonics and trauma, not long after a talk considering the drawing practice of Joan Jonas, given by Rodenbeck. The conversation was recorded on June 9, 2016, in Ojai, California; during the audio session, two workers from Pacific Gas and Electric climbed into the neighboring canopy of one-hundred-year old oaks to prune.

Play of Context (after Virginia Errázuriz), 2017
Ink, color pencil, and graphite on Takefu washi, 63.4 x 96.5 cm / 25 x 38 in

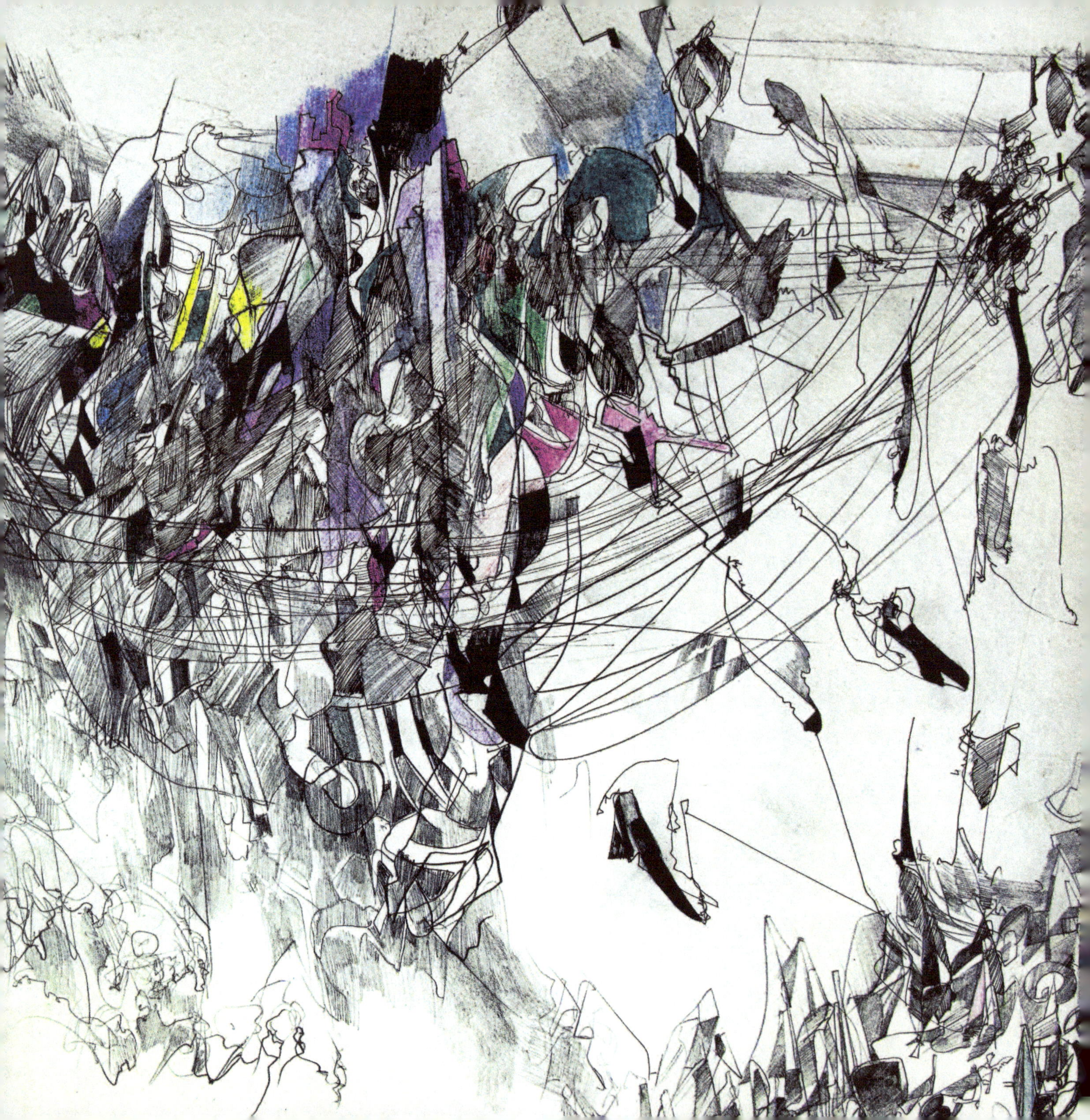

CM Reflecting on your recent discussion of Joan Jonas's installation, *They Come to Us Without a Word*, for the 2015 United States Pavilion at the Venice Biennale—you describe how she presents a techne, in the form of an imaging of transmission, to children of the future. Against this sense of an apocalyptic future, is there, in the action of her drawing, itself, a flow, that's almost like a material form of hope, or a material transmission of a type of knowledge? I'm thinking specifically of how one moves images into a plane where they can be accessible in a time of chaos. This is a projection of what my desires are in drawing.

JR Part of what I see happening there—and we'll use Joan Jonas as a reference point for me—is that Jonas/the drawing agent is acting as a kind of channel for mark-making, on the one hand, in a given type of material and a set of substrates, where that mark-making (and its strata) is thought both concretely and then more abstractly. There's a through-line to aspects of Jonas's oeuvre, and the through-line becomes really visible in the Venice project in its conjoining of environmental and trans-personal concerns. This is an artist who is very particular, and who has very particular ways of working; these latter are hard to parse, idiosyncratic, hard to read, and that idiosyncracy is often read as rendering the artist as magus, or exterior, eccentric to the social world. And yet, what is happening in that work, at the very same time this otherworldly conjuring is taking place, is the making of a socius. Working with these children, who come more or less—they come to us without a word, they come without prejudgements—in the workshops with the kids, the kids take up Jonas dance moves, Jonas drawing moves, Jonas animal moves, but it's not her training them to be Joan Jonas, but rather, engaging them in an open space.

CM Right, it's a transmission.

JR That [transmission] becomes clear when you juxtapose the work, with the young people, with the ghost stories that she's recording from a variety of places. So there's a way in which the process of drawing itself (as idiosyncratic, as personal as that might be in terms of the mark and the process) is also trans-individual. I was thinking about things you've said to me and in your writing about your work and ways you articulate things like seismic fields and transfers not only in naming suites of drawings but also in kinds of procedure that are actually seismic, both in terms of individual marks and in terms of layering. That layering is profoundly geological, it's metaphorical, it's real.

CM I'm making an outlandish, or in-land-ish claim, on the part of an anyone/artist to draw, but as a transmission in feedback loop system with Earth itself. For example, I draw between seismicity and post-traumatic stress disorder. As with visualizing seismicity, drawing layers of shifting, there's a groundedness...or is there? There's a shifting—

JR Where's the starting point? There isn't one, right?

CM There isn't one, right, and so each of these objects that I make, or performance works that I do, have frames or bounds, but it's almost as if it's just a film still from within some larger sequence.

JR Let's just say that's the temporal frame—

CM Do the drawings exhibit a temporal constraint?

JR Well, you finish them, there's that. But as perceptual objects they're pretty temporally dense. I want to press on this seismicity as metaphor and as what is one's lived experience, and what is the expression of—well, now I'm backing myself into a corner, saying that any artwork is an expression of experience.

CM Drawing could be a kind of knowledge production, but the production is not autobiographical. Sometimes, people want me to reveal particular experiences that have led me to do *xyz*, and then an interpretation can set up a grounding through a causal chain.

Detail, *Play of Context (after Virginia Errázuriz)*, 2017

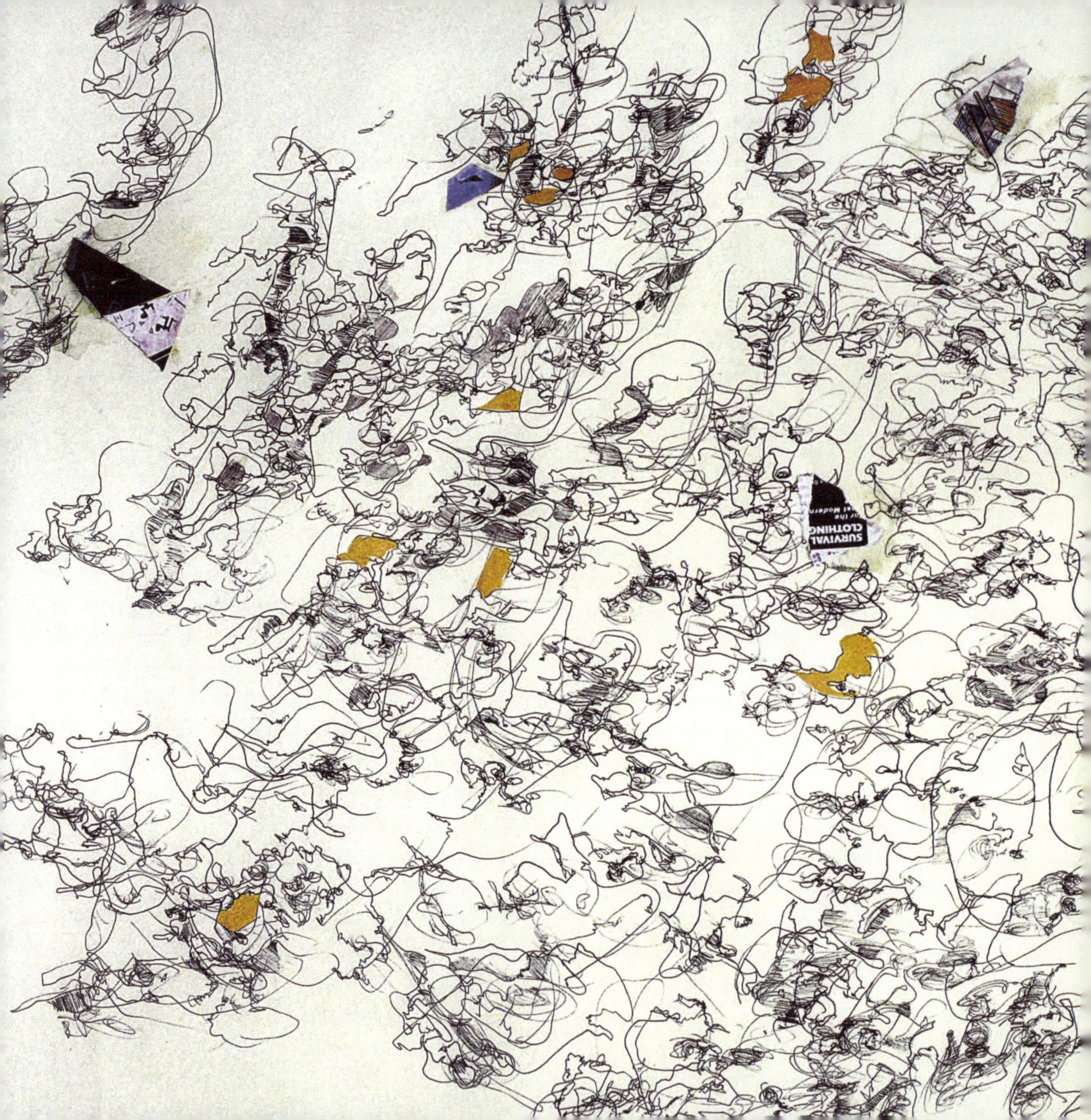
SURVIVAL
CLOTHING

JR The causal notion is the one that is the problem, certainly with something as open-ended as an art work…

CM A recourse to biography.

JR A hunting-back of causal links—this is one of the problems of neuro-aesthetics in my mind: and so if we discover that the brain is wired in such and such a way, to look at or to produce art, and—

CM Just design an artificial intelligence apparatus to reproduce that and then we could have art.

JR Isn't it so great that I invited you back here, because it would be so quiet, and here this guy is cutting the limbs of this hundred-year-old oak tree thirty feet over our heads and today of all days? Gregory Bateson says about the self, you know, we think in common parlance of something like a "self," as bounded by skin and nervous structure; he says it's a total fiction, that we're in continuum with, not just other beings, but the elements around us. If we take that approach, the idea of obviously legible, biographical, or narrative causality becomes difficult to sustain.

CM People talk about art made as if to communicate to or for machines, so, to eliminate the "human." I work outside that opposition.

JR So we'll say unframing, unframing that can operate in a variety of ways. Here's the interesting thing about your drawing: one of the things that struck me when we first met was that you were working with the Sydney-based online list-serv discussion forum,*-empyre-*, , but then you also had a really "primal" drawing process.

CM And at that time, it was really secret.

JR You were a closet draw-er.

JR I say primal, but I'm kind of putting that in quotes, because the implication is that it's primary and all this other stuff is add-on. It's basic, it's fundamental, it's "everything draws," right?

CM There's that great title of a book, by Gloria Anzaldúa, *This Bridge We Call Home*. She wrote this beautiful book about activism, and I love that architectural image; it reminds me, too, of a rock climber sending out a belay—so the line becomes the thing you can actually walk on to get to the next space.

JR It makes the next space…and (working the belay) the retrieval—proceed and retrieve, in a way—

CM When I think about retrieving content out of crushed drawings, or when I work a painting—because if you rely on this generative-line method, then often the material object will fail—it's not being constructed primarily as an object to begin with, so if it's lucky it may end up as a thing, but it may not. As I shoot photographs of the drawings, and then manipulate the photographic digital files as drawings; what then? Then I'm in…is it recuperation? That sounds like a health thing. Recapture? Connaissance? In French, that's "to apprehend" wisdom?

JR Connaissance is knowledge, in an old fashioned way—deep knowledge. Glissant talks about connaisance as co-naissance, right, born together, so it's that kind of knowledge—

CM Now we're getting at it…

JR Well, this idea of being born together, however one wants to take that, is a way of thinking about knowing, if you want to deal with issues of process and how one is with a process, and we're really

Detail, *Survival Clothing;* full image, p. 134

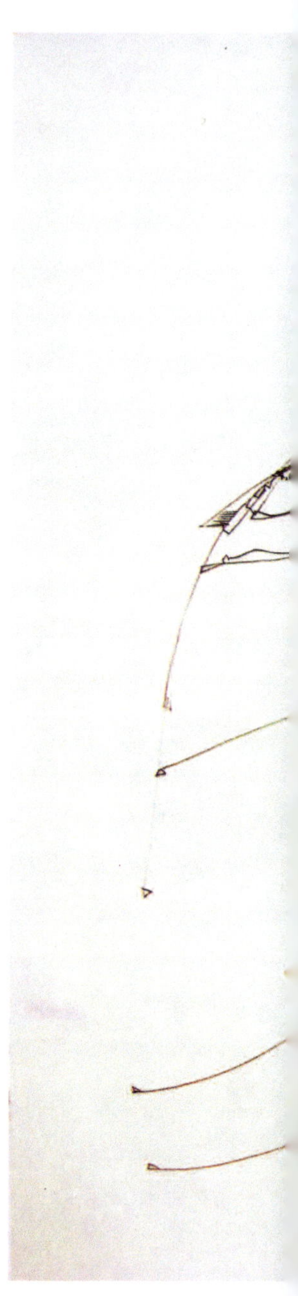

Study for Flesh Turned to Atoms, 2016
Ink, color pencil, and graphite on Takefu washi, 63.4 x 96.5 cm / 25 x 38 in

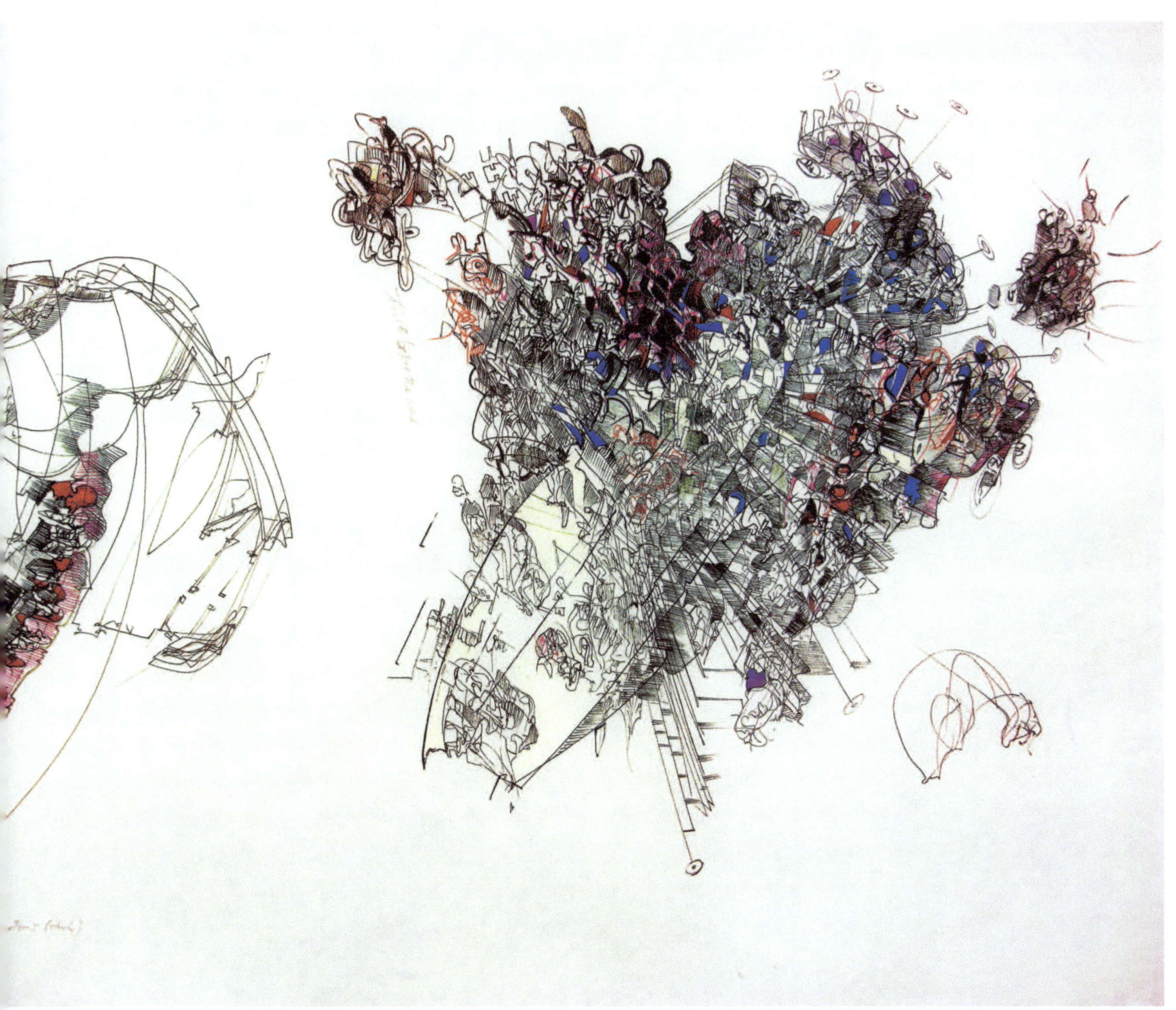

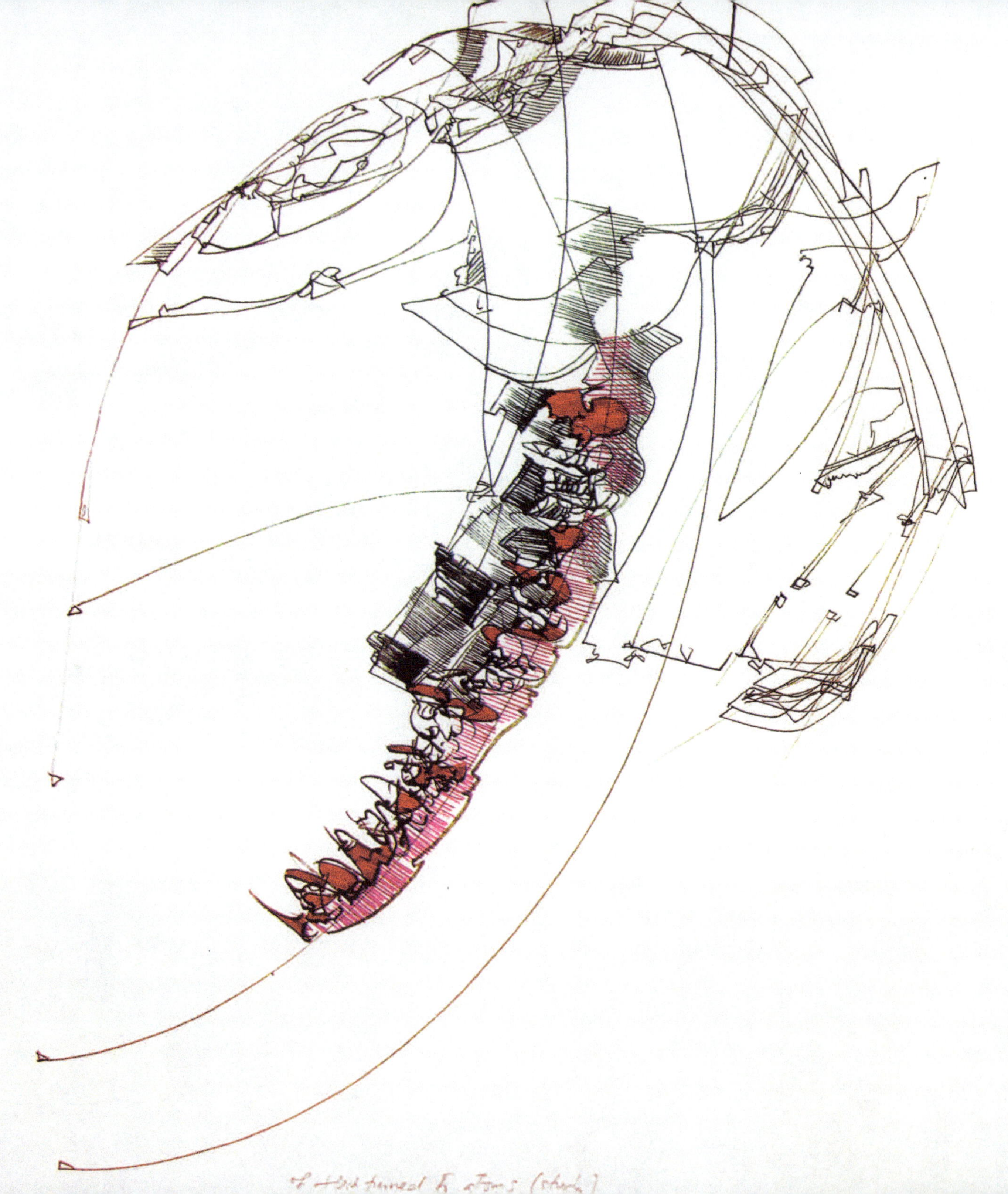

talking about your drawing: I'm remembering the piece you did with Pamela Z (*Carbon Song Cycle*, 2013). There's that moment when you're actively working, you were lying on the floor and drawing, fully inhabiting this space of the line so that the mark made was secondary to this other thing that was made, not quite dance, but something else, and that to me is this co-naissance idea.

CM I was listening to the musicians, simultaneously drawing, using the relay of light from my mobile phone to draw what I was hearing. Then the electronic expression of my drawing motion, that's what the musicians were playing.It was a triple cycle going on.

JR A triple axel.

CM A triple axel (yeah, right!), immediately I think about autopoiesis and...enclosed....homeostasis...drawings as temporally bound. In the performance of *Carbon Song Cycle*, nearly simultaneously, the musicians read and perform my live drawing as a score.

JR It's an open score. So say more about autopoesis. There's an engagement that's been ongoing for you, if I'm not wrong, with language around the concept of autopoiesis.

CM Autopoeisis calls up, to me, an imaging of a world, a giant world or a tiny world, full of infinite moving parts that are self-generating. Before *Carbon Song Cycle*, I was working on the *Tesserae of Venus* project, in 2009; I was drawing the tectonics of Venus, which are characterized by complex ridged folds, or tesserae. Allegorically speaking, if our terrestrial climate got hotter and hotter, like Venus, one might imagine that the tectonics of Venus would start to appear, here on Earth, complete with folded-ridge terrains; as if climate could shift geologic plates, or supersede them. I made models (using folded paper drawings) of how this was going to (somehow) look. It was a fantasy apocalypse. Against this, autopoiesis implies there's no end, or, a "world without end." We think that our world is changing and falling away from us, or taking leave of us, or we of it. A continuous sensation of loss relates to our experience of being mortal.

JR Self-consciousness—

CM Consciousness itself is based in loss, but sometimes drawing teaches me there is no loss; for the processes of autopoiesis, loss is subsumed within a full, complete set of possibilities. That's comedy as paradise. Right now, the Pacific Gas and Electric technician is liberating power lines from tree limbs with a buzz saw, while we're trying to do this thing: maybe our conversation in the midst of sawing is a little comic bit, a bit of paradise right now. That sounds a little like Annie Besant!

JR So here you are [in Ojai!].Speaking of Besant, when you look at the early twentieth century, there are a number of figures dealing with issues of repetition across time, transhistorical and transcultural repetitions, Aby Warburg and his *pathosformel*, for instance. I like to think about Warburg being connected to someone like Kubler, with his braids of time and form. Those thinkers, then, allow one to imagine that form (let's say) expresses itself through individuals: that we're expressing form, which, in a sense, performs us. And that's another way of getting away from the causal version of art. One of the things that I so appreciate about your drawing, and one of the things that got me into thinking about Jonas as well, was to ask, what does it mean to return— and return is the wrong idea—

CM—Reconnoiter—

Detail, *Study for Flesh Turned To Atoms*

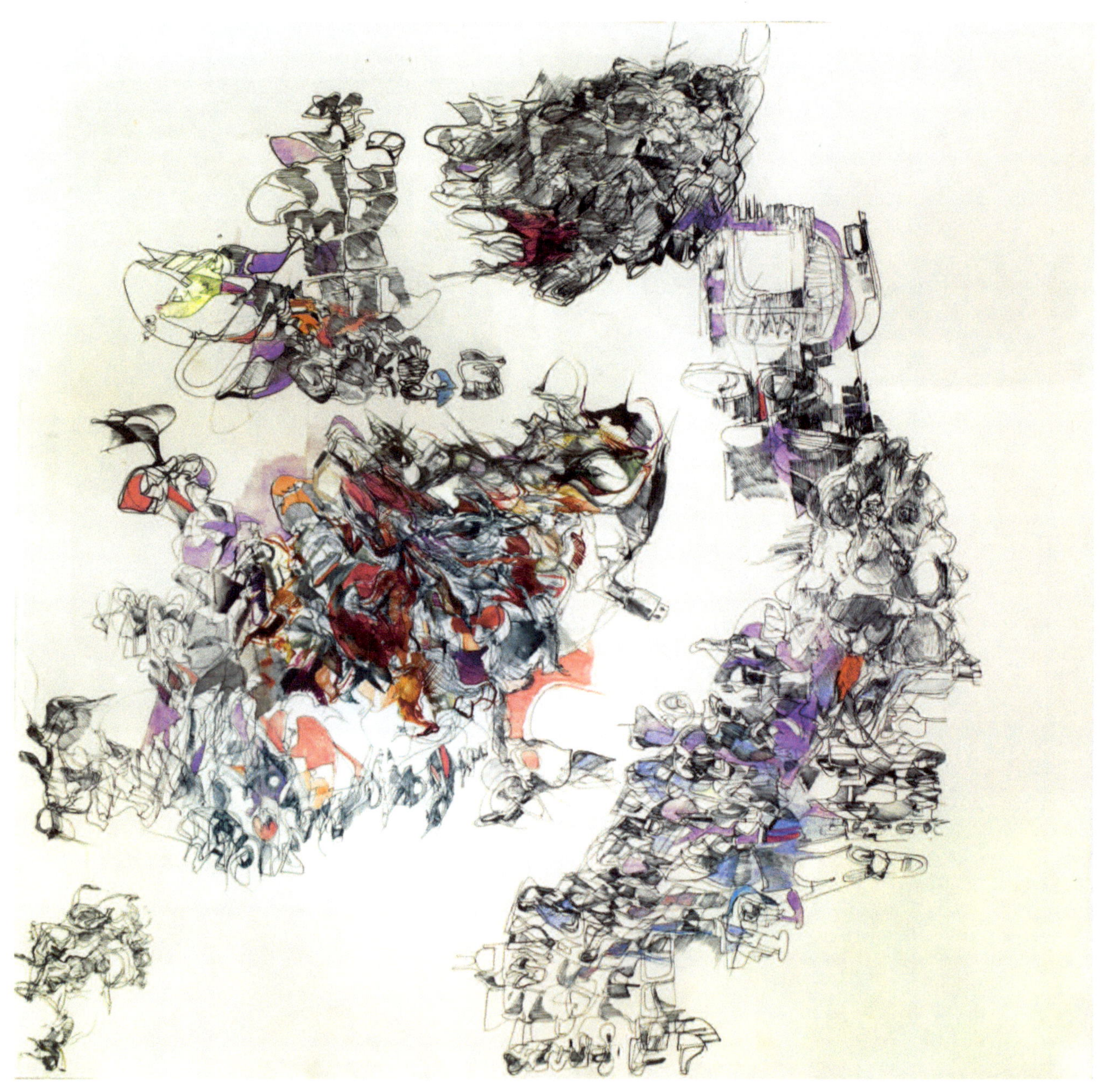

JR Reconnoiter (or even reconnaitre), to fold oneself back into a fundamental creaturely mark-making, in an era in which everything is made of electronics, is about the instantaneous and trivial, zeros and ones. In such a context, a relatively devalued practice like drawing is not trivial at all.

CM No, quite the opposite. There's something about the primacy, in drawing...that, well, there's no time-edge...the drawings may generate their own 'real' in my lifetime and after; somehow that's a resource for hope. It's not like I have a message.

JR You're not Annie Besant—

CM No, the work can make itself available in and create its own times and places, beyond whatever small world I happen to inhabit.

JR This is provocative when considering the Anthropocene, and thinking about how to convey the topic to young people. For instance, we are going through this election season (2016), and for many of us it's a moment of profound concern about the nature of discourse in the United States. You talk to young people and they're excited or they're not excited or they're engaged or not engaged, however they approach their being in the political world; but their memories are short. Their knowledge of history is slim. It's not that the world renews, or recycles, it's a brand new thing for them. Their experience of the world is that this is simply how it is. There is student debt, this is just the way it is; there is a level of discourse that is abysmal—and they haven't lived through something different than that. So thinking in terms of the Anthropocene is also asking us to think in terms that are not dictated by three score and ten, the average lifespan, or a set of family relationships that are within knowledge, but rather detaching one's "self" from that sort of timescale, going scalar.

CM That's another thing I want drawings to do: drawings are constantly involved in movements of scale. Integrating tiny threads of diagrammatic content and glyphic content into large compositors, from within a six foot frame, towards the millimeter differentials—I find tiny pivots or switches in drawing. Lines cluster into small tesserated planes, with an accumulation, almost to a point of collapse: a certain angle of repose is about to fail, and a cascade of marks is about to slip.

JR Well there's this filigreed quality to some of what you're doing but it's deliberate, it's not decorative, it's—

CM Skeining—-

JR The way in which you are working both with deliberation and automatism is quite provocative.

CM Well I think that's it.

JR I leave you with that, provocative.

CM That's a great way to stop.

Dragonfruit USB, 2015
Watercolor, ink, color pencil and graphite on paper,57.1 x 57.1 cm 22.5 x 22.5 in

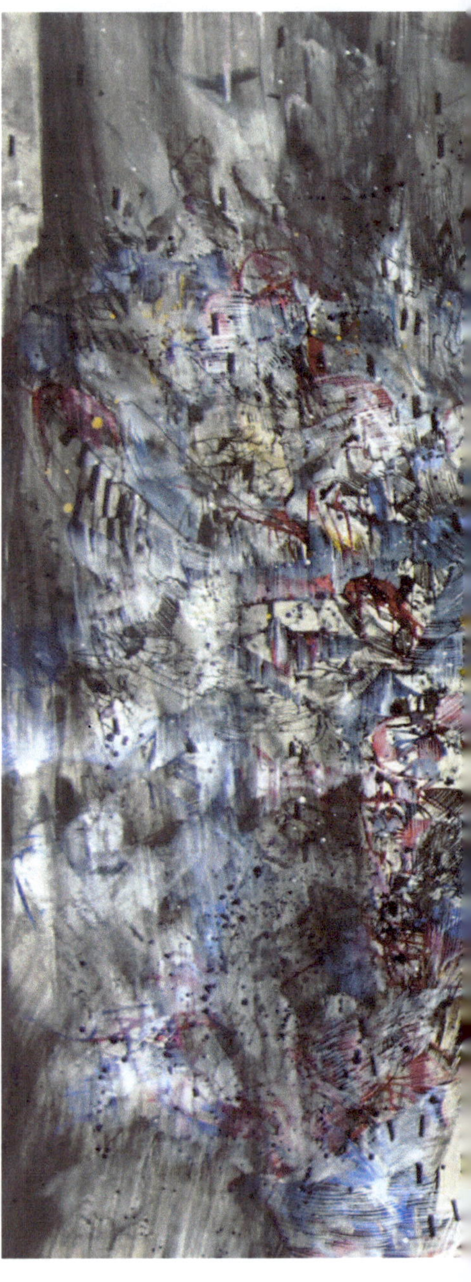

Weary Blues (After Langston Hughes), November, 2016
Ink, dye, oil, and graphite on canvas, 99 x 165.1 x 6.3 cm / 39 x 65 x 2.5 in

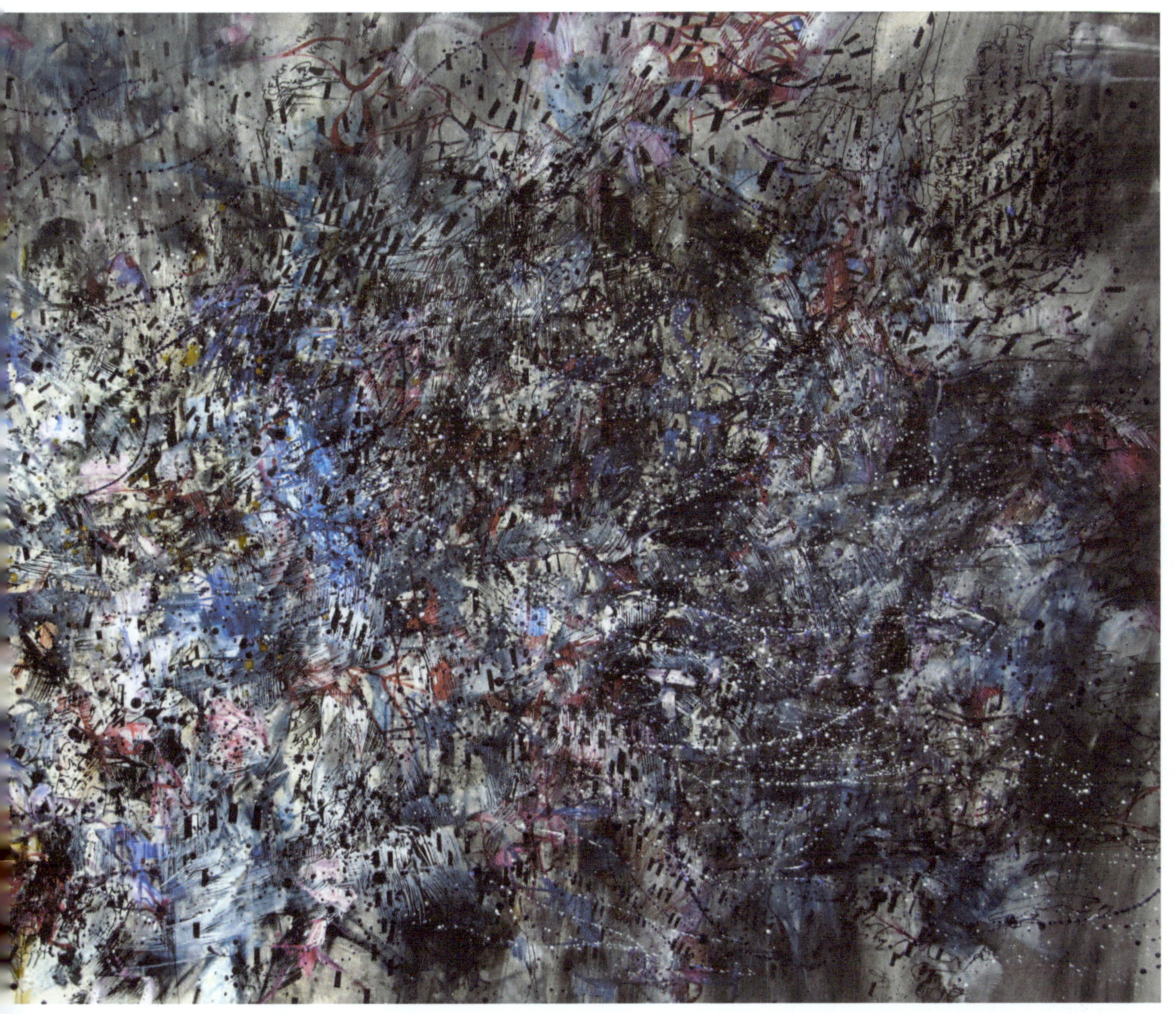

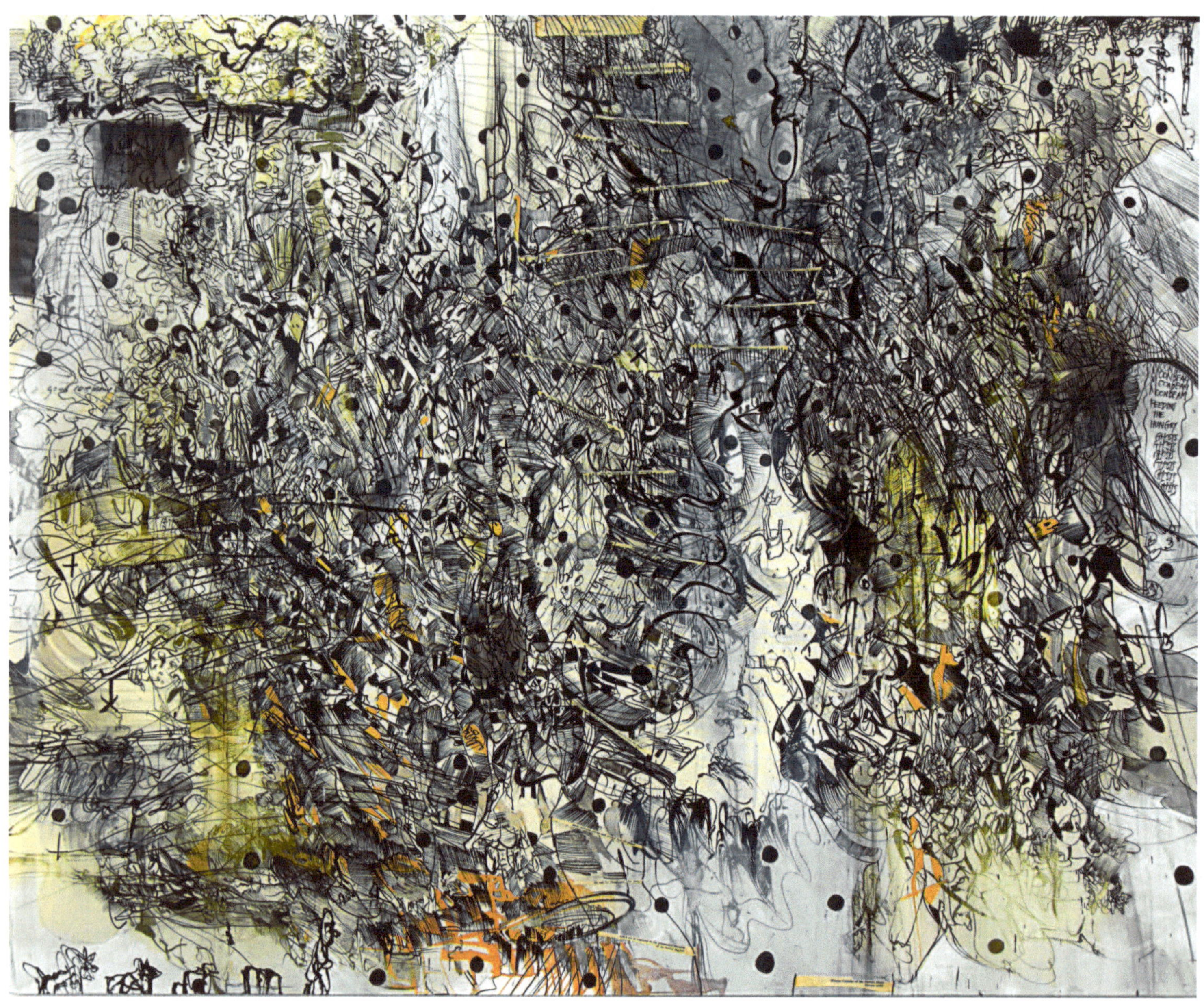
MOONBEAM
FEEDING THE HUNGRY

Hungry Ghosts (Evil Desires the Key to Vertigo, After Tristan Tzara), 2016
Shellac-based, sumi and acrylic inks; flashe, watercolor, and graphite on canvas, 137.1 x 167.5 x 6.3 cm / 54 x 65.75 x 2.5 in

Detail, *Hungry Ghosts,* 2016

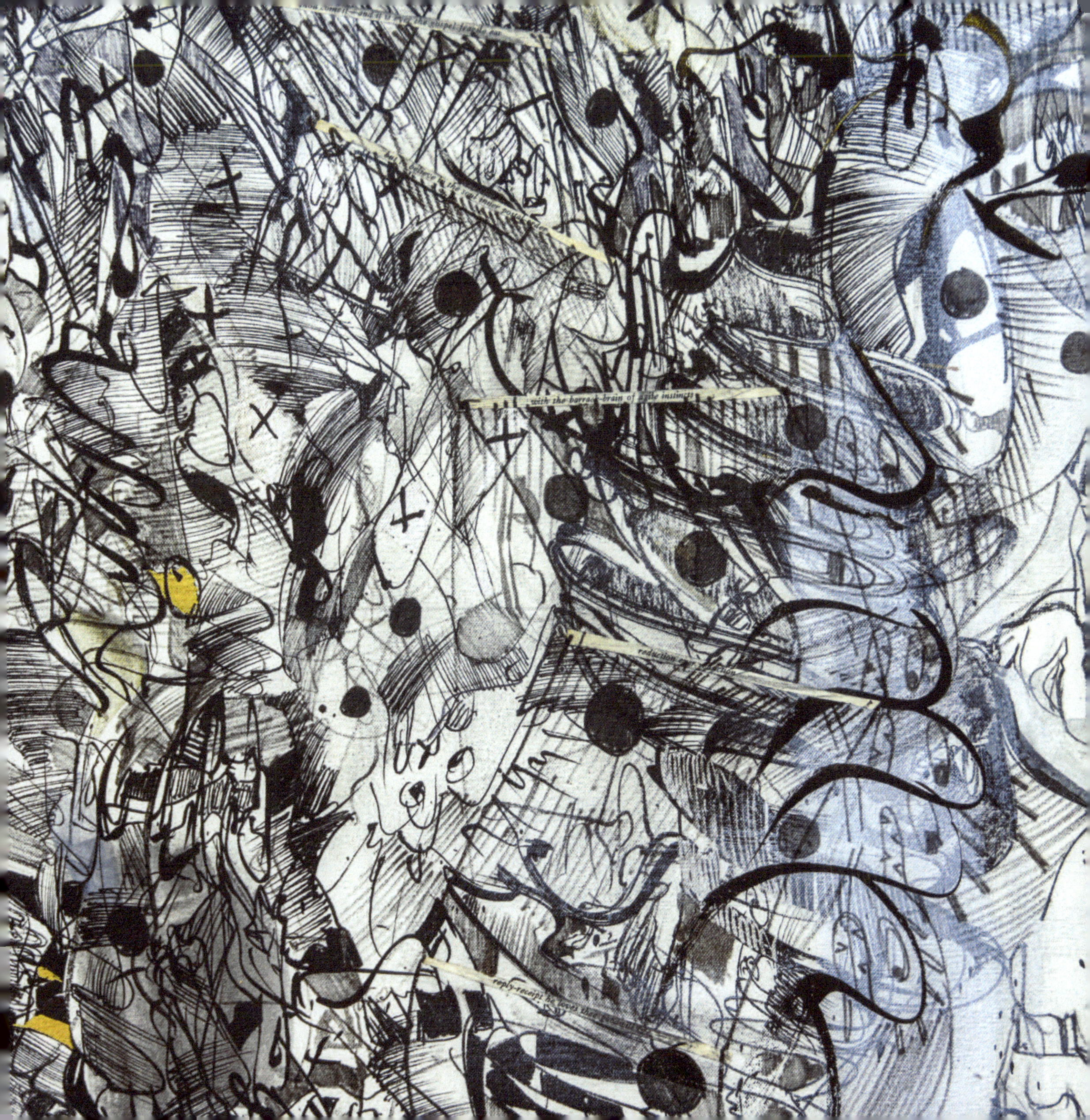

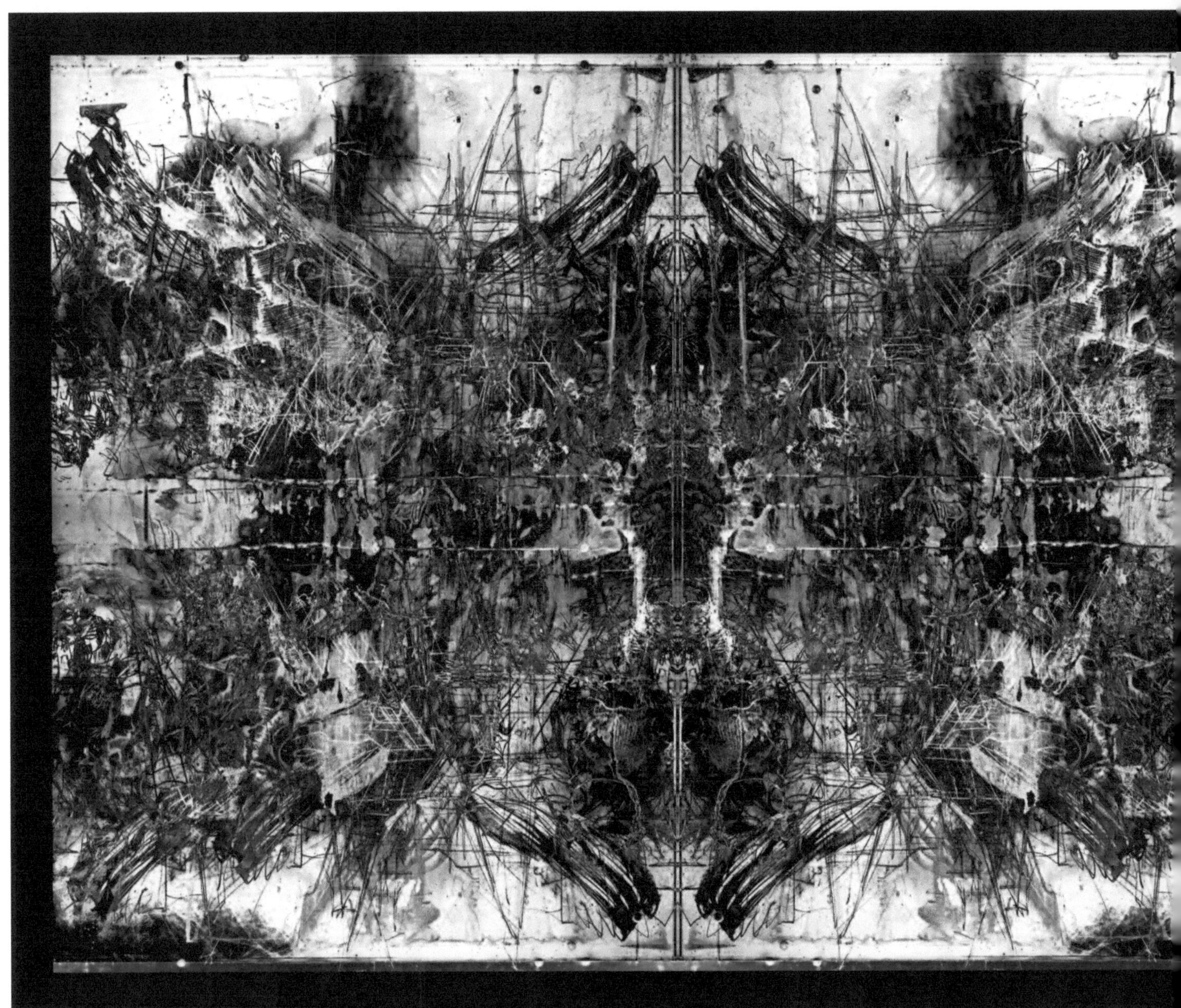

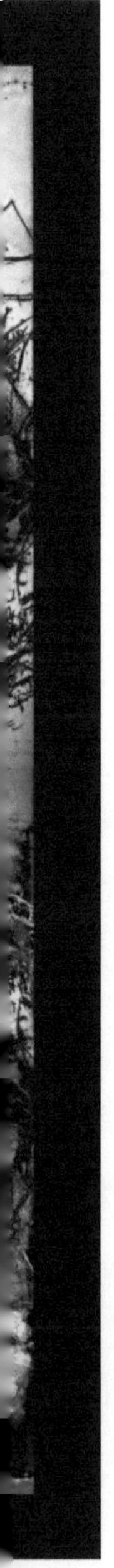

Double Blind Study 36, 2012
Gelatin silver print on archival paper, 76.8 x 101.6 cm / 30 x 40 in

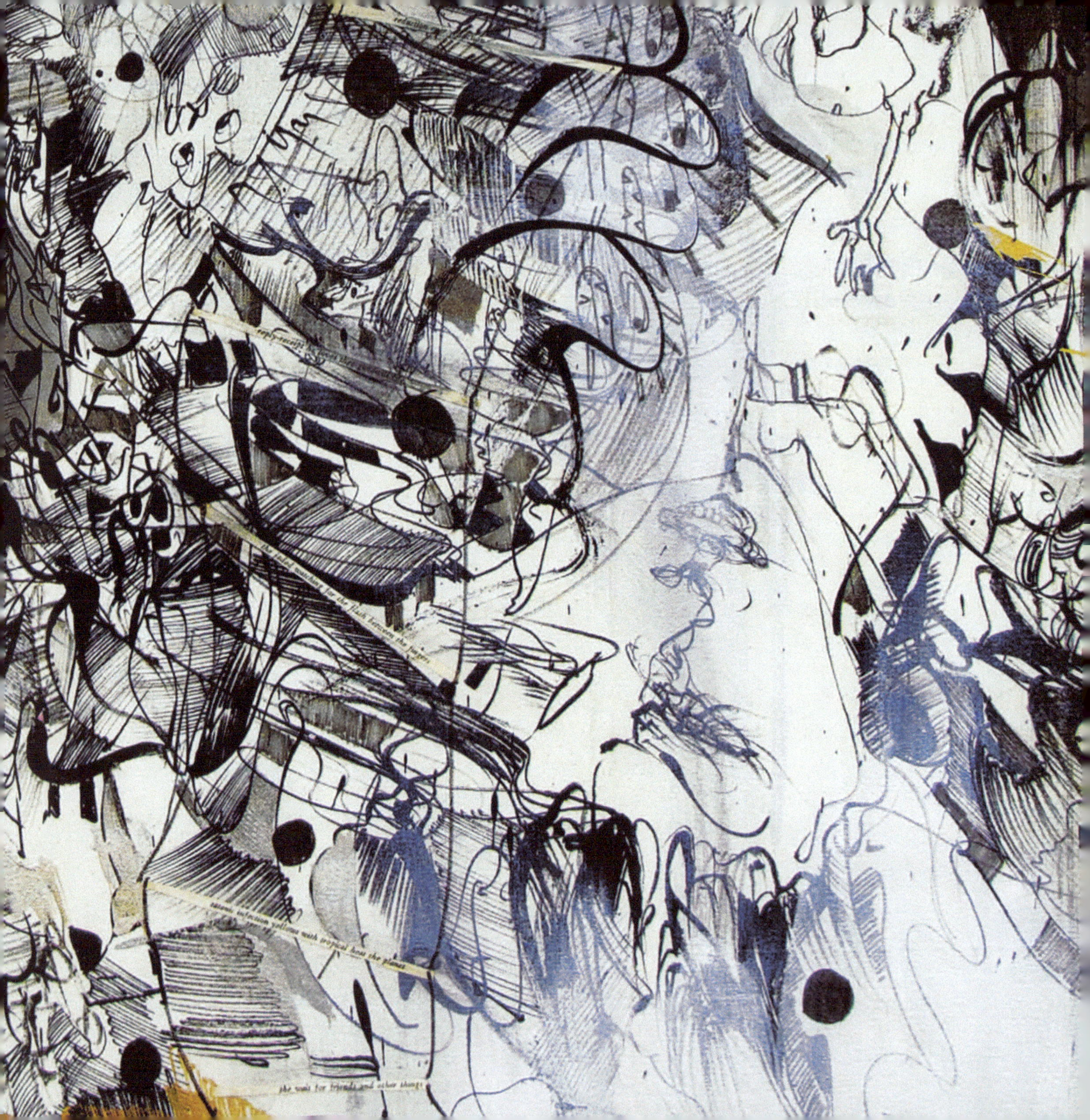
the faded watching for the flash between the fingers
she waits for friends and other things

STUDIO VISIT
PHIL KING

I've seen Christina McPhee's work in the flesh a number of times now and often find myself compelled to write about those experiences. On a recent visit to her temporary Oakland studio, two drawings in particular captured my attention, and then my imagination. I was initially hesitant; the stylizations somehow held me at bay, the style of some of the lines were reminiscent of things unfathomably unholy to any residue that might have remained of my sense of taste, reminders of arts for which I have maintained a horrified and perhaps deviant feeling of enthusiasm. Forgotten interests. I couldn't shake the feeling of Roberto Matta lurking in the drawing, perhaps even defining it. I told Christina this and she, laughing, responded with an ironic mention of Georges Mathieu, and I knew then that I was hooked.

Chains of relevant associations followed. Some were immediately shared and swapped in conversation with her, others emerged later as part of a dream of how artists can evoke and bring back to life forgotten but uncannily vital worlds, often through the slightest twists of style and handling. A certain cross hatch calls Van Gogh to mind, a run of ink, Michaux; a dark shape queasily animates a sense of Beardsley. I think that the force of a developed yet experimental body of work such as hers is profoundly associative, and therefore open to the uncanny and questionable multiplicity of art as a disjunctive whole while giving access to a genuine sense of consistency. I feel that in her case everything reinforces everything in an amazing and ongoing display of fecund and untimely movement that cuts across the boundaries of limited tastes and actually enables us (in reverie) to reach a breathless Blakean threshold.

This visionary fluidity is one with the kind of shadow world in which her paintings participate. Literally, on a visit to her tree-shaded garden studio, the California light speckled the surfaces of her canvases. Thick paint overwhelms and reveals the fine drawing; heterogeneous gluts of brute matter are not excluded from the strength and knowledge of these works. A lucid grimness plays a part here too. Paintings become screens for a play of light and shadow, or possible frames that could release their contents in animations, into animated worlds, such as her video drawing/paintings.

Detail, *Hungry Ghosts,* 2016

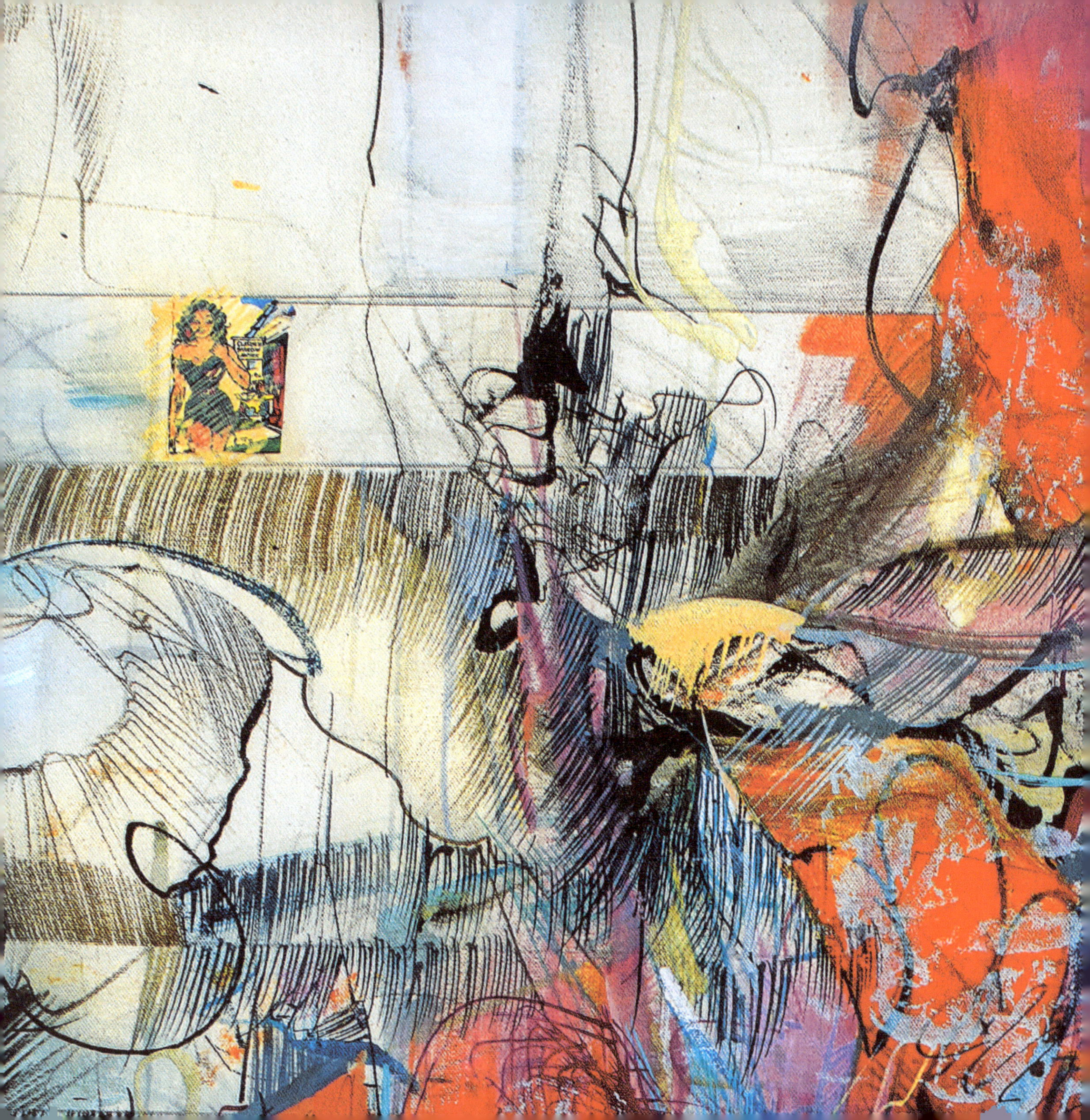

Shed Cubed, at Krowswork in Oakland, involved four looped sound and video projections emulating the four walls of her drawing studio, the original Shed. Speeding up long term video documentation of her everyday drawing activity, *Shed Cubed* auto-records how the drawings themselves abandon fixed mentalities, and expand to leave behind first points of reference. Shadow play shifts, unbidden, through a frenetic, visionary calligraphic graphism. In the Oakland installation, the sounds of eighteen months' passage were compressed into an aural texture, which served to intensify the spatial and temporal slippage between a four channel video loop of layered, animated footage of the Shed, projected onto the gallery's four walls. This is contingency as a form of painterly light, a motley inclusion that begins to define the edge of surprising differences, differences whose *son et lumiere* take us somewhere else. Christina said that she liked the Keystone Cops effect of the speeded up film, and there was, indeed, a comic element at play. As she spoke, I noticed people craning to hear her speak and felt impressed at their curiosity, the fact that the work had a genuine interest and puzzling effect for people, that things were going on that they didn't quite understand but wanted to know more about. Some representation was at play but held in abeyance. As a document of activity somewhere else, doubly caught in a different time, the time captured and the accelerated vision, *Shed Cubed* demanded that we lose our moorings and so, in time, we begin to slip into a kind of engaged reverie in which the drawing itself becomes a kind of murmuring.

Her new paintings also begin to forcefully embody all these differences, not encyclopedically in any way: theirs is a place of fugitive light and sounds, variously collected tectonics of different responses and reflections. They also confront us terribly as matters of fact. Here is the affect whose flow persists as I write this—a figural, diagrammatic affect whose ungrounded work becomes truly enveloping, a sort of ungrounded sub-language of the disintegrating and body of gesture, pushed by the complexity of the artist's realization into a developing out of body experience. Becoming out of all this graphic architecture is a multi-dimensional multiplicity of lost experience. Both the possibility and the actuality of such loss is made fact. This is painting, a painting capable of moving me to the edge of genuine loss of identity, to a loss that, in oil paint, draws and grounds the light of new thresholds, where despair and hope hold hands.

Detail, *Strange Legacy*; full image, overleaf

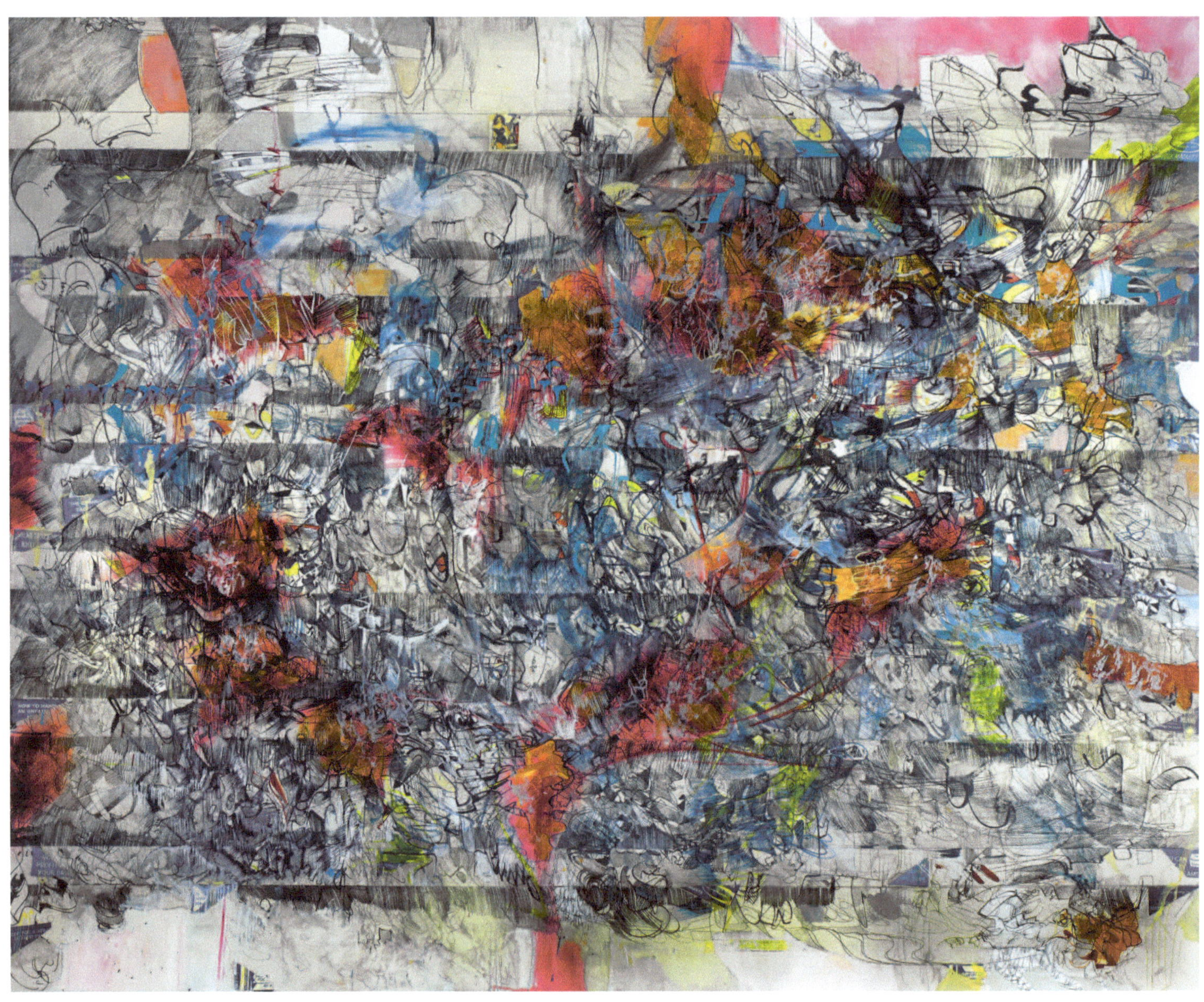

Strange Legacy (after Moonbeam McSwine in the New York Mirror), 2017
Shellac-based, sumi and acrylic inks; flashe, oil, and graphite on canvas, 137.1 x 167.5 x 6.3 cm / 54 x 65.75 x 2.5 in; detail, overleaf

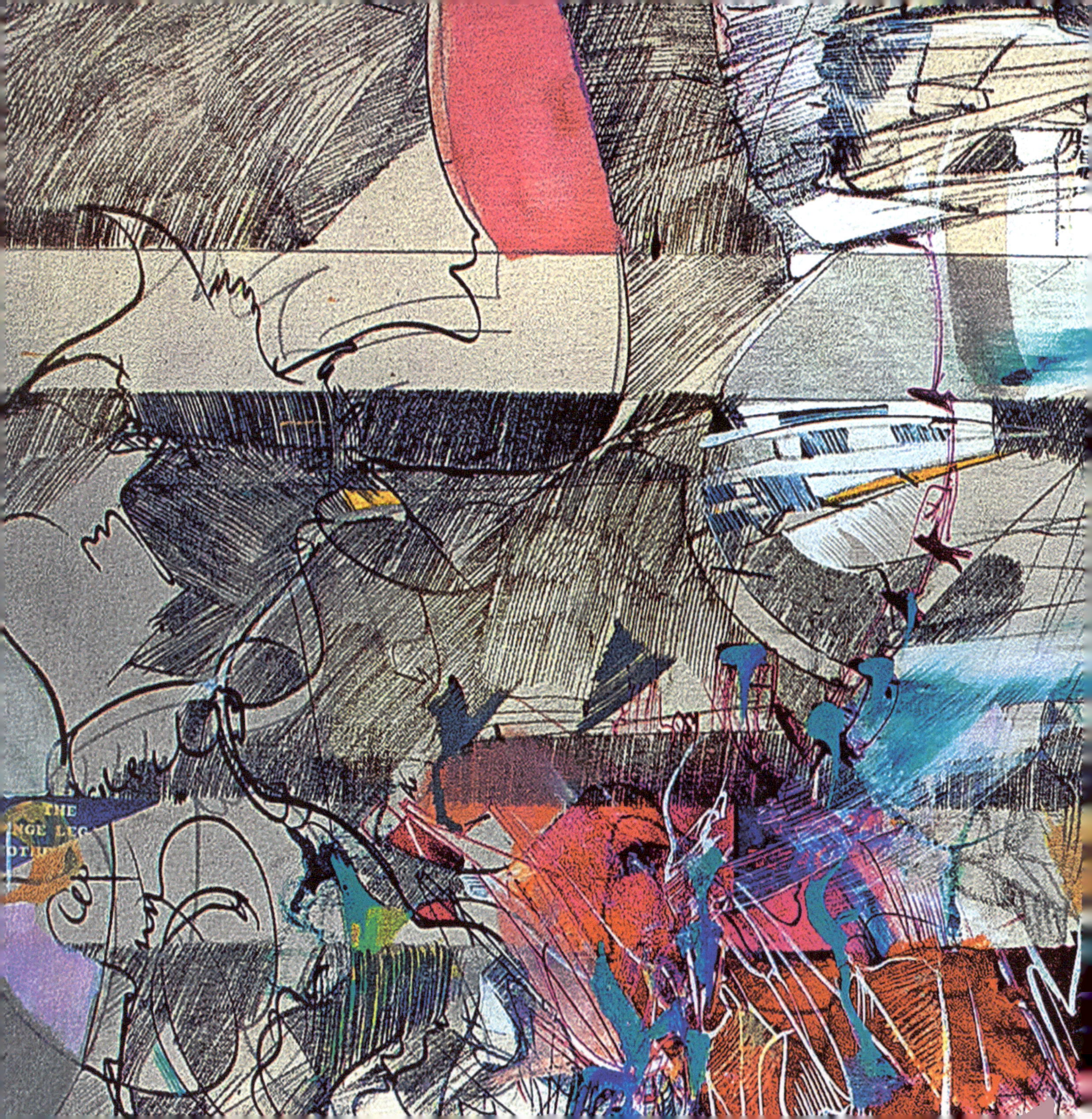

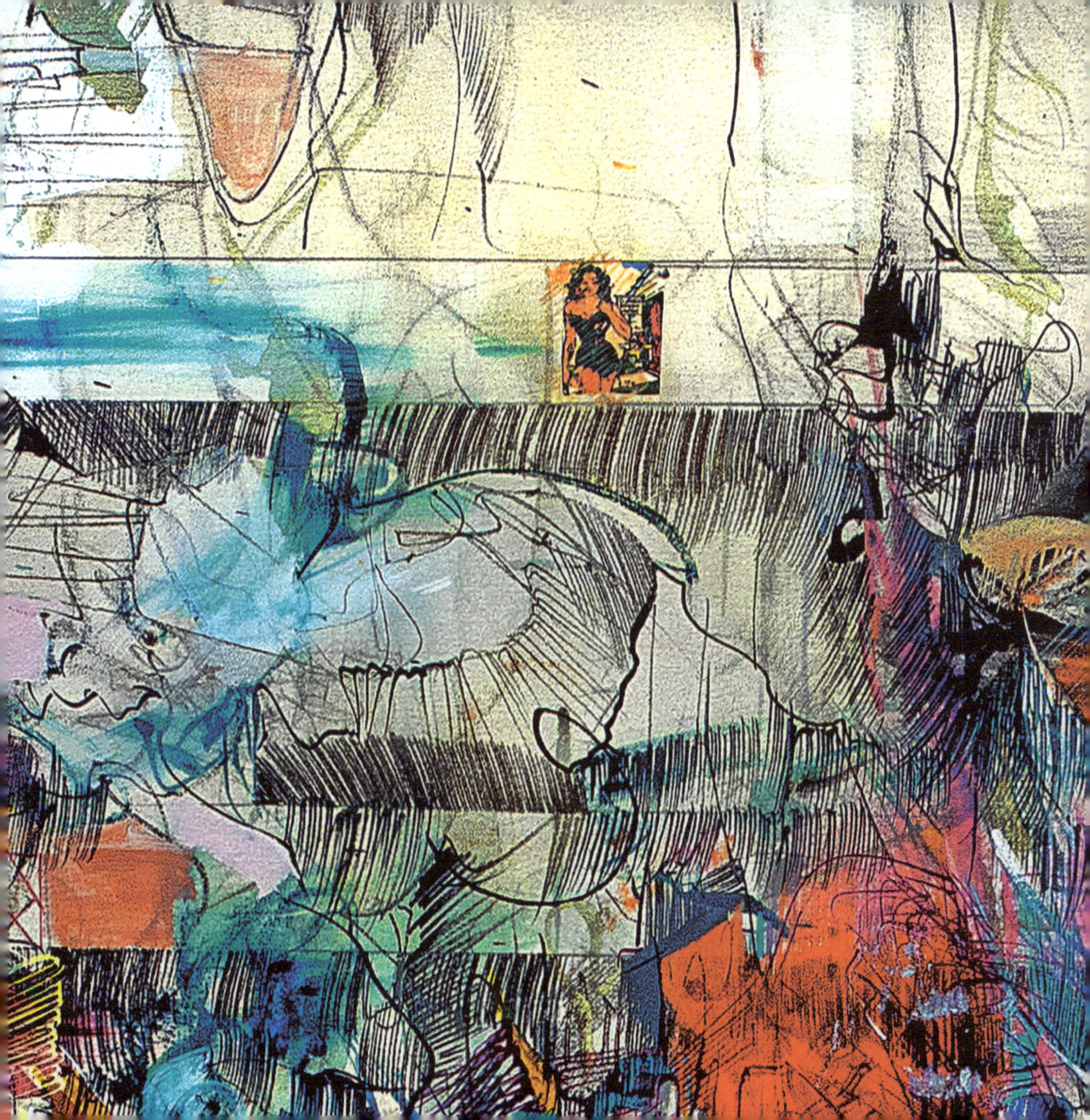

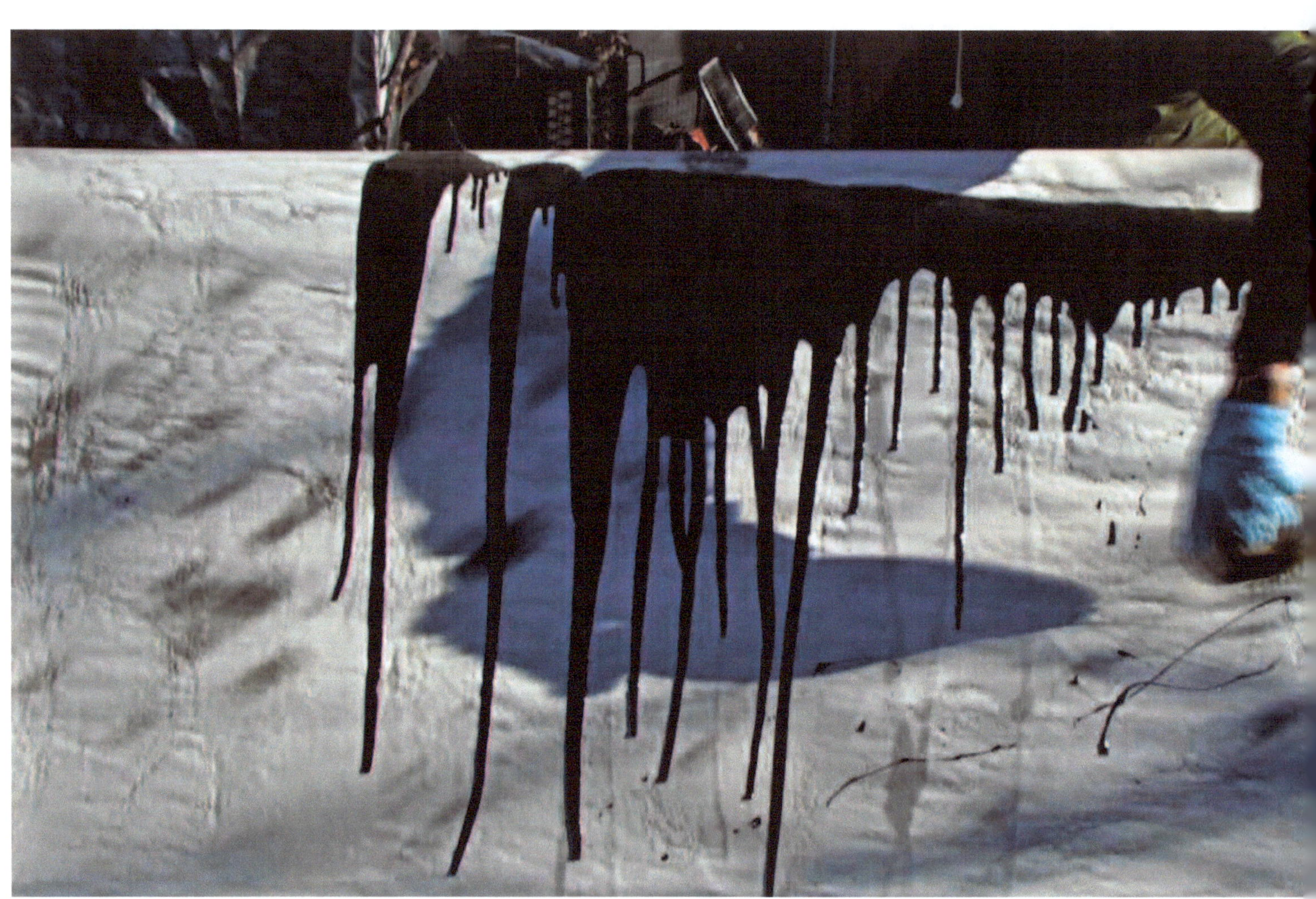

CARBON IMMEDIATE

FRAZER WARD

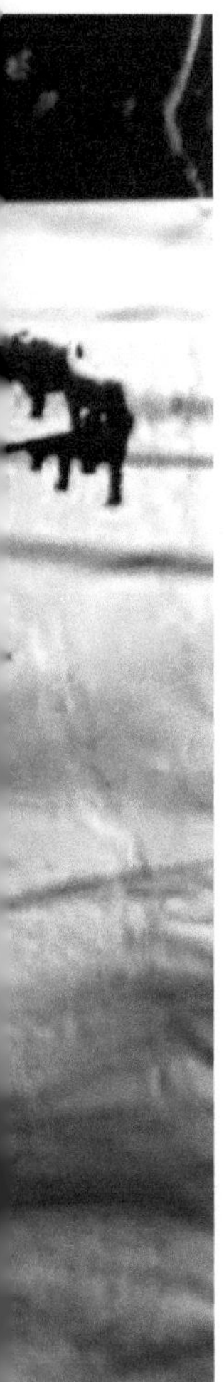

A sequence of musical notes can be a line. Three successive notes in Dmitri Shostakovich's *String Quartet No. 7*—written in 1960, by which time Shostakovich's relation to the Soviet Union was gothic in its ambiguities—are said to represent the NKVD/KGB knocking at the door. The line of notes is mimetic, but it is also a translation, from one register of sound to another; and it is an abstraction, insofar as it condenses the totalitarian percussion and accompanying affect (say, dread) into the terms of a compositional system, the rules of which are at least partly autonomous from the organization of Soviet society at the time (this is the case, even if Shostakovich was a Stalinist stooge, as some would have it). Within that compositional system, the three notes cannot only—and cannot necessarily—represent the inevitable knocking. In this instance, the sequence of notes—the line—is not only something that traverses levels or layers (the set of horizontal lines of the musical staff), it is also already a compression or layering, itself. Christina McPhee invoked Shostakovich's process in the Q&A following a 2013 performance in Brooklyn of *Carbon Song Cycle*, her work in collaboration with composer and vocalist Pamela Z, and she had referred to it in the essay of 2006 that accompanies her project, *La Conchita mon Amour*, documenting the multiple and poignant ways in which the residents of La Conchita have made their own the 2005 mudslide that ruined much of their southern Californian town.[1] *Carbon Song Cycle* montages together footage of industrial and natural energy production (e.g. geothermal plants, volcanic activity), footage from the Gulf of Mexico after the BP oil spill, or scientific visualizations of climate change (charts and graphs, more sets of crisscrossing lines). Finally, she writes,

> *[L]ive performance drawing is brought into the time-images. These performances involve burning pomegranates from our garden to make charcoal; then using the charcoal to make drawings for animation in the film…distilling liquid carbon from axle grease and pouring it onto translucent muslin stretched canvas, to emulate oil spills as painting… raku-firing ceramic urns in garbage cans filled with newspaper.*[2]

At an early moment in the performance of *Carbon Song Cycle*, McPhee draws over projected images with the light of her cell phone, casting lines across scientific visualizations of carbon concentrations. To the extent that McPhee's practice is undergirded by drawing, her home-made

Detail, *Carbon Song Cycle*, multi-channel video ensemble with music by Pamela Z, drawing performance by Christina McPhee, 2013 charcoal, for drawing, and distilled carbon, for pouring, suggest a relation between pressure and release that is important in her work, and expressed in the scribble and swoop of her line. Look at the drawings among the montage works in *La Conchita mon amour,* or the *Teorema* drawings, where fleet lines occasionally seem to escape from agitated, dense passages. If the video components of *Carbon Song Cycle* document the production of drawing's materials, McPhee's drawings themselves register the duration of their own performance intensely, which provides them with much of their drama.

McPhee's practice holds together drawing with home-made charcoal and with a cell phone; in fact, it seems to insist that they are on a continuum, from carbon to petrochemical derivatives, for her work articulates the tactility of drawing with the visualization of various kinds of data sets, especially ones related to economic globalization and environmental degradation (examples include climate change data, maps of carbon concentrations, geomorphological data following earthquakes, research tracking the effects on biodiversity of the BP oil spill, or sixteenth-century bank documents that speak to the deep history of globalization). In the context that McPhee provides, every line—charcoal, musical notes, cell phone light—embodies the expenditure of resources and energy necessary for the forms of capture and condensation that representation requires. As though metaphor were to be measured in kilojoules.

There are art historical precedents for this kind of work, often produced in collaboration with other kinds of researchers and using mixed technological means. These include work by the Gutai group in Japan following World War II, by Robert Rauschenberg and collaborators in the US in the fifties and sixties, or the intermedia and expanded cinema artists of the sixties and seventies. What McPhee brings to this loose genealogy, though, is an urgent concern with the effects of globalization on the environment. Many of the ways in which she condenses and articulates her own research and the work of scientific collaborators seem largely unprecedented. The densely-layered surfaces that she produces—whether in drawings, paintings, collages, moving-image or multimedia works involving soundscapes and live performance—ask us to rethink our environmental situation, which is at the same time to say our relation to walls of data, the lines of ones and zeros that now flicker insistently, as if they had embedded themselves beneath the skin of the phenomenal world.

Double Blind Study 33, 2012
Gelatin silver print on archival paper, 76.8 x 101.6 cm / 30 x 40 in

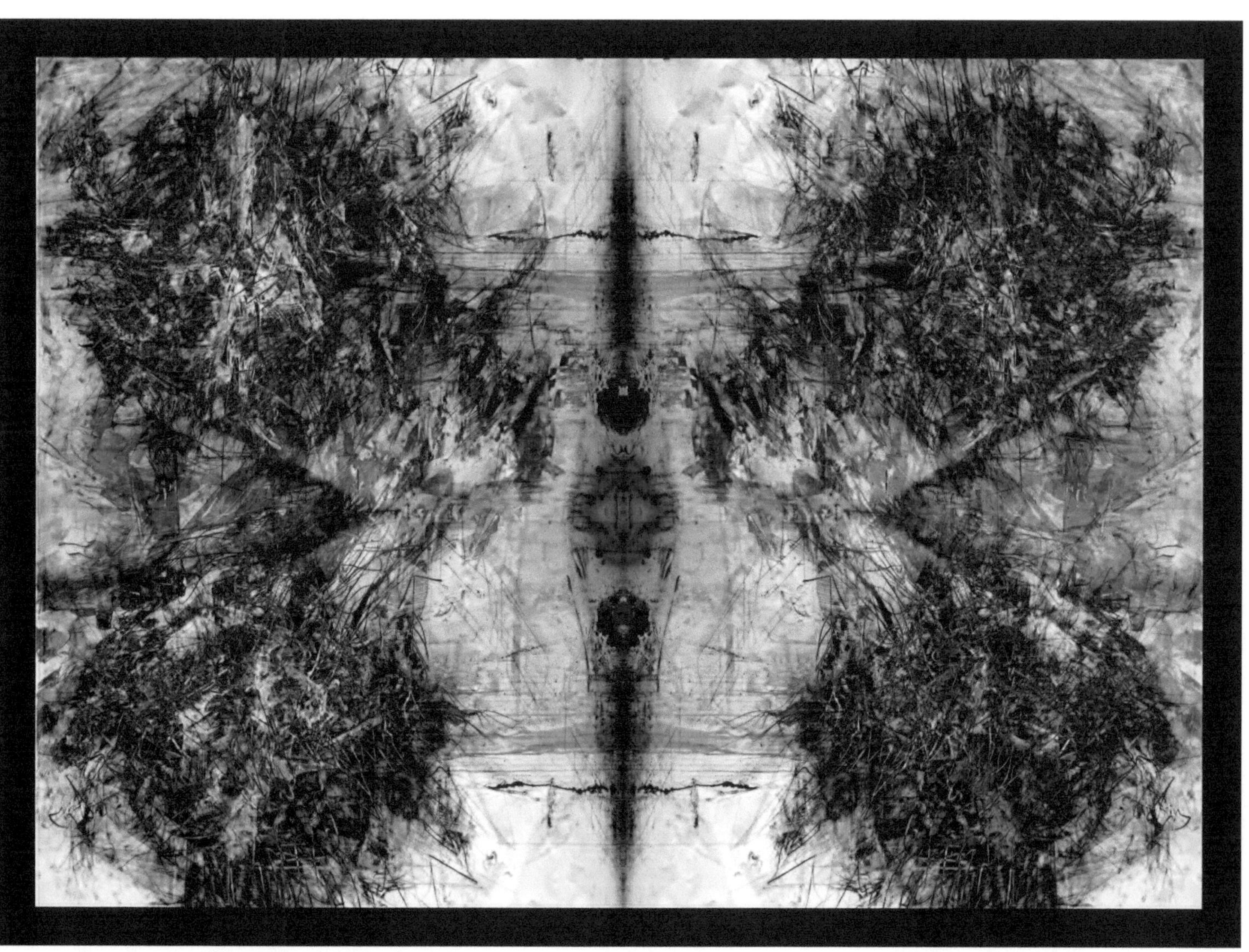

Yet even McPhee's most highly mediated works maintain a sense of immediacy. Perhaps this derives from the way that drawing remains a touchstone in her work. As much as some of her works might refer to geological time, they typically insist on the fragility of embodied time. Here one might think at the level of content of the disarmingly direct documents of La Conchita, or at the level of making of the jagging lines of her drawings, or the audible breath of Pamela Z in performance, inhaled and exhaled against McPhee's projected images of energy uses that endanger that fundamental little exchange of oxygen for carbon dioxide. This sense of vulnerability stems from the aspect of McPhee's work that reimagines drawing as energetic in a broad sense, as fully imbricated in the carbon cycle, the abuses of which are increasingly breath-taking. The line drawn on a surface (or over in the case of the cell phone light), perhaps especially the charcoal line, requiring both combustion and respiration, appears in a new strange light: a thing at once excessive, quixotic, and necessary.

[1] "In his trios and quartets, Shostakovich recast the dread of the KGB into complex motives that (...) mimetically refer to the actions of the KGB (the pounding on the door, the breakdown of the door). Shostakovich displaces those motives into fugue structures that reconstitute into architectonic reverberations both predictive and memorializing," Christina McPhee, *La Conchita mon amour* (New York: Sara Tecchia, 2006), 19.

[2] Christina McPhee, "A deep ecology of performance, landscape, and scientific visualization in *Carbon Song Cycle* and related films," www.christinamcphee.net/artists-statement-a-deep-ecology-of-performance-landscape-and-scientific-visualization-in-carbon-song-cycle-and-related-films/

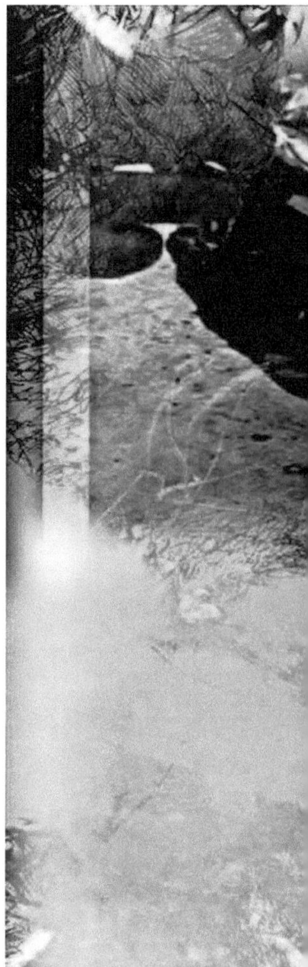

Detail, *Carbon Song Cycle*, multi-channel video ensemble with music by Pamela Z, charcoal-making performance by Caitlin Berrigan, 2013

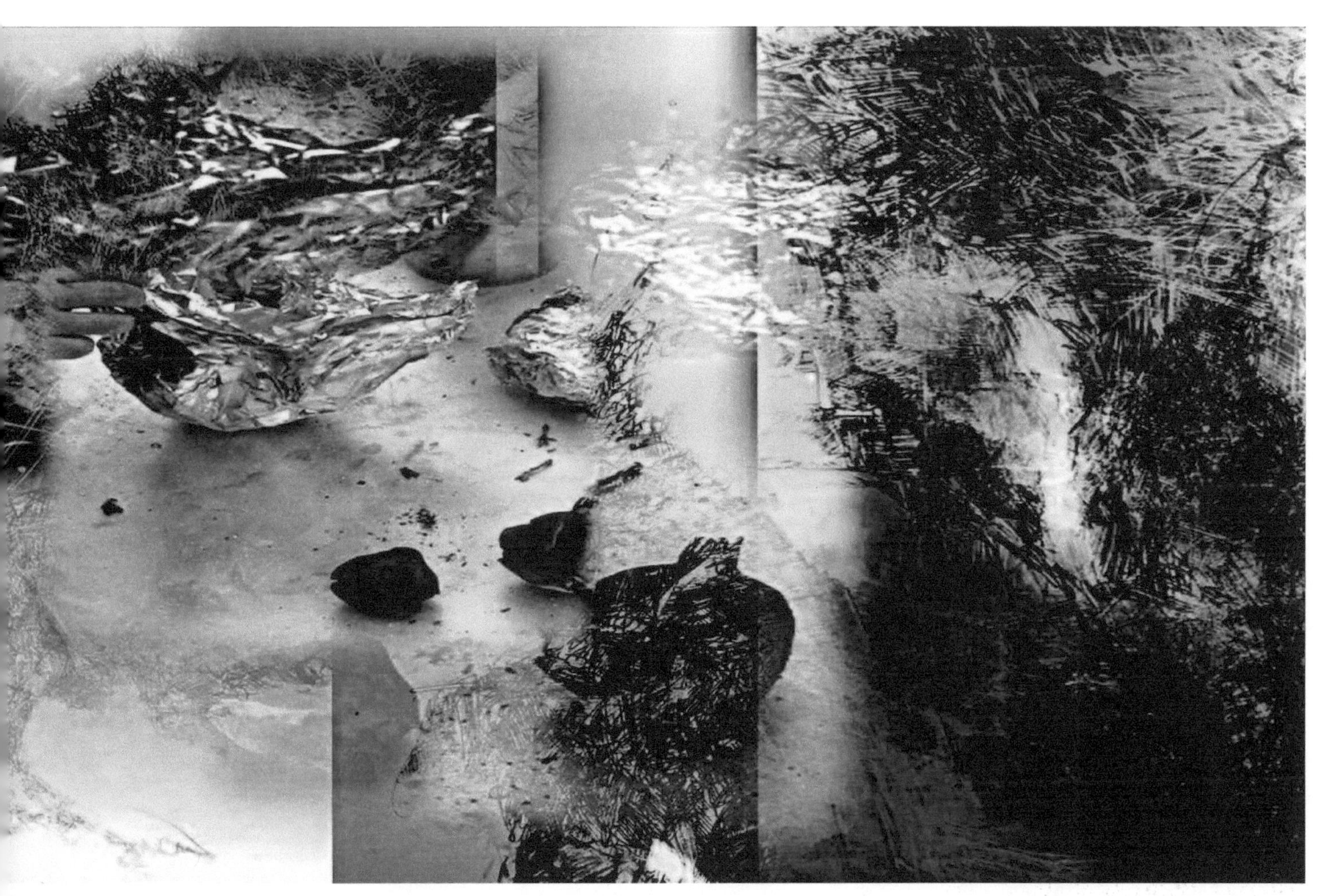

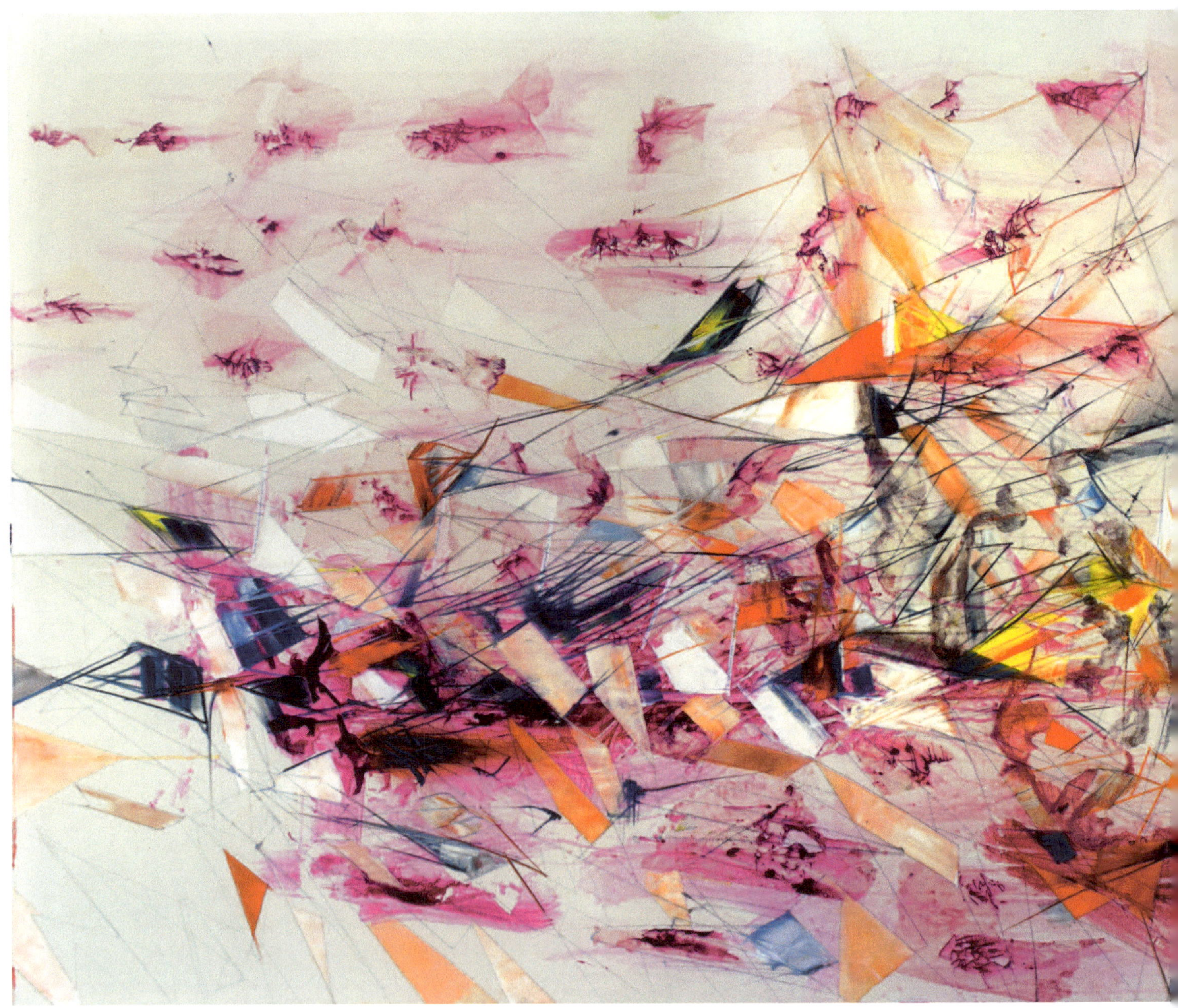

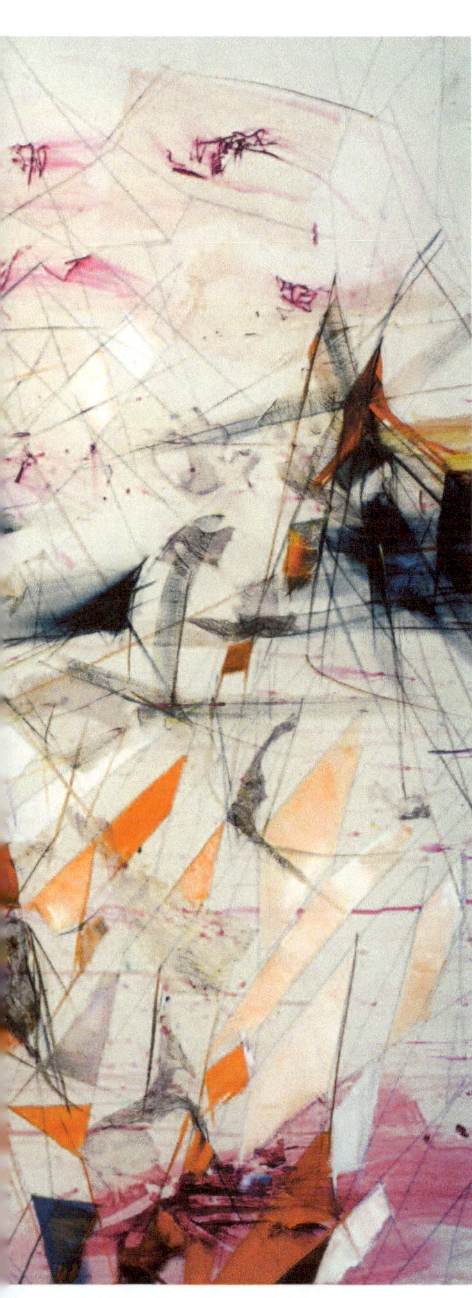

Crush Pomegranates Inseminate Agents, 2015
Ink, dye, oil, and graphite on canvas, 99 x 165.1 x 6.3 cm / 39 x 65 x 2.5 in

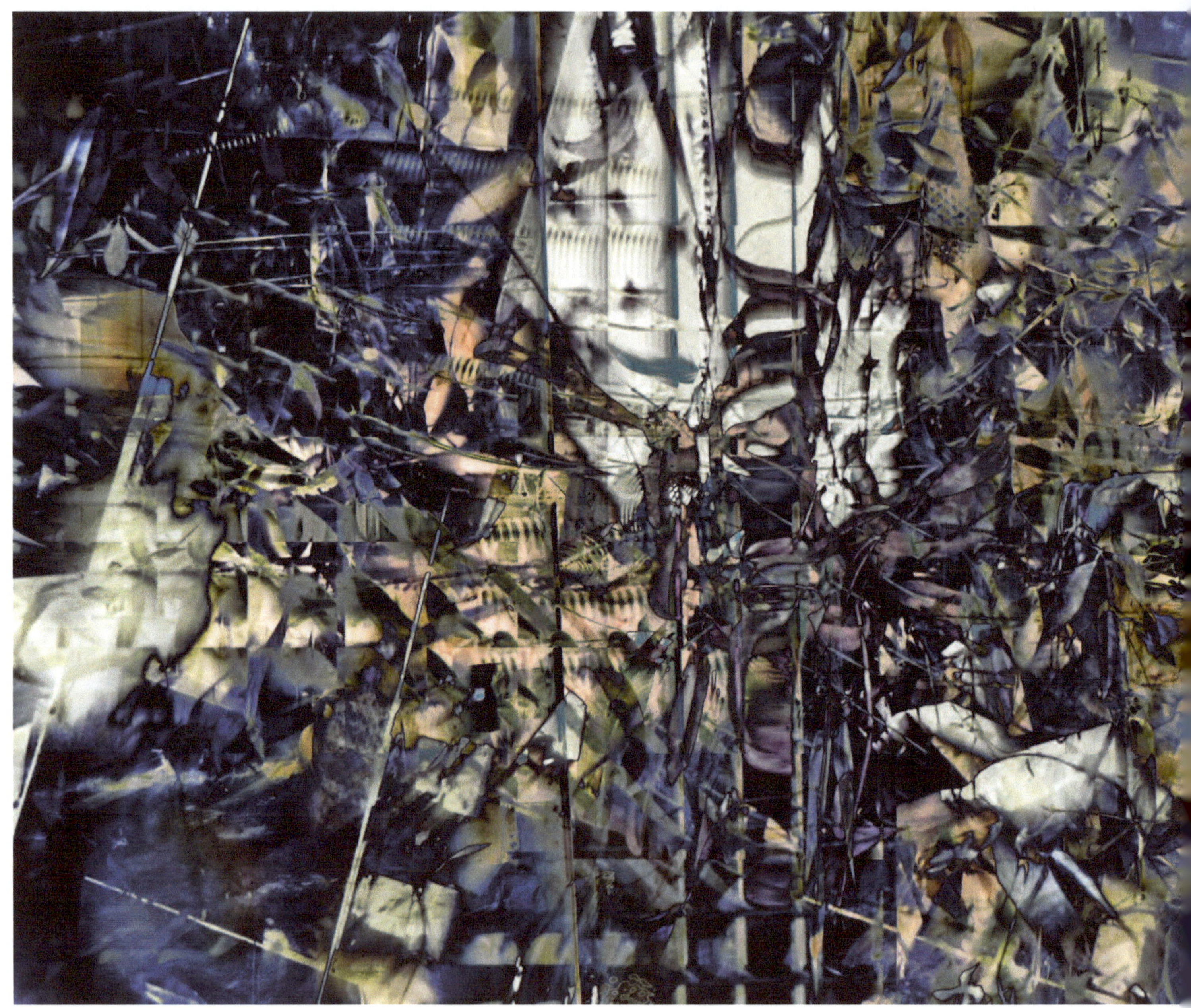

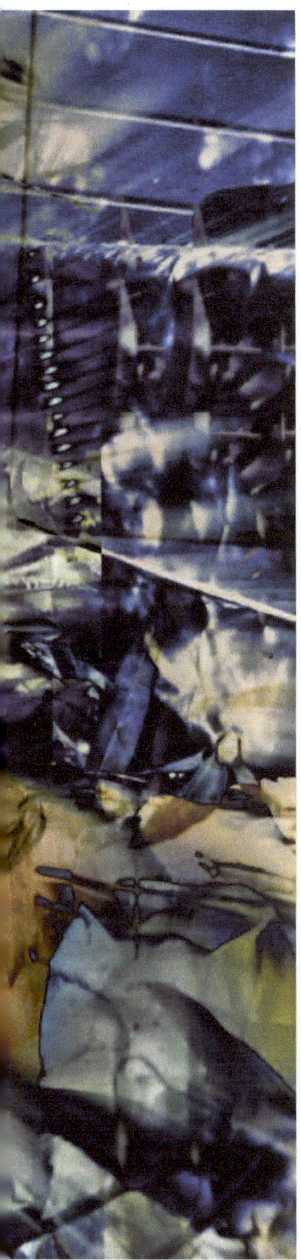

MINERAL BELIEF

INA BLOM

Two ecological moments in the history of video art. On the one hand, there is Bill Viola, discussing the animistic qualities of non-organic materials. " It is not hard to see why a great leap of the imagination is required to recognize that the material essence of the tools we engage in contemporary life, our telephones, color TVs, VCRs, and computers, are of the earth. All of these devices come from the ground, created from 'nothing', the conforming of an immaterial idea onto raw materials, animal, vegetable and mineral, gathered and distilled from the raw earth. Hidden presences all, from the metals in the chassis frame to the petroleum distillates that composed the tape and cassette boxes."[1] A "leap of imagination" is needed, since the black-boxing of media technologies make us imagine that their apparent animation, as well as their memory capacities, are essentially the effects of human input and human perceptual responses that are supported by, but in the end unrelated to, the materiality of machines as such. Such anthropocentrism was easier to uphold as long as film was the key reference, since the animation of the figures in the sequence of still images that make up a filmstrip is an illusion of the human eye/brain. With the increasing presence of electronic, signal-based technologies, such as video, temporalization and mobilization appear as an ontological condition that exists irrespective of human vision. In particular, with the emerging 1970's industry of time-based correctors and dynamic tracking technologies, the habitual focus on "visual works" or media products would temporarily get blurred by a new realm of opened-up machines, asserting a variety of microtemporalities and material processes. At the time, many had high hopes for videotape as a new archival tool for cultural memory: ultimately, the product of video was enhanced storage capacity. Viola, for his part, saw this memory in starkly "mineral" terms, as part of larger cycles of earthly transformations. The growing stacks of rapidly deteriorating videotapes signaled, to him, not just the historical archive as information overload, but, more pertinently, "a magnetic city dump."[2]

Detail, *Swampthing Industrial Soundglass,* single-channel video, with sound by Quinn Dougherty, 2017

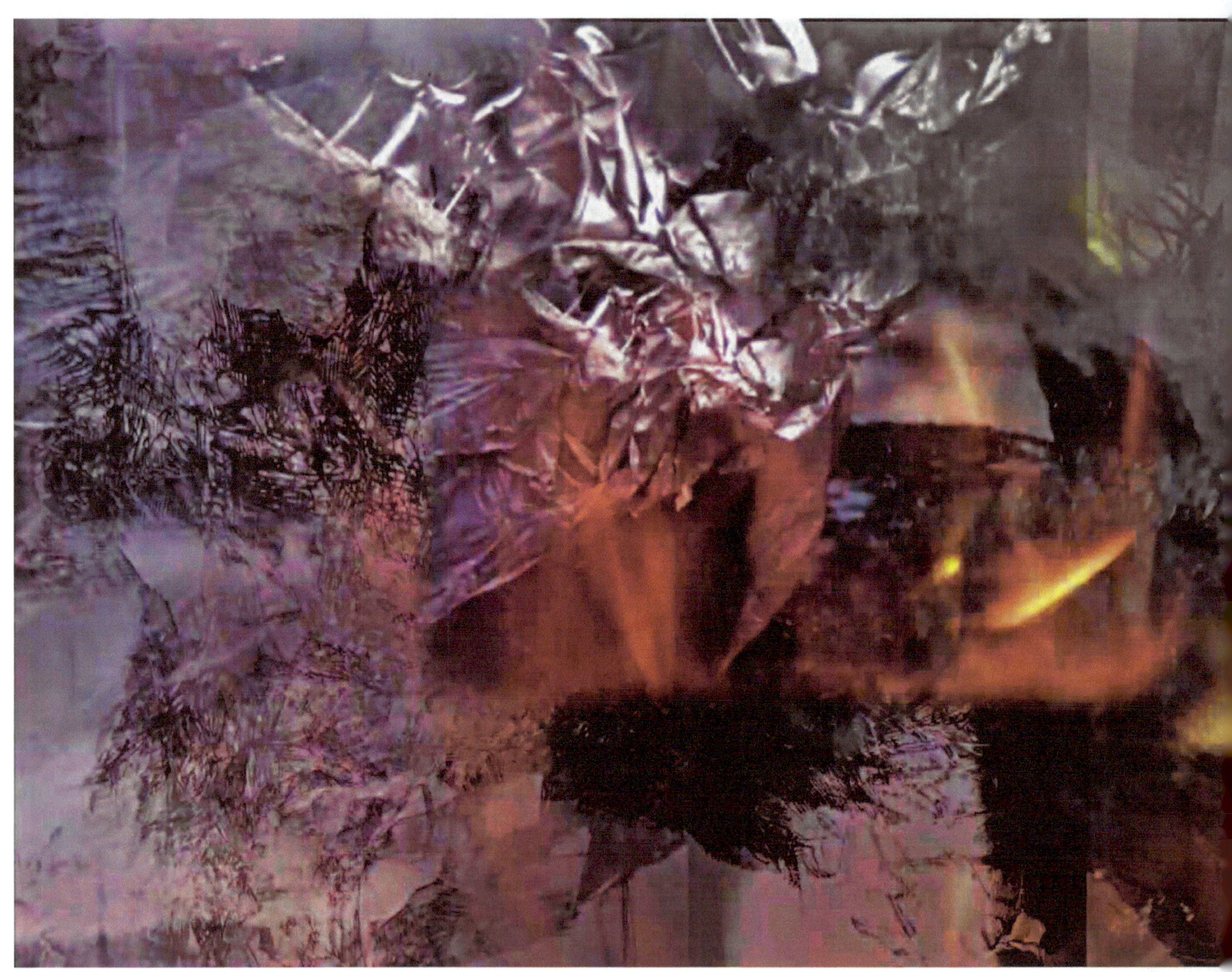

On the other hand, there is Frank Gillette, one of the founders of *Radical Software* magazine, using video as a way of positing emergent continuities between electronic and biological forms of life. "Nature" was, in other words, aligned with micro-temporalities and techniques of frequency modulation, at odds with human perception and (consequently) any traditional sense of ecopolitical "attention" directed toward known natural entities.[3] What was at stake in this strategy, was an acute emphasis on the possibility of producing new collective individuations that cut across usually separated spheres of political influence, the division between a "voiceless" nature and "vocal" political activists. Technology, here, was metaphysical or meta-technical in Buckminster Fuller's sense of the word—a globally integrative tool rather than the "destruction machinery" it had become. In the political context of the 1970's, where strategic emphasis was on the critique, subversion and guerilla action, Gillette's use of video stood out in being explicitly based on a dynamics of belief: a mode of mental formatting or infrastructure organizes the intuitions through which the future acts on the present. Belief is essentially a navigational tool, which is why Gillette spoke of video's connective affordances as a "self-organizing topology of beliefs" and associated it with the relational logic of cybernetic models.[4] But, more significantly still, belief is per definition collective in the non-contained or distributive sense of the term: it attests to the contagious dynamics of imitation and invention that, according to Gabriel de Tarde, extends across all forms of being, from the smallest mineral composites to interhuman relations.[5]

The work of Christina McPhee is in many ways a sophisticated amalgamation of these two moments, put to work in the eco-political present. Technics of various kinds conjure up a genuinely political animation of the earth itself by engaging concrete instances of mineral or biological productivity in projective dynamics of imitation or belief across media (McPhee uses the term telemimesis[6]). The general context is one of imminent crisis, evoked through reference to a number of concrete sites of energy production, destruction, or research and analysis: volcanic landscapes, oil fields in the Salinas Valley, lime kilns in Big Sur, the Konza Prairie grasslands, the Gulf of Mexico following the BP oil spills. However, the most pervasive technical mediator in this work is not electronic or digital systems, but drawing—a form of drawing characterized by expanding and contracting webs of thin lines, dotted with scattered explosions of color as if to demarcate particularly critical points of action or intersection. For this is a form of drawing that is essentially energetic: it does not provide forms and figures as much as mobilities, precarious leaps of connection from one point to another, tense thickets of activity and slower, lonelier, lines of release. If mathematics may at times use arrows to visualize the essentially abstract properties of vectorial functions or forces, McPhee's restless lines often seem to evoke similar issues of visualization. One gets the sense that the image conjured up is all at once a particular, individual, material composite (colored ink, graphite, paper, the skills of a hand) and a precarious, temporary, expression of forces for which no

Detail, *Seismic Aquifer,* single-channel video,with sound by Quinn Dougherty, 2014

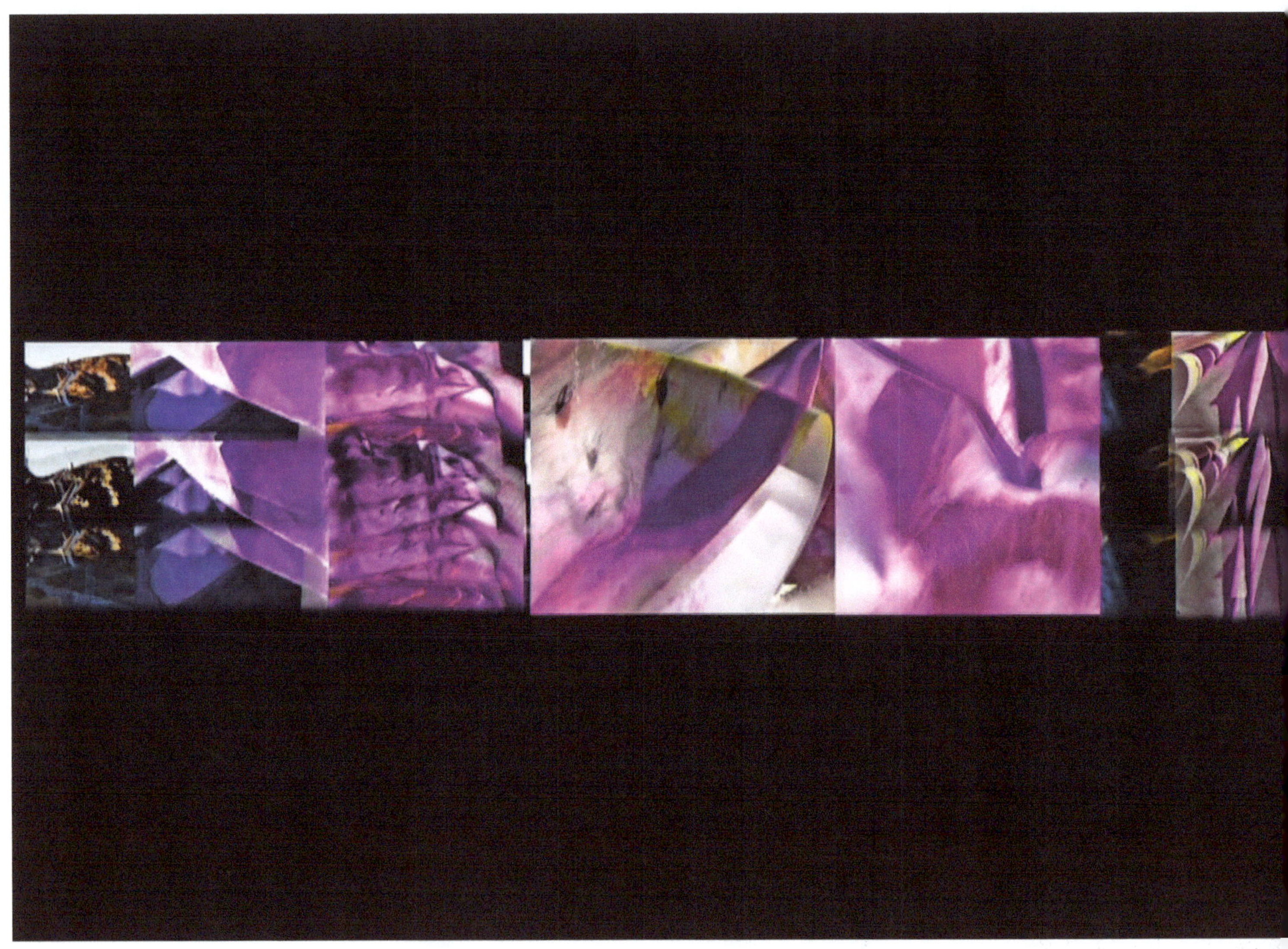

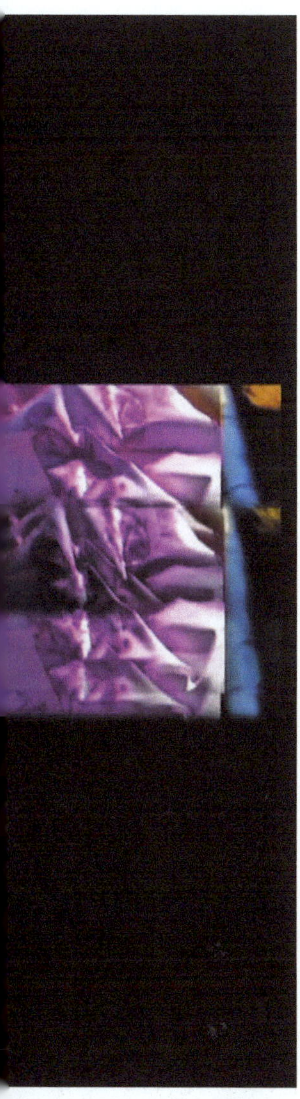

adequate, human-readable language exists. The question of drawing's mobilities is thus a question of expressive sympathy, imitation and belief in some kind of connection or association to other mobilities, however fraught or tentative. Yet it is at this level that drawing also enters into alliance with new media technologies, inasmuch as these are often seen as quasi-living forces, based on feedback circuits and vectorial operations that have the capacity of either simulating or visualizing life below the threshold of human attention. There is, however, no simplistic positing of life forms here. As the frontier of biological knowledge hovers uncertainly between genetic and computer codes, life itself is, as Eugene Thacker has shown, in any case a troubling and contradictory concept, whose metamorphic quality is witnessed in the essentialist concept of "life itself" as in formation, as well as in the proliferation of vitalisms and the pervasive politicization of all life.[7] McPhee's drawing, extended to and infiltrated with digital video, seems to outline a different and stranger project: that of creating as yet unknown material composites by aligning the rapid time-processing of our nervous systems with the emergent natures at actual sites of energy production or extraction. These are, as she explains in a note to the single channel installation video *Tesserae of Venus: Ghostdance* (2009), usually rejected or neglected natural areas, like marginal streambeds, riverbeds, swamps or sloughs in estuaries near the ocean, places that provide the large amounts of water needed for cooling. In such places, things are decomposed and recomposed: assemblages of disconnected elements are thrown together, their point of contact making up a kairotic moment that can be mimed and propagated by video montage. Thanks to video, the promise and desperation of these sites—their striving—can be "condensed," "extracted," and reanimated. This is a distinctly futurist form of eco-sensitivity, a state of affective engagement that is less attuned to the condition of existent beings (however important they may be) than to the sense of future crisis that colonizes the present moment. An acute feeling for an event that has already not yet happened produces some sudden and unfamiliar sedimentations—present in almost all of her work but perhaps most explicitly articulated in the project that takes as its inspiration the complex ridged folds or deformations that mark the planet Venus—a planet that does not have the Earth's tectonic strike-slip faults, and whose generative land building may possibly be an effect of its heavy, ninety-six percent carbon dioxide atmosphere. Strange folding events, propagating across a number of media and sites in McPhee's work, from inside electronic equipment to crumpled paper surfaces, may thus be a visitation from a carbon-intensive future. What we have here are, essentially, geological leaps of imagination, or belief, taking place within and through the mineral worlds that are at any time hard at work in video and sound technologies, as well as in pencil, paper and liquid airbrush paint.

Detail, *Tesserae of Venus (Ghostdance)*, single channel video, with sound by Pauline Oliveros, 2009

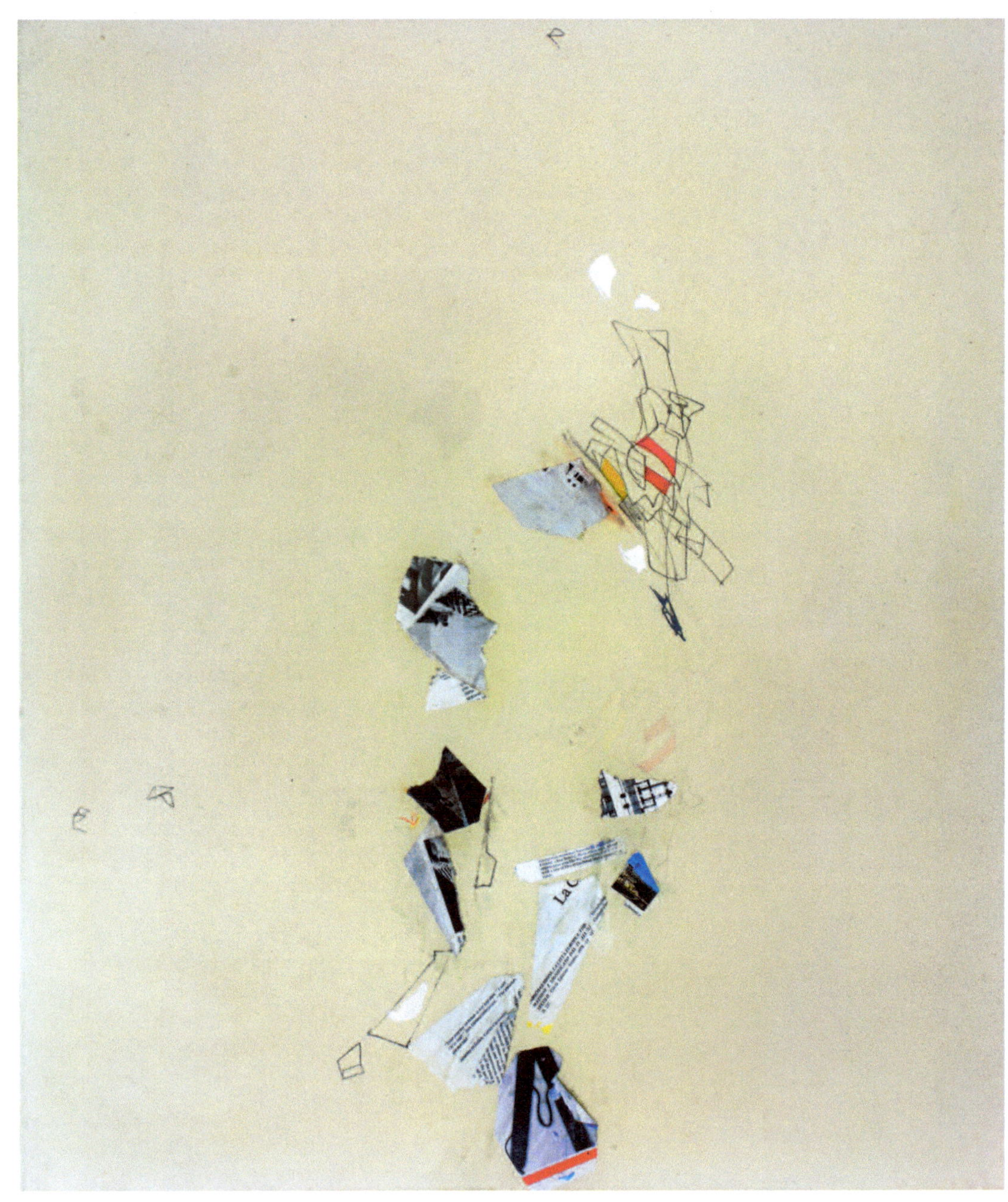

[1] Bill Viola, "Landscape as Metaphor" (response to questions from Martin Friedman, 1993), *Reasons for Knocking at an Empty House: Writings 1973-1994* (Cambridge: MIT Press, 1995), 254. Similar intuitions inform many technocentric texts of the period, among others Gene Youngblood's *Expanded Cinema* (New York: P. Dutton & Co, 1970), 53: "What happens to our definitions of 'material' and 'spiritual' when science has found no boundary between the two? Although it is still popularly assumed that the world is divided into animate and inanimate phenomena, virologists working at the supposed threshold between life and non-life at the virus level have in fact discovered no such boundary. 'Both animate and inanimate have persisted right across yesterday's supposed threshold in both directions...subsequently what was animate has become foggier and foggier...no life, per se, has been isolated.'" The quote at the end is taken from Buckminster Fuller's "Planetary Planning," the Jawaharlal Nehru Memorial Lecture, New Delhi, India, November 13, 1969.

[2] Viola, 125 ("History, 10 Years, and the Dreamtime").

[3] Key examples are works such as *Quidditas* (1974-75) and *Symptomatic Syntax* (1981).

[4] Frank Gillette, *Between Paradigms: The Mood and its Purpose* (New York: Gordon & Breach, 1973).

[5] Gabriel de Tarde, *On Communication and Social Influence: Selected Essays*, ed. Terry N. Clark (Chicago: University of Chicago Press, 1969), 177–208; and *Social Laws. An Outline of Sociology* (London: Macmillan, 1899).

[6] Christina McPhee, "Sense of Place and Sonic Topologies: Towards a Telemimetic Sublime in the Data Landscape," http://www.christinamcphee.net/texts/slipsonictopos.htm.

[7] Eugene Thacker, *After Life*. (Chicago: University of Chicago Press, 2010), ix–xvi.

Line of Flax in His Hand, 2017
aper collage from *Archetype* and *Domus*, ink, oil paint and graphite on canvas, 97.7 x 81.2 cm / 38.5 x 32 in

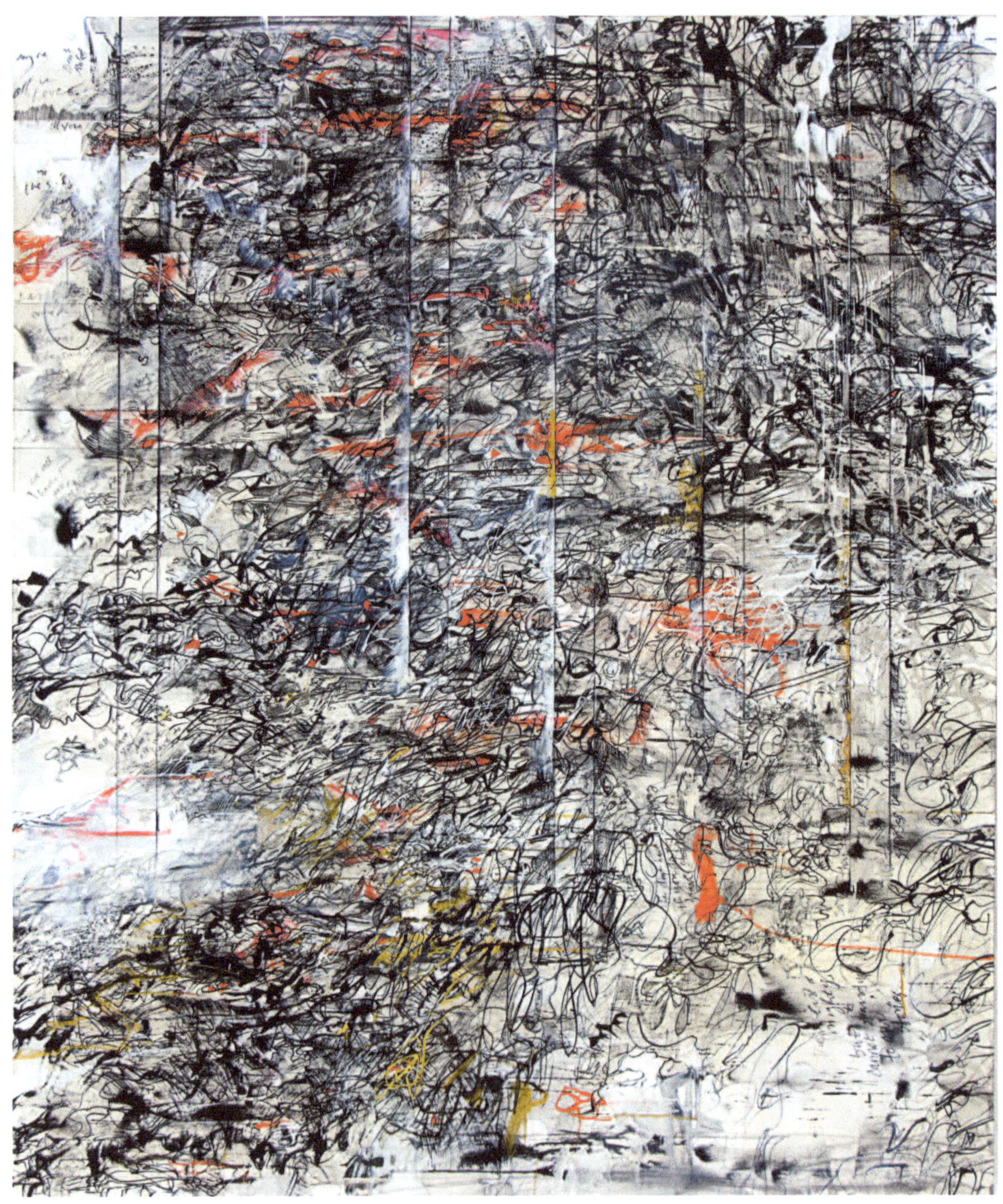

Moonbeam Redaction (After Leslie Marmon Silko), 2016
Ink, flashe, watercolor, graphite, rabbit skin glue on canvas, 167.5 x 137.1 cm / 65.75 x 54 in

Detail, opposite and overleaf,, *Moonbeam Redaction*

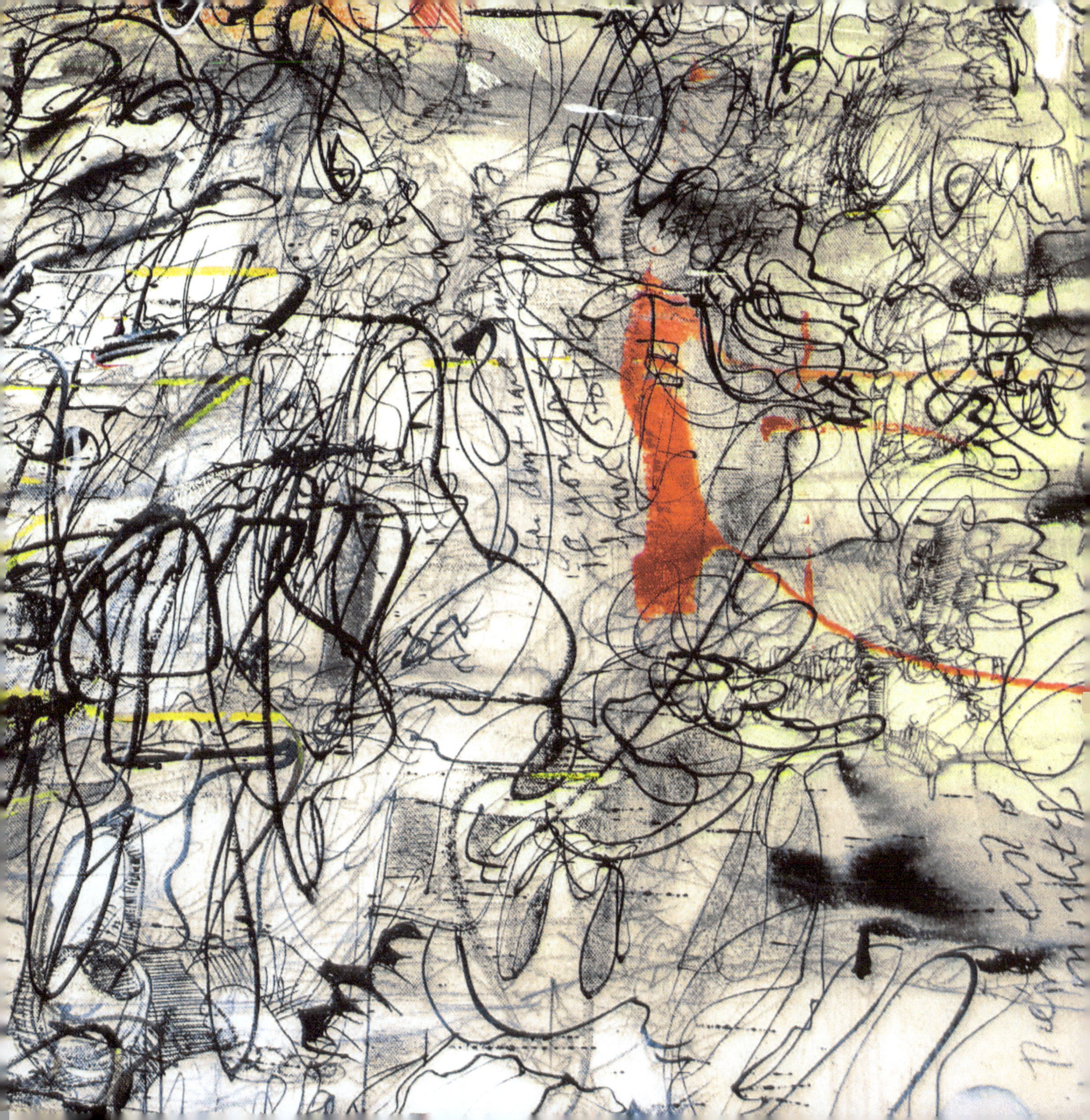

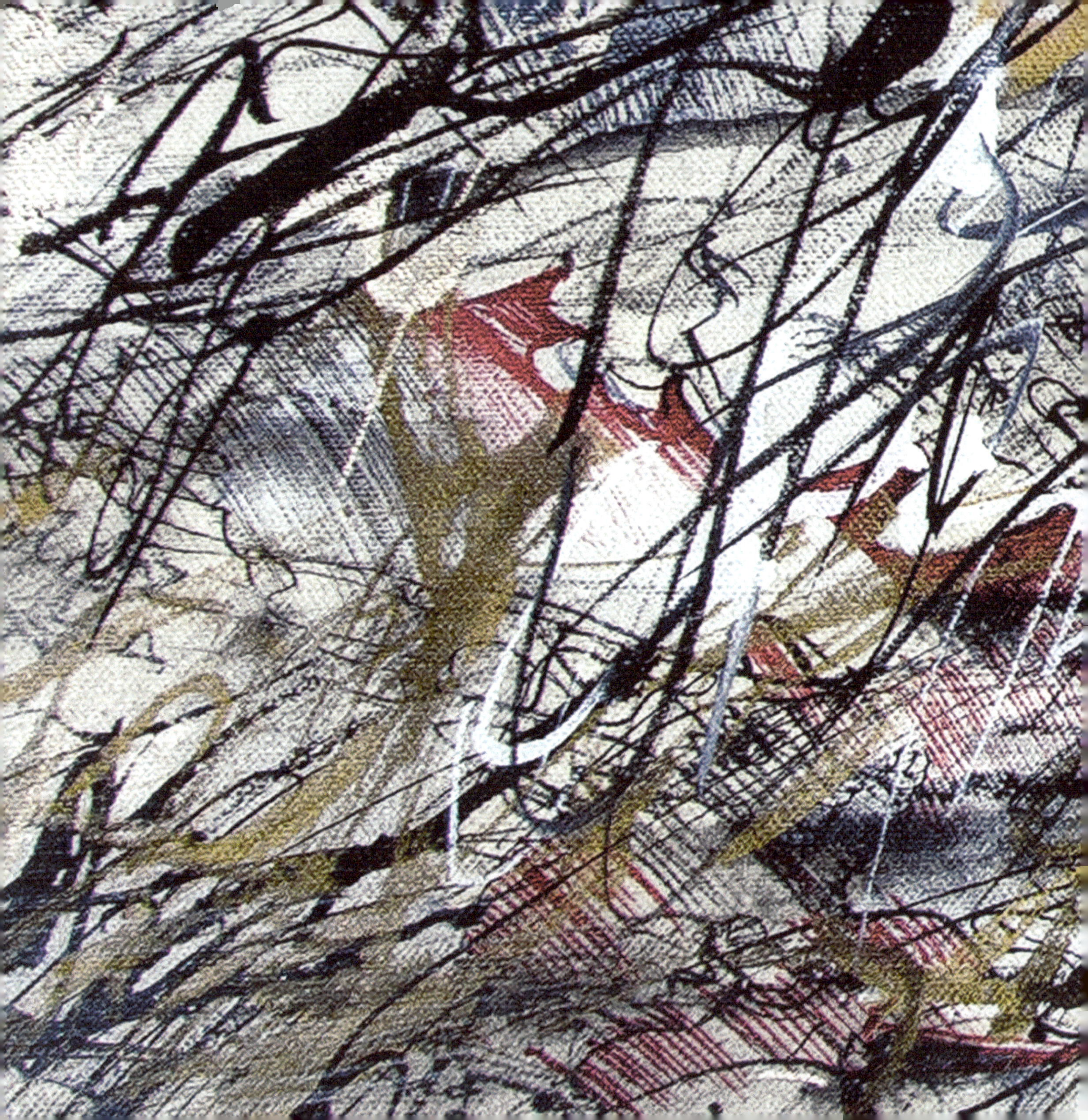

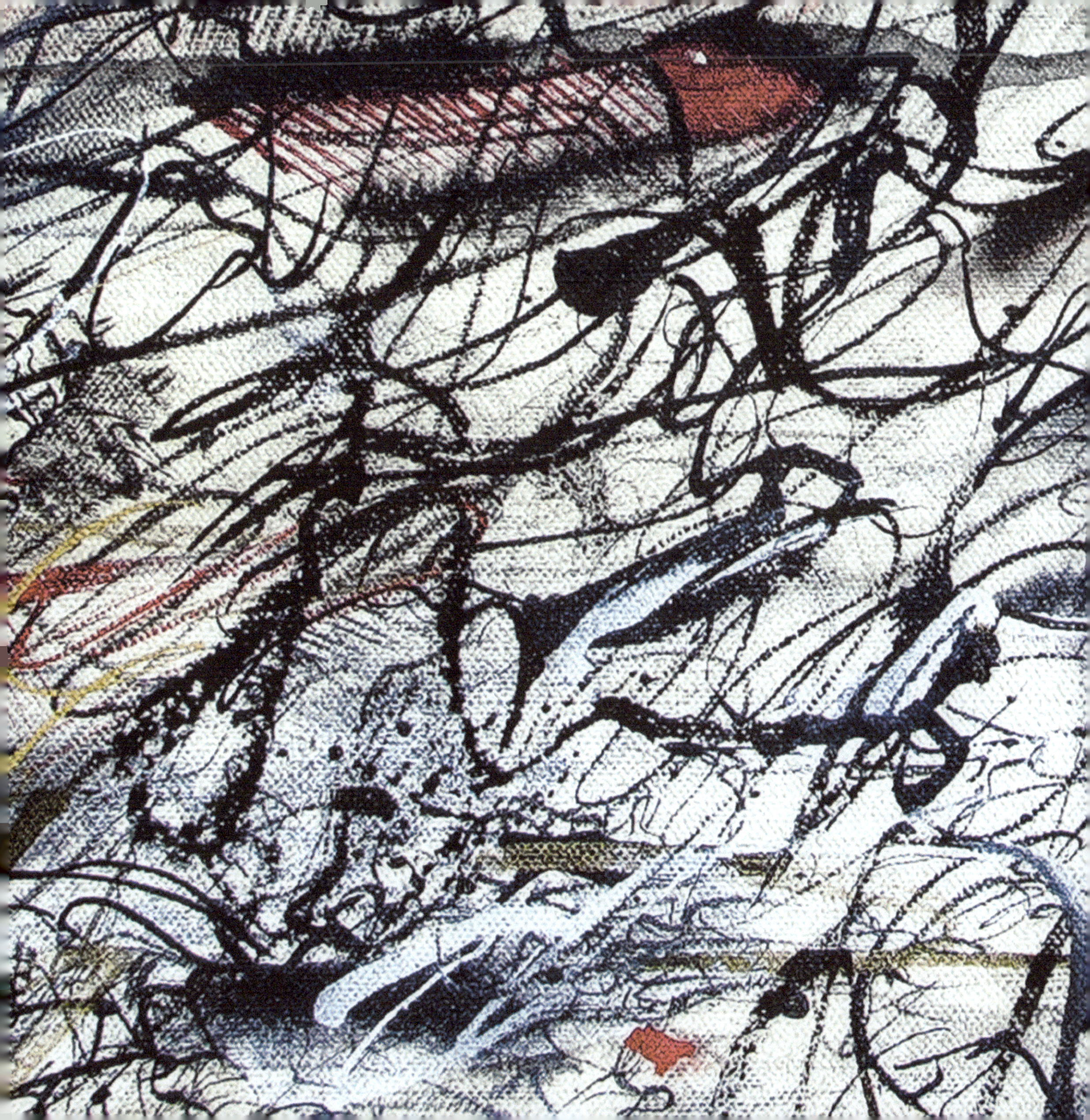

Double Blind Study 21, 2012
Gelatin silver print on archival paper, 76.8 x 101.6 cm / 30 x 40 in

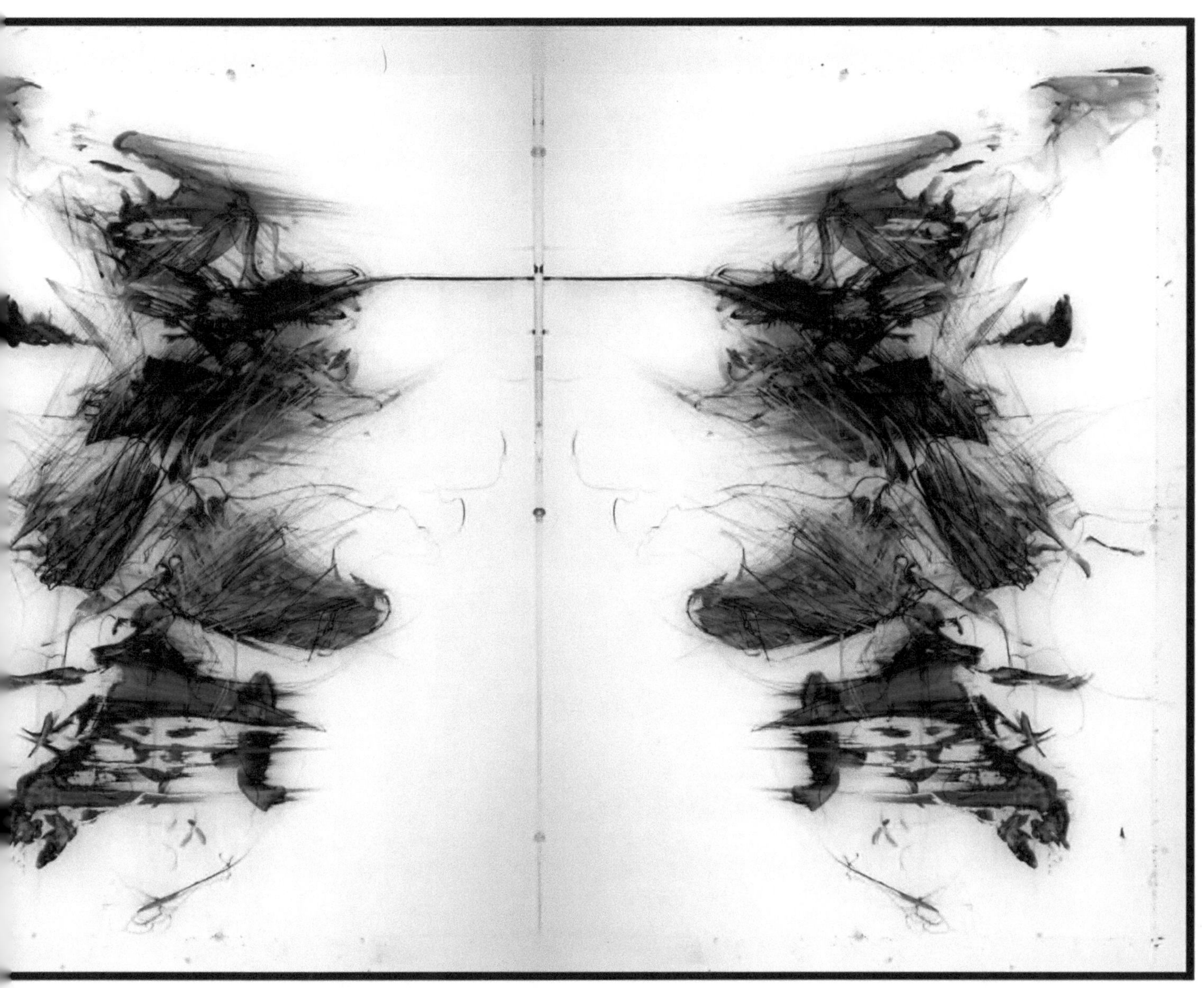

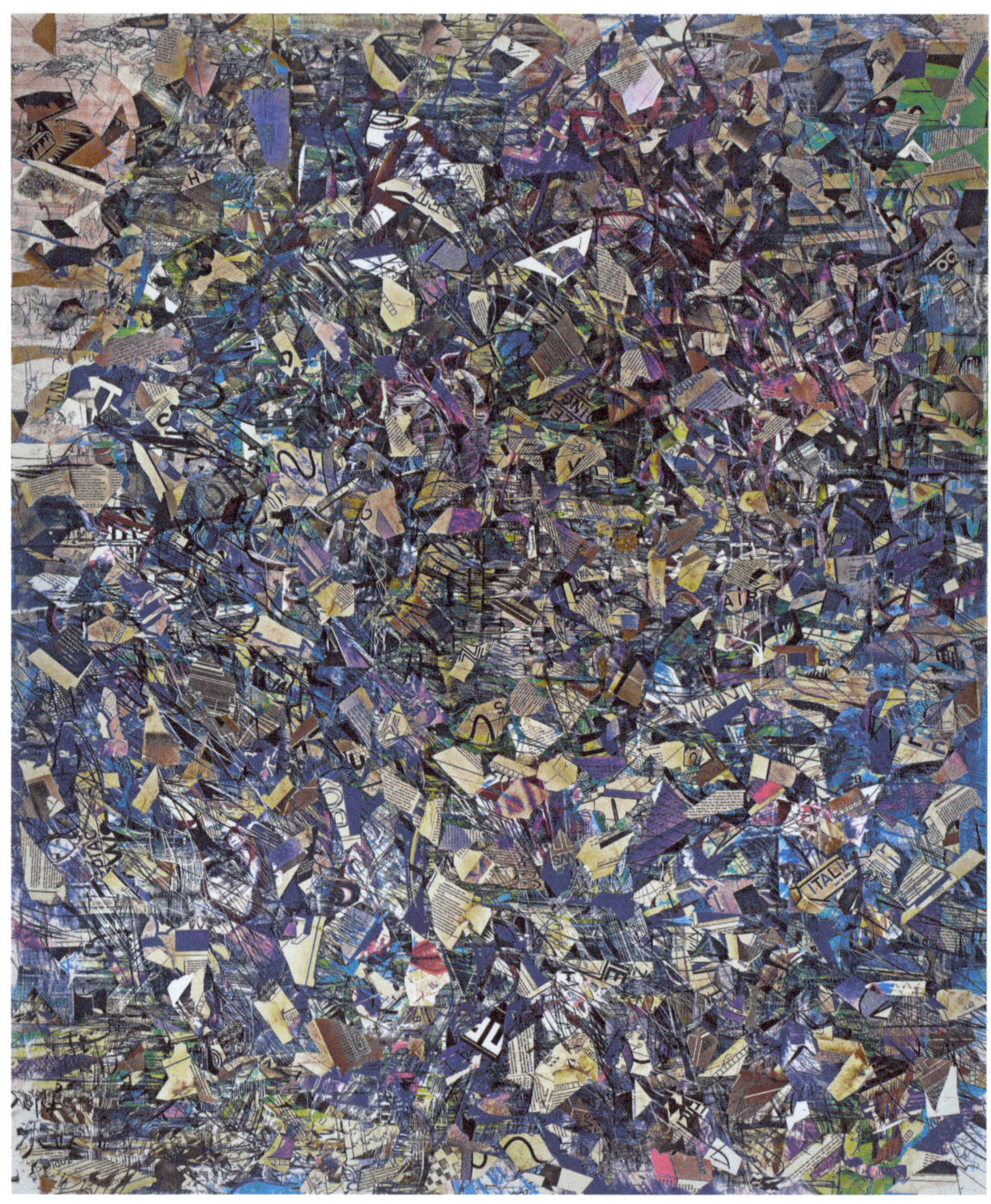

Aliens Rivulet, 2017
Ink, oil and acrylic paint, paper collage from *Wet Magazine*, 1980, on canvas, 165.7 x 137.6 x 6.3 cm / 65.25 x 54 x 2.5 in

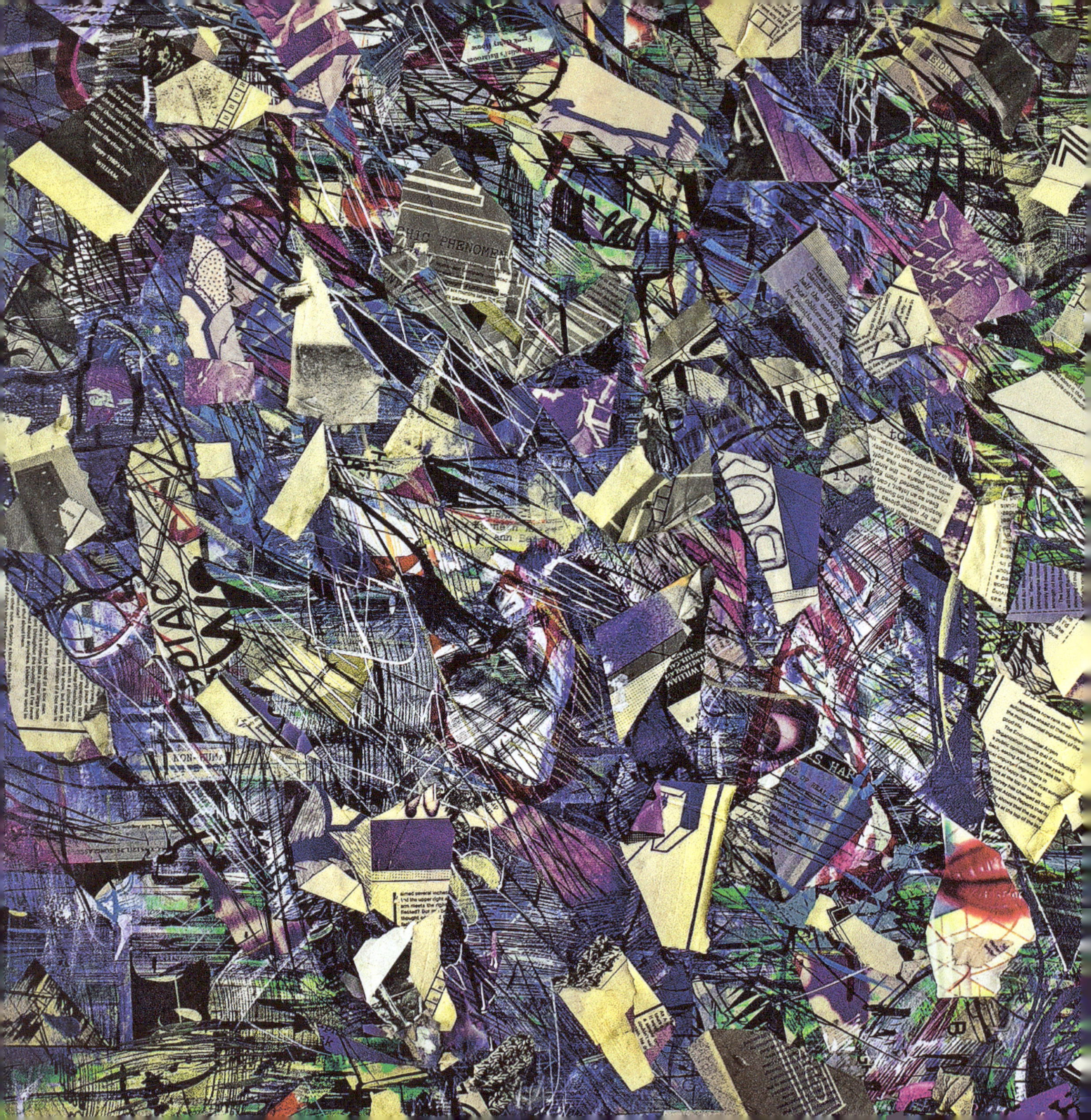

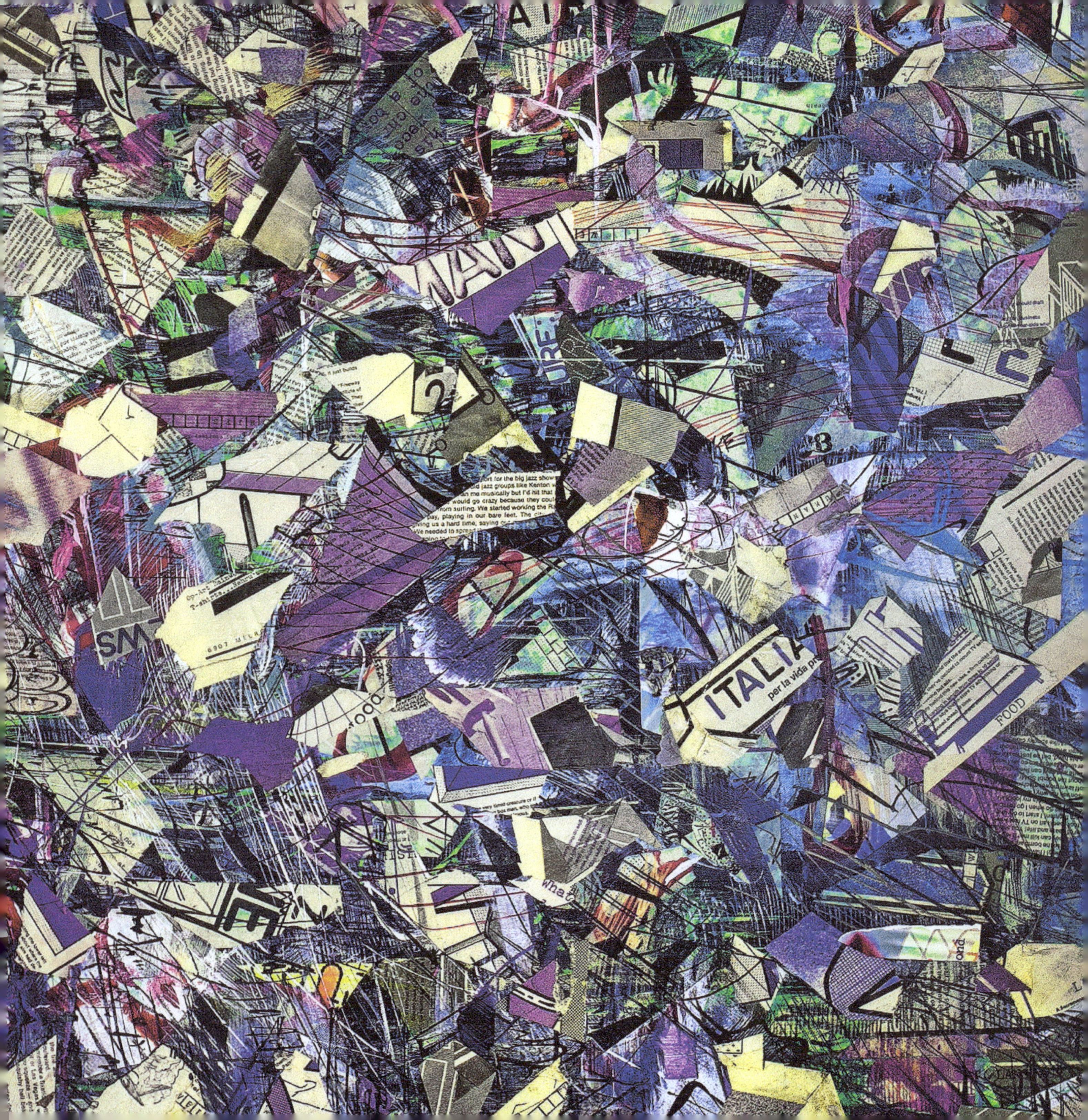

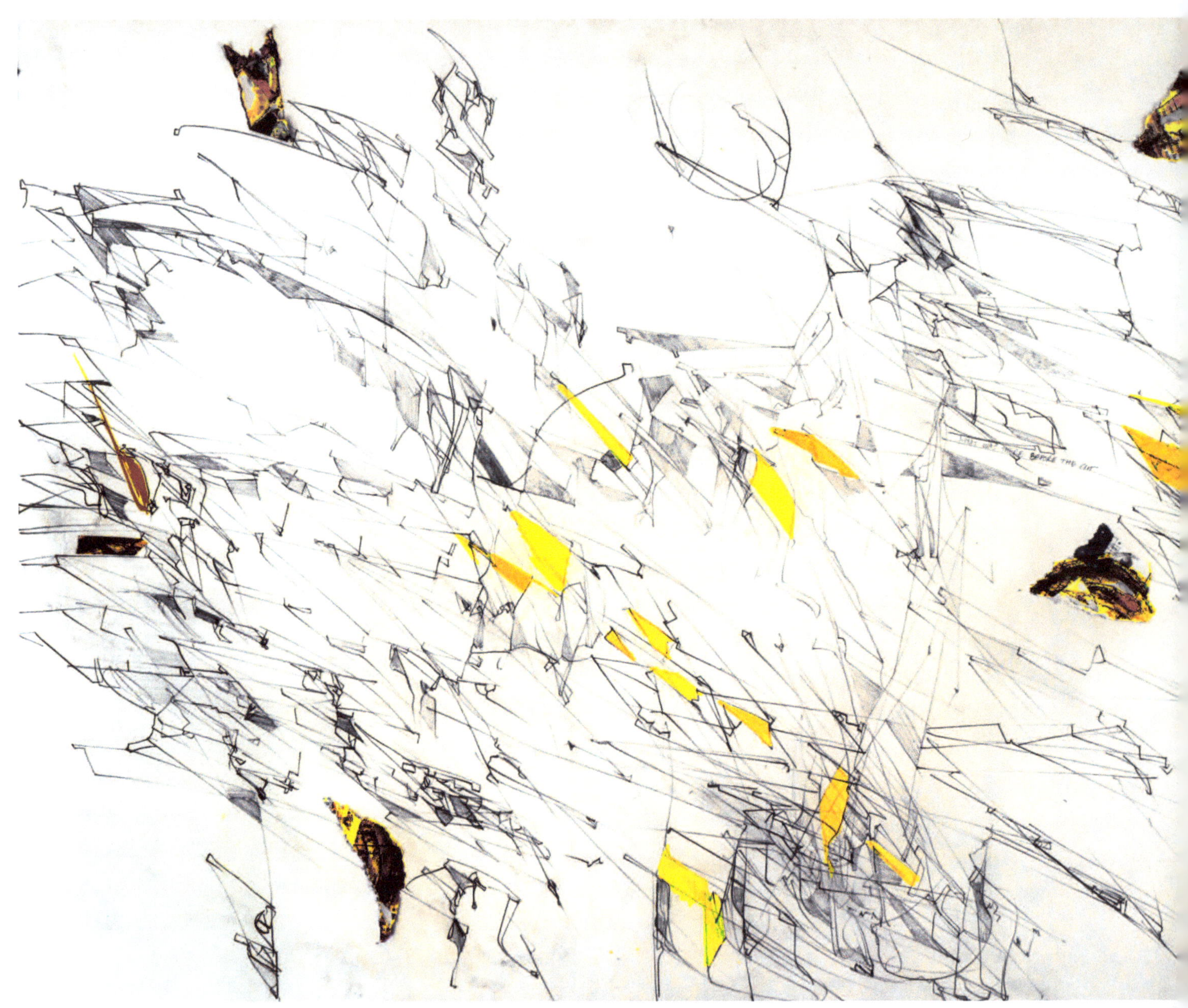

Before the Cut (After Annie Proulx), 2017
Graphite, crayon, ink, and found magazine collage, 55.8 x 76.2 cm / 22 x 30 in

Double Blind Study 49, 2014
Gelatin silver print on archival paper, 76.8 x 101.6 cm / 30 x 40 in

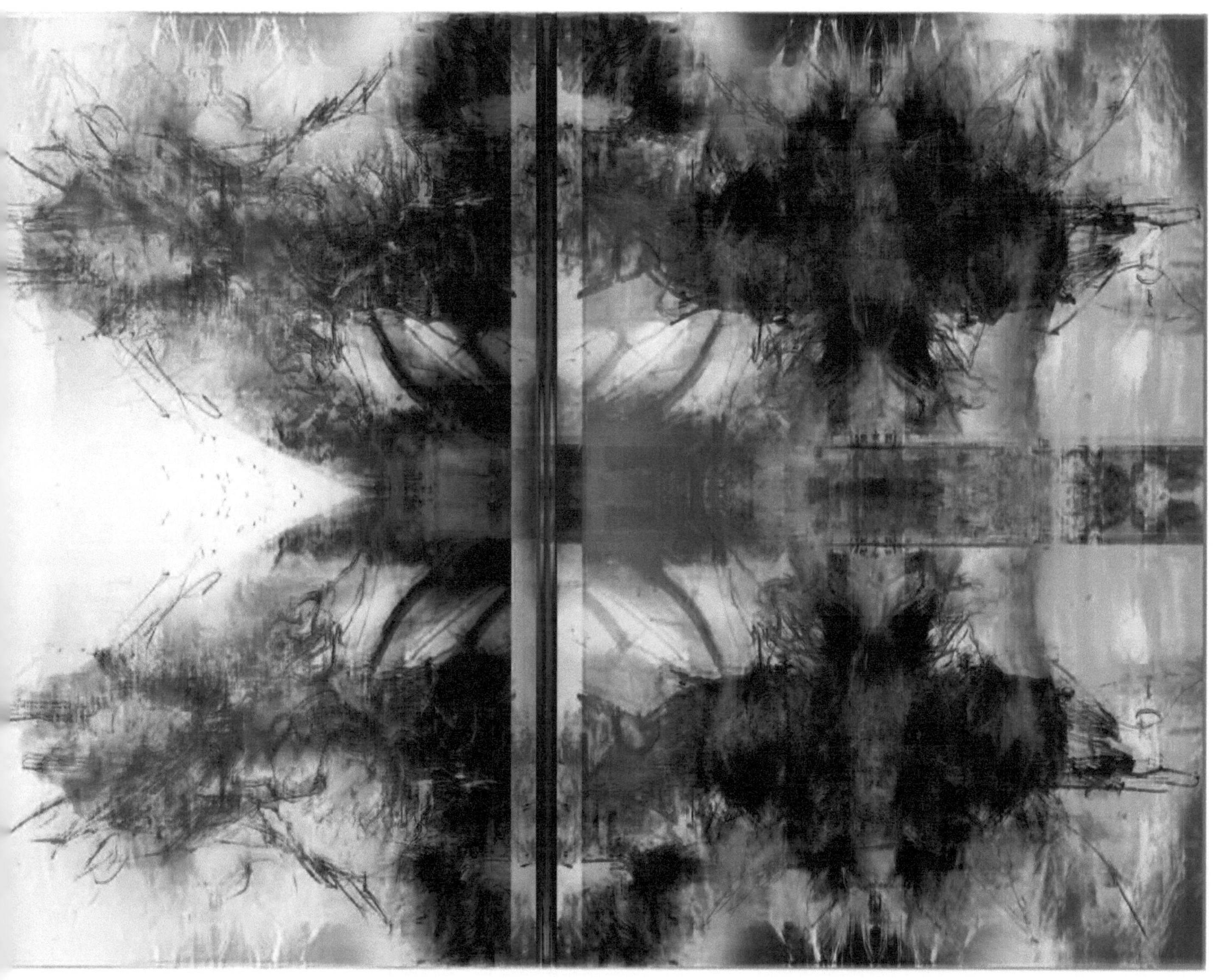

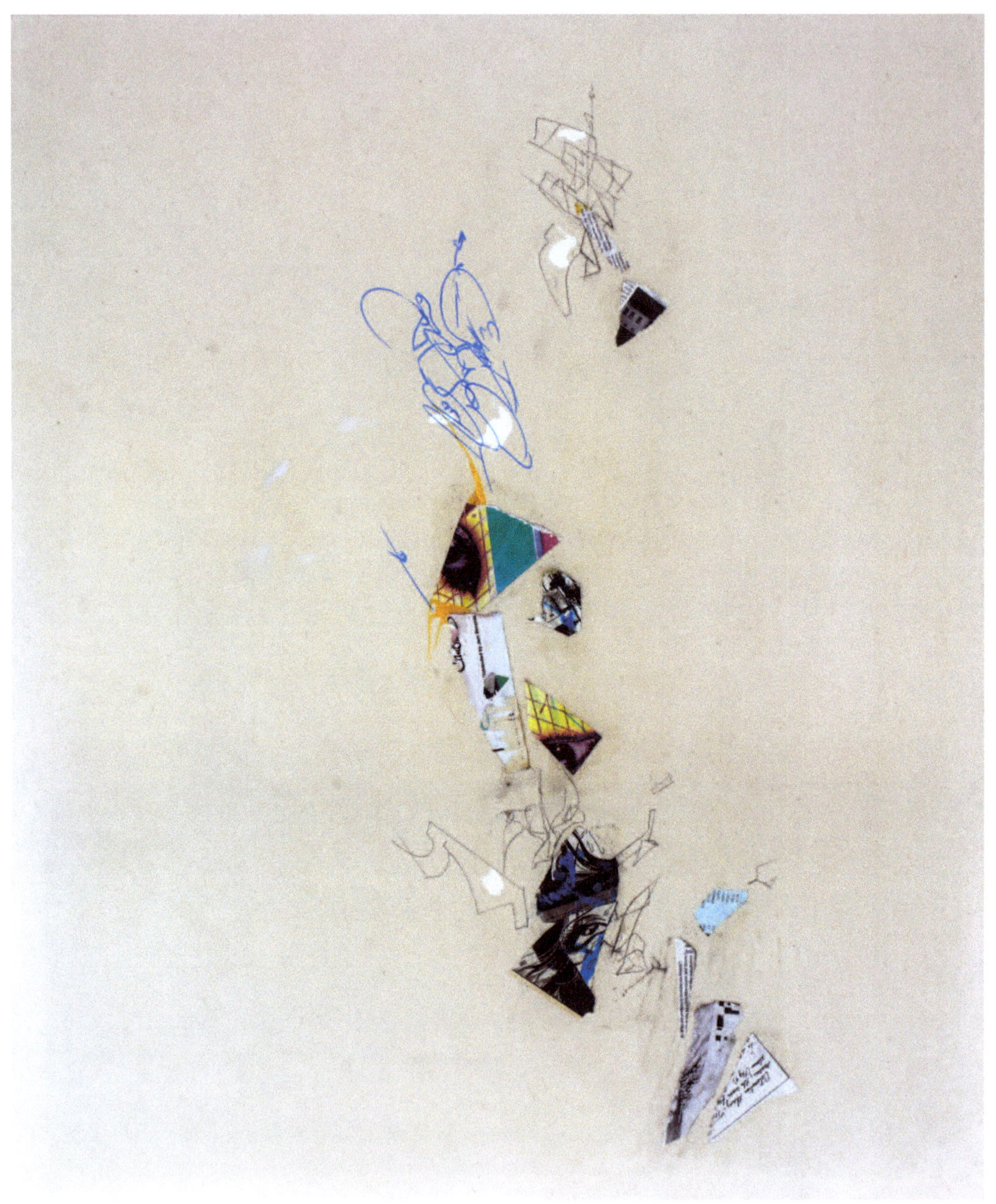

INTERVIEW: THE POLITICAL AESTHETICS OF NATURE

DONATA MARLETTA WITH CHRISTINA MCPHEE

This interview was first published on *Digicult* in February 2017.
Permalink: http://www.digicult.it/news/christina-mcphee-political-aesthetics-nature/, Italiano/English, translation by Donata Marletta.

The Eyes of All Wait, 2017
Paper collage from *WET Magazine*, ink, oil paint, and graphite on canvas, 97.7 x 81.2 cm / 38.5 x 32 in

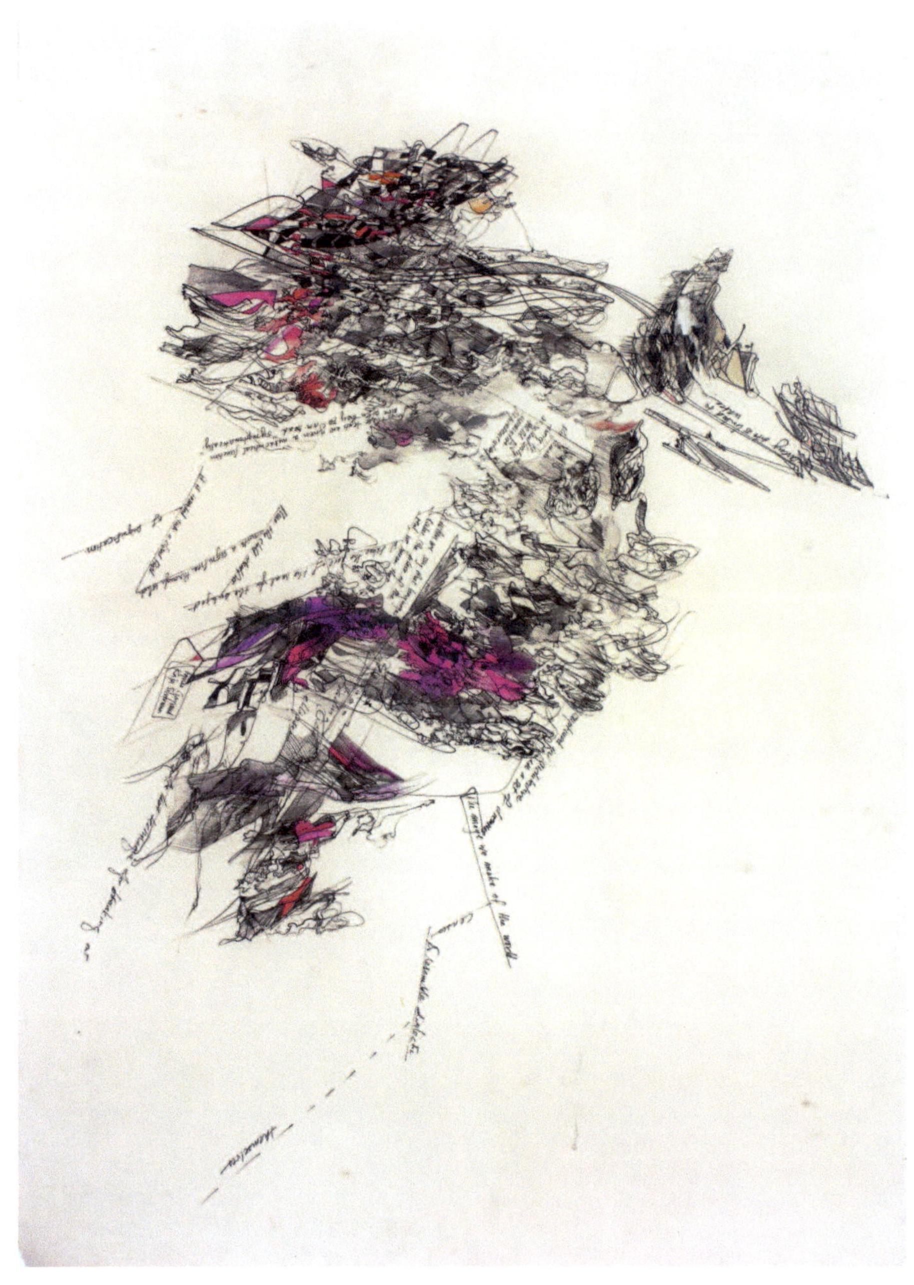

DM [...] What follows is an insight into her inner and outer worlds, where themes such as nature, landscapes, climate change, feminism, and politics are translated into her works through performance, paintings, drawings, data visualizations, photography and video installations.

DM What are the key references that have influenced your artistic view and production? And how your Californian roots have informed your tight bond with nature?

CM A strain of American drawing and painting and performance charges to the sensations of the visual world an account of a witnessing body, the artist as a sensing receptor—I respect a combination of traumatic drama and *stupor mundi*—amazement at the wonder of the world, in diverse works from Joan Mitchell to Vija Celmins, Philip Guston to Lebbeus Woods, Edward Hopper to Lee Bontecou. Haunted, also, by canvasses by the post war Italian artists, especially Marisa Merz's drawings and structures, and Alberto Burri's collaged canvasses, I notice how and where traumatic sensation stores itself inside materialities of support and surface, through overlays and slash and mark making. The performance works of Joan Jonas and Trisha Brown use drawing as choreographic fields to foretell or, nearly, prophetically foreshadow future states of life. I love the visual music of Len Lye, Jordan Belson, and the cutting aesthetic of Chris Marker's *Sans Soleil*.

When I was a kid of seven, our family moved from Los Angeles to the middle of the continent, in the tallgrass prairie country. Here was this weird lonely sea of land, a place of intensity in extremes, with dullness in the middle range. The prairie attuned me to how the smallest curve of a feather might connect visually to a cumulous cloud towering overhead. I taught myself to draw out in the countryside, while a social 'real world' of school and home was a tough game of warfare, boys against girls, or vice versa— the rough tumble of mid-twentieth century sexual violence and repression. The world seemed ripped to shreds. Drawing on my own made things integrate. When I returned to California to live, it was coming home, to a rural landscape visibly marked by the San Andreas Fault. I made work in photography and video, resonating between traumatic memory visualization and scientific images of seismicity—'seismic memory'.

DM As I was born in the eastern part of Sicily, a place where earthquakes and volcanic eruptions represent a routine, I'm particularly fascinated with your explorations of the ephemeral power of nature. How did natural events and processes first inspire you?

CM 'Nature' has materiality, rawness, is the same as my hand, even the same as the digital keyboard upon which I write here and now. 'Natural' is a cluster of swerves, of now you see it, now you don't. Now you access a truth beyond reason and perspective, now you lose it. Nothing is predetermined, no perspective is optimal, no subjectivity commands authority. I like this kind of space even if it's imaginary. It's a math and music space like a series of polyphonies by Hildegard of Bingen, in her *Origin of Fire*, which I 've been listening to in studio while working on a painting about arrhythmias. A perfect analogy for this situation of 'nature', if it is a subject for art or the other way around—is the trope of the earthquake. Scientifically, it's not possible (yet) to predict precisely when earthquakes come. The blurred edges of vision contain the force of these events hurtling towards us from the future. Post-traumatic visualization—in nightmares—is a site in the brain, in the inner vision behind the retina. I want to snap to attention at the first signs or traces of a future disruption, or a break in the fabric of the everyday. An everyday practice involves a searching line.

I remember studying, at five or six, a catalog of Vincent van Gogh at Auvers. I still have the catalog in my library. In the color reproductions, the marks moved from sensation to sensation, the artist matching his move to the move of a tree branch, a pile of dirt in the road, a scuttling cloud. That drawing is not a view of, but is inside a time, the time of Vincent drawing the drawing. I assumed 'art' was a correlation to 'being there being here' from within spatial layers of time. Art objects held time in a sensual volume, or, could release time from within that volume. What if time seeps out from local objects? A magical thinking moment, but if you can imagine the space/time curve as a surface, then gravity is a curved surface, then perhaps gravity is a function of time, or, operations around objects

The Last Technique for Breaking Out (after Agnès Gayraud and Kaja Silverman), 2016
Ink and graphite on Fabriano Rosaspina paper, 68.6 x 50.8 cm / 27 x 20 in; detail, overleaf

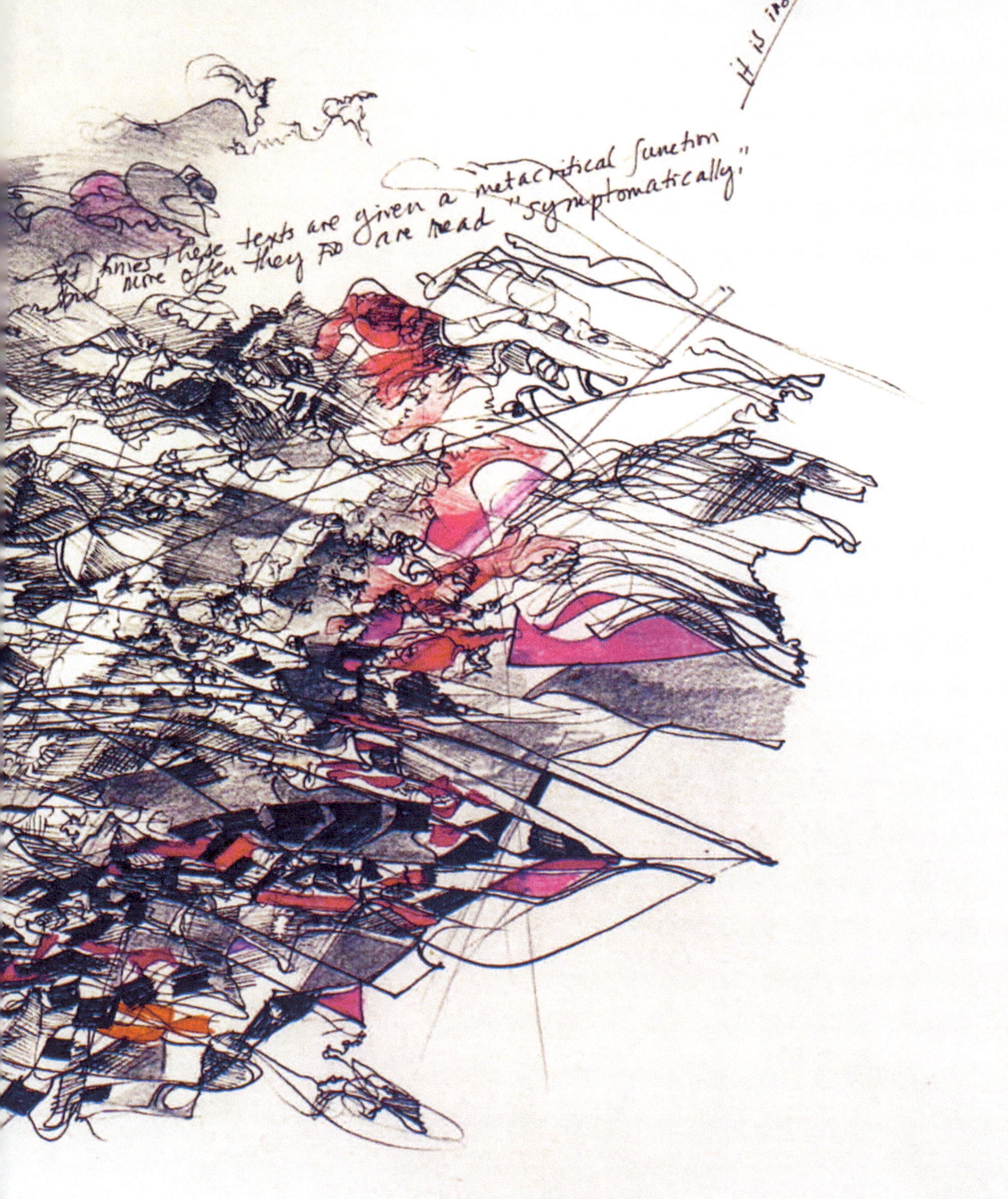
At times these texts are given a metacritical function
but more often they too are read "symptomatically."
It is inse

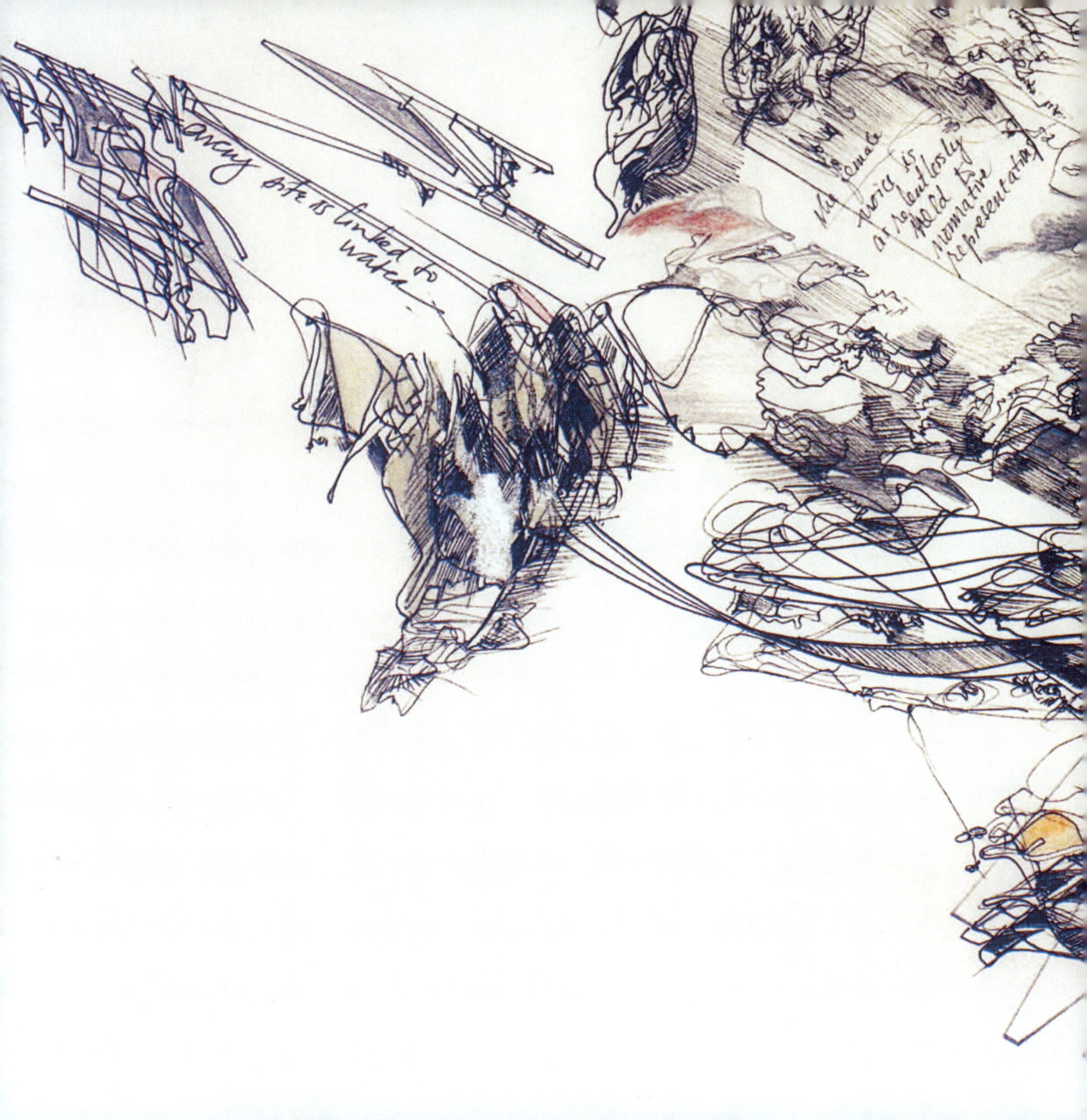
site is linked to water
held to normative representation

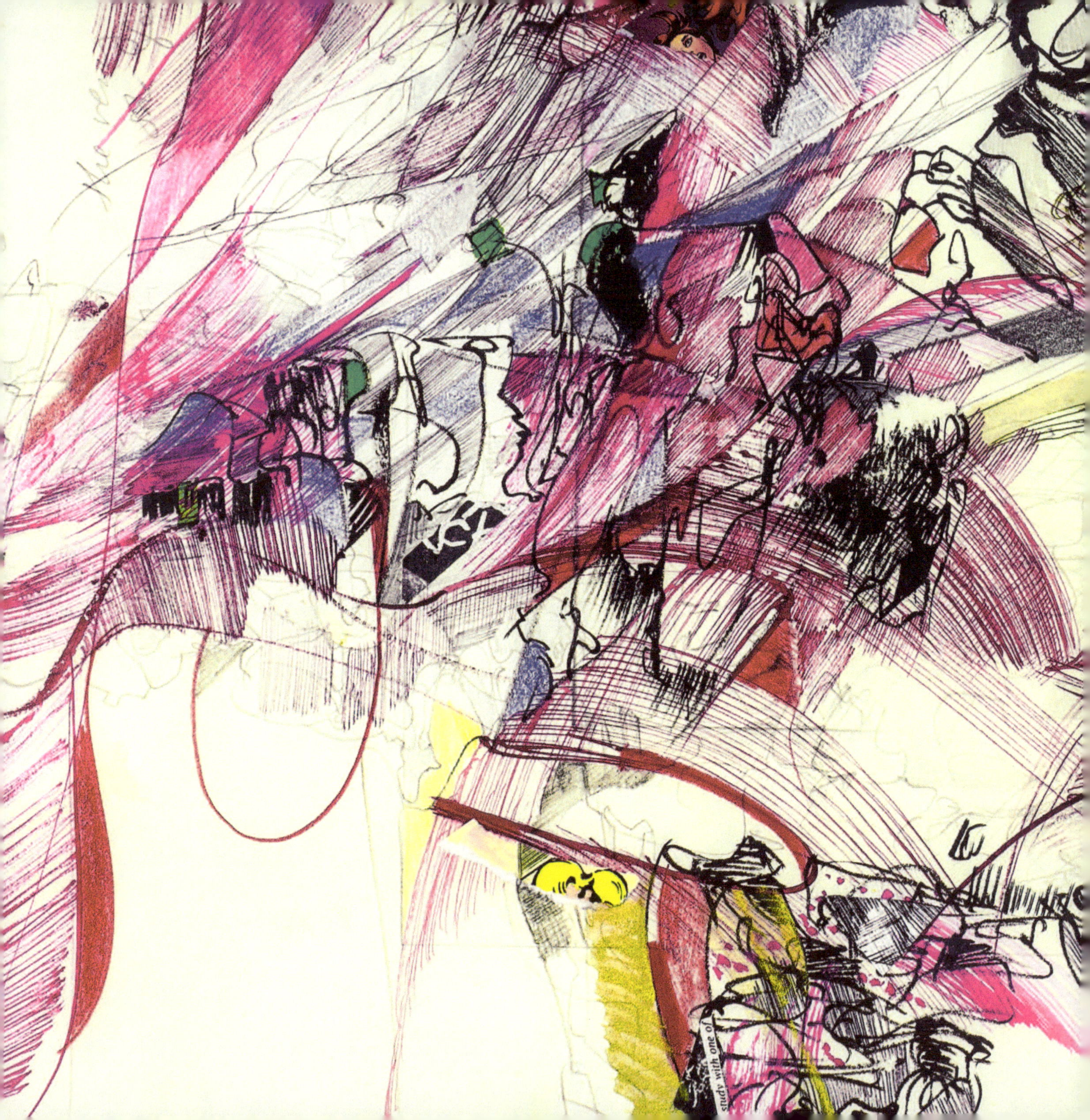

'bend' the curve of time. If geologic layers are saturations of time, I'm marking local nodes or sequences of nodes, like a musical score. In the nineties, I made repeated visits to Mauna Kea volcano on the Big Island of Hawaii. I started lifting emulsions of photographs shot at the volcano and setting them into monotype prints. The print medium felt as if it were a way to take or capture an impression of the explosions both visible and under the earth that were happening in the Pacific Ring of Fire.

DM It seems that you act as a sort of catalyst, activating a sequence of reactions between natural and digital elements/tools. How do you position yourself within these practices?

CM Yes, a catalyst, within a matrix where there are constant differentials flowing between mark making and energetic forces external to, and yet also integrated inside the mark-making. That's a weird description, I know. To unpack things a little, imagine tools as outlets that sort of release or seize upon and then release time. Erotically, to pun on 'tool' as sexual. In English, there's an insult, 'Oh he's such a tool.' I like the negative implication of the insult. Insults are resistant. I love the contradiction of the negative label. 'Digital' and 'natural' are stereotypes set in a binary, against one another. This never has made sense to me. Nothing is 'not' natural, nothing is 'not' digital, for me, it's all drawing. Drawing is energetic. It doesn't have to respond to the exclusively sighted or programmed. Drawing is making a world through receptivity, to phenomena in a certain place; making presence to the awareness of having already lost sight of something. Drawings for me seem 'complete' whenever they reach thresholds of what may appear'off-screen' in future. Ephemeral processing, referring to what's not identifiable, what is yet to come, suggests that any kind of sign language can become the subject of a drawing too — like predictive graphs of risk.

DM How do you approach the sites of your installations and audio-visual works? What's your relationship with these places?

CM When you ask about the approach, I'm grateful how you phrase this, to emphasize 'approach' sites, the approach comes through drift, as I am moving around, through a kind of casting process, like casting a line. Casting a line out. I'm attracted to sites where the biosphere is in flagrant tension with large-scale technologies. A recent video work, *Microswarm Patchwalk*, rescales the technologic event to my own retina, after surgery. Remember Luis Camnitzer's self portrait of his profile as a 'site' with little houses and toy animals clustered around his eyes? I wanted to make a video about a site being at the retinal level, inside the eye, when the eye is patched because the retina is hurt, torn, and damaged. A walk on the beach while semi-blindfolded. Sight and sightlessness collide. At the beach, the film offers a visual and sonic field of imaginary numbers rising from the ocean's edge.

For *Double Blind Studies*, I made a series of photographic prints generate in analog format (gelatin silver prints) out of drawings of marine animals. Not literally descriptive of taxa, rather the drawings emerged from the video footagė I shot on board a research vessel with biodiversity scientists in the Gulf of Mexico during and after the BP oil spill of 2010. I shot digital photographs of the drawings, then turned them into Rohrsach-like symmetrical images through layering, resulting in a digital negative, from which a print, in gelatin silver processing is made, by hand.

DM In your ongoing guerrilla-style interventions – such as the *Tesserae of Venus* and *Carbon Song Cycle* videos, you have filmed in discarded areas that you have defined as "bastard spaces" – spaces where decomposition and re-composition are possible. Could you tell us more about the symbolic value that these places have within your body of work?

CM Well, I've thought of these spaces as bastard, not in a pejorative sense, but in the sense of the kairotic—the incalculable, chance encounter. The ancient writer Lucretius talks about the swerve, or clinamen, that creates new things. Just as drawing might comprehend all kinds of bits of information, or shards of data, or phenomenon, in its questing task to trace, note, make a mark, so I also look for places or spaces that could be taken as, or deeply appreciated, as possible sites of the 'new things'. The word 'swerve' is slang for saying 'no' to a

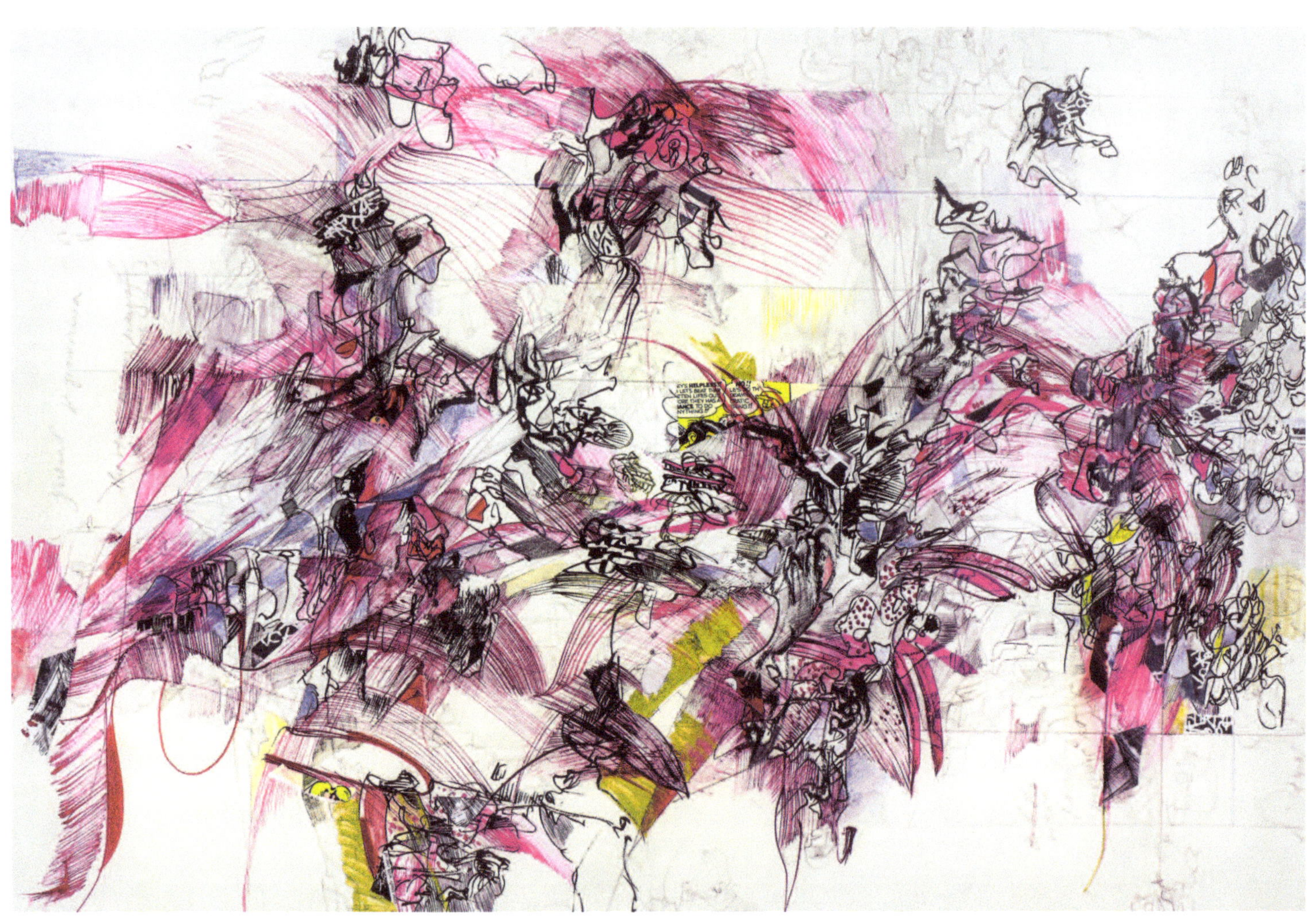

request, especially an unreasonable one. And to 'swerve on' is to get in the mood for a party, for swing time, a mutual flow-rhythm without concern for ends, to party on. To dance is to pattern structures that mix one's life into and within the lives of unknowable others, a process linguistically and narratively produced on one level (in time based media) and on another in the still moment between the slip of one image-still and the next, and those levels together make a new thing, as Zadie Smith's novel, *Swing Time*, suggests. For *e-flux Journal* a few years ago, Hito Steyerl anticipates free fall, or a situation of groundlessness, as a condition of culture, unremarked, even unconscious. Maybe to dance is to mark out the rhythms of free fall. This is an oblique, or even bleak view of such a mix-up everything is falling into disorder, mayhem, and dissolution. How absurd, to montage a space of recomposition. I think of the absurd, the negative way, the *via negativa*, where every fall can be taken as a defiance against necessity: I made a drawing, *Arm of the Starfish: Temeridad* after one of the *Enigmas* of Juana de la Cruz, the Mexican Baroque poet. In phrases nearly impossible to translate into English, she demands:

> *¿Cuál es la temeridad*
> *de tan alta presunción*
> *que, pudiendo ser razón,*
> *pretende ser necedad?*

My drawing's title also checks into *Arm of the Startfish*, a novel by Madeleine L'Engle, which I read as a girl. That book is about regeneration.

DM Time is a power that we can't control. It is also a recurrent theme in some of your works – such as: *SALT*, *Shed Cubed*, *Deep Horizon* and *Double Blind Studies*. How do you deal with the concept of 'time'?

CM Probably my work takes on rhythms, it counts time, like music, participates just in time, stops to face the possibility of endless time, wonders about the world beyond human time, plays a melody in counterpoint to a signature of measured time, this last usually through repetition of cuts. Holes. Time warps. Tesseracts. Places you can't find

counterpoint to a signature of measured time, this last usually through repetition of cuts. Holes. Time warps. Tesseracts. Places you can't find
on a map because they are to come, or are disappeared. Places where the sound environment is cyclical and rhythmic. Machines, like oil derricks, creaking as they move up and down. Sucking up the oil, which is hidden in the tubes, lines and tanks of the oil field. At sea, the drift of oil down through the photosynthetic layer, down to the benthic layer where the crustacean live, and the sightless fish. Casting topologies, this process of tracing indeterminate and forces without predicate, without objective. The digital-analog 'divide' is subsumed under my process that wants to move against the certain positive identification, the surveillance-derived identity.

DM I find highly compelling the overlapping lines and the shadowy representation in most of your drawings and printed works – e.g. *Double Blind Studies*, *Persons of Interest*, *Moonbeam Redaction*, *Hungry Ghosts*, etc. What can you tell us about the light/shadow dichotomy?

CM One must try to 'shadow-forth' (to borrow a made up verb from the English poet, Hopkins) modes of comprehending a site, whether it's textual, or it's around a comic strip, or if it's a Moebius strip, or if it's a physical place… when learning or knowing a space means risking being outside of comfort—in the wild—in the countryside of a world that's not objective, but rather is speaking or shadowing-forth towards us— we understand in parts. In architecture, the term 'parti' denotes the decisive decision that is a matter of taking the part of, a certain design direction for the future built form. I love the play of 'taking part' with 'taking apart' and the 'part taken up'—implication being, that you must, in the image, rely on a partial comprehension, there's always something that exceeds the 'parti', which will be a built thing—the full realization of something as yet in shadow. I'm happy I can actually see, for real: but what I see I can't really grasp except through this shadow play. I often think of the surface of a work, whether it's a painting, a drawing or a photo or a video still, as projections or residue-traces of projections of something via a screen. Kaja Silverman, in her recent, magisterial book on photography, *The Miracle of Analogy*, comes to the end of describing a dialectical relationship between projected image of the ocean from within the

Demmycratic Thing (after Moonbeam McSwine), 1958)
Ink, graphite, watercolor, and paper collage from the New York Mirror), 50.1 x 71.1 cm / 19.75 x 28 in

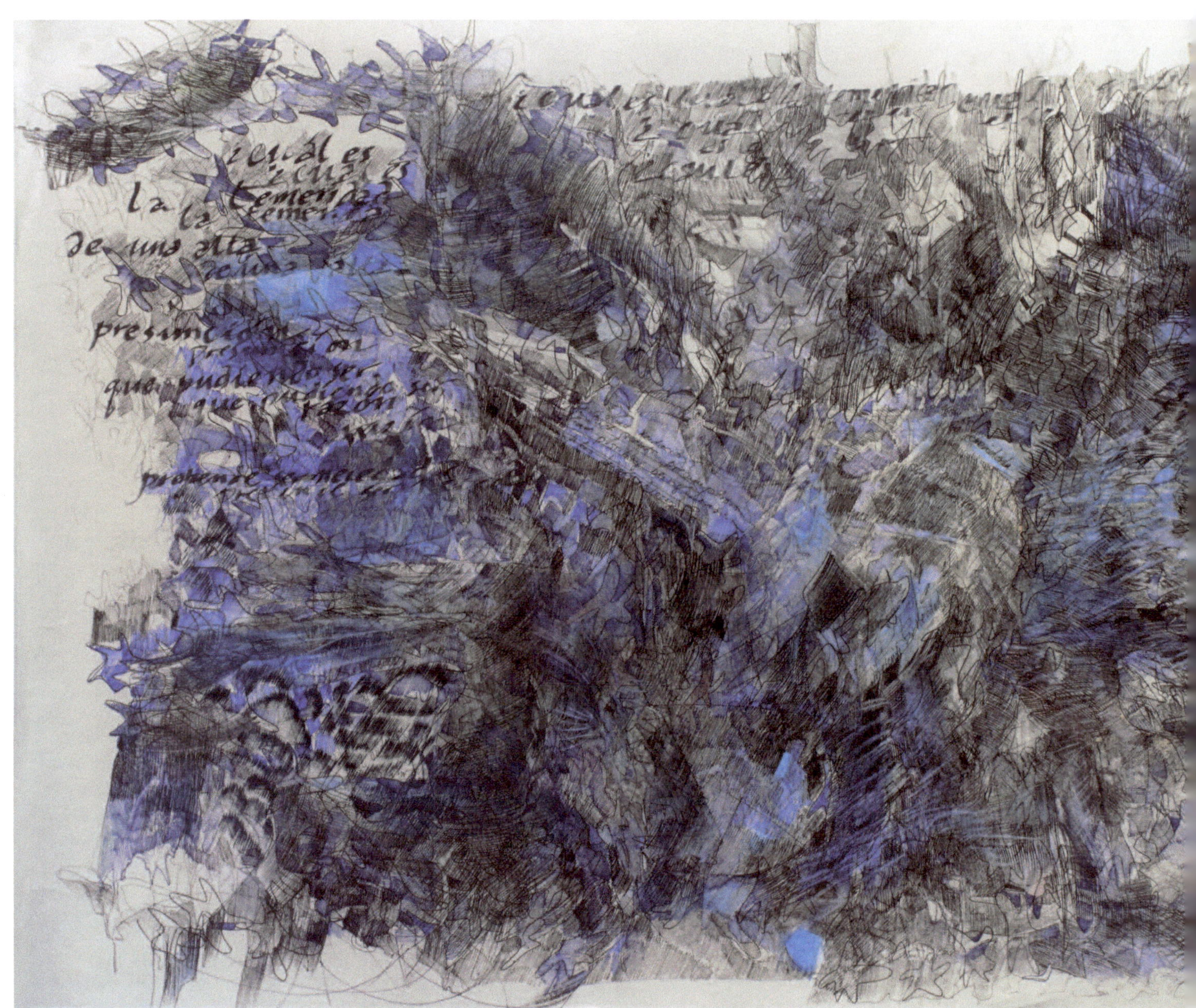
¿cuál es
de una alta

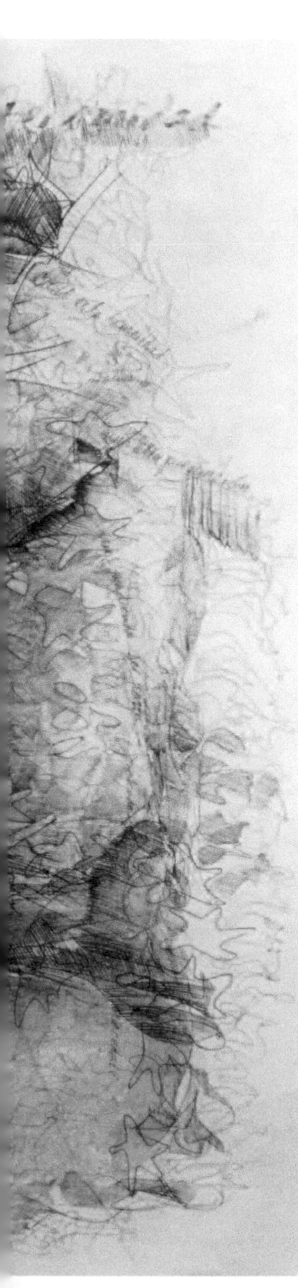

Arm of the Starfish (Temeridad)(after Sor Juana de la Cruz), 2016
Ink, color pencil, and graphite on Takefu washi, 63.4 x 96.5 cm / 25 x 38 in

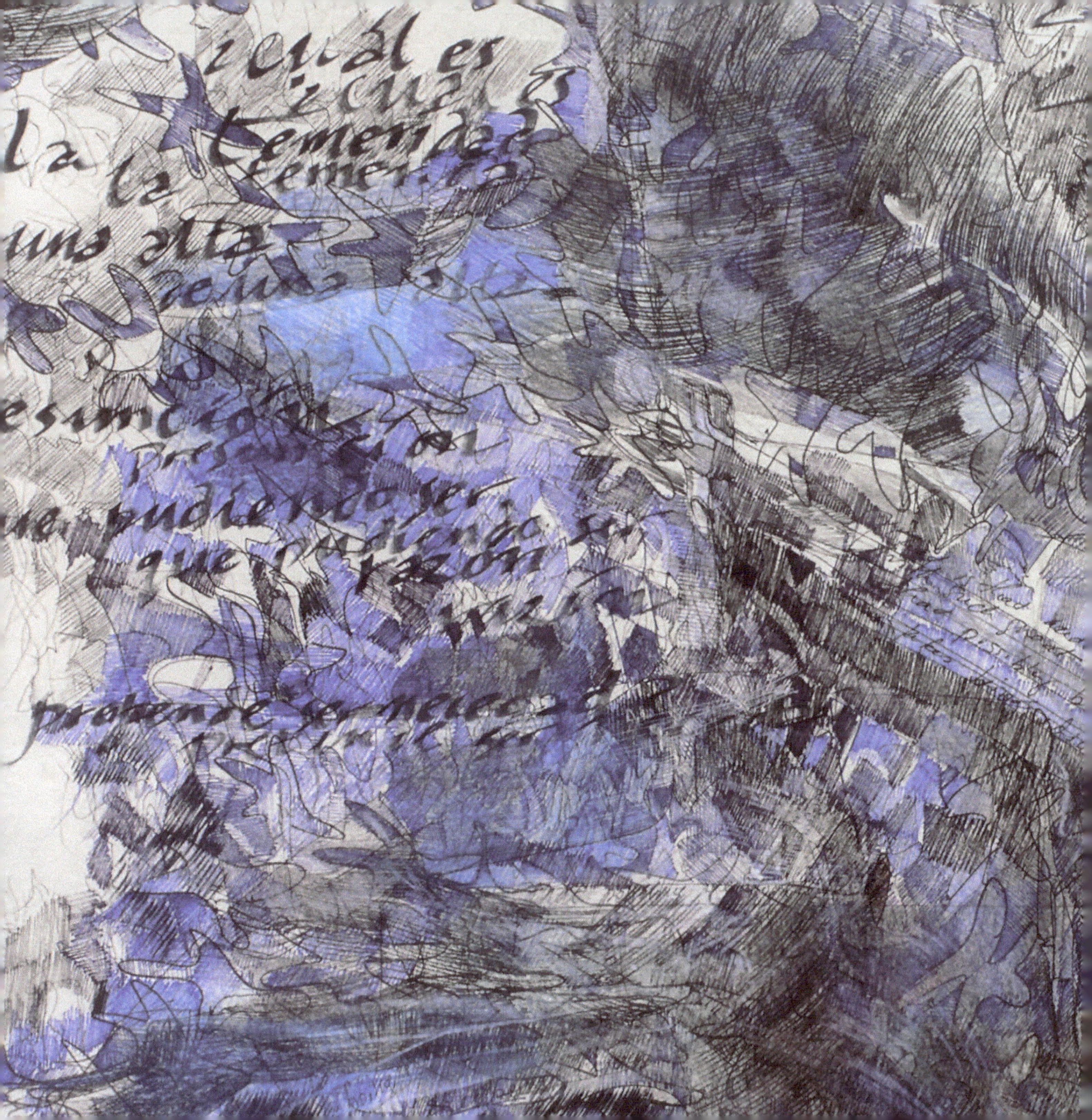
¿cuál es
pudiendo ser

'spaceship in the film *Solaris*, by Andre Tarkovsky, and a possibility that photography captures a projection from outside us, when she surprises us with this amazing comment, core to her argument about how images work: "Like Tarkovsky's scientists, we have secured ourselves 'behind a barrier of perfectly engineered glass,' so that we can 'study' an oceanic planet without getting 'wet.' This planet is as 'intelligent' as the one in *Solaris*, and it also communicates with us through images. Like the hallucinations in Tarkovsky's film, these images are ontological calling cards: a summons to relationality. This oceanic planet, however, is our world, and it is through photography—rather than hallucinations—that it speaks to us."

DM I'm interested in the ways you physically engage, combine, and re-invent different media and techniques. Could you give us an insight into your creative process? Is it an individual or a team-based process?

CM Most often I work alone, in the physical sense, in a studio-based and field-based practice, but a community of friends and family all around, through virtual connections and real life, make this creative process deeply and structurally networked and supported. In this sense, I never work alone. I sense we are in a community of making, even as we are also diving deep under the veil of being watched or watching. In camouflage. Under the radar. Wanting to be with the overwhelming 'is-ness' of the world coming at us and through us. Honoring a sensibility of trust and compassion as we stand face to face with each other in a 'nature' – world that is both intimate to us in our very cells and molecule, exceeds us at every turn, and communicates through us. Do I think of recombination, invention, and engagement differently than I could have long ago, as a child drawing next to her bicycle in the countryside? Yes, now, making an object around place or the sense of place is a relation of face to face, even virtually, across vast divides, and happens with the participation of many hearts and minds — it's as if we are all bringing works into being, of which some emerge in this place or that studio, in my studio. If I remember rightly, the philosopher Emmanuel Levinas accounts for the human, the creation of the human, whatever that can be, only and always in the moment of facing one another. Sites or places, and my network are alive to me in the moment of mutual face-time. The practice unfolds in the relation. The material trace of that is the 'body of work'. In video or drawing or painting or photomontage or even video installation. This is a lot harder to talk about than it is to engage in through media — I feel the difficulty of trying to speak of this. The meaning of what's made arises contextually.

DM In light of the latest political developments in the US, could you tell us your thoughts on how this turning point will change the ways a female artist approaches environmental and socio-political issues?

CM For my new project, *Moonbeam*, this year, 2017, I'm painting topological collages work as if from the point of view of Moonbeam McSwine. Moonbeam, a forties and fifties cartoon figure who is the only literate denizen of Dogpatch, USA and lives in a pigsty, was the name my mother taunted me with when I was in high school. Flipping identity politics, I'm making paintings from within the screen filter of Moonbeam's mind, so the paintings are analogies to a screening of her satirical observations and remixes of literary scrawls, manga-like fragments, and scrambled titles. I'm 'occupying' as Moonbeam McSwine and delivering gridded topologic feedback, in the spirit of the 2016 meme, 'Pussy Grabs Back.' They are medium-large canvasses, in oil paint, flashe, ink, graphite, and dye on canvas; and drawings. Moonbeam 'reads' texts and data of various kinds, from cardiac arrhythmias in electrocardiograms, to brain scans, to feminist texts, folklore, and her own comics. *Moonbeam* sets up a visual system for imagining common futures, paths not taken, open paths.

DM Have you ever thought of creating a piece in a place outside the US that presents similar characteristics to your local area?

CM During the time I was shooting video and photography for the seismic memory project, *Carrizo-Parkfield Diaries*, scientists from around the world had gathered in the first days after a 6.0 quake struck along the 'moving section' of the San Andreas Fault, at Parkfield, California in 2004. They were at the San Andreas Fault Observatory at Depth, as guests of the US Geological Service. There, I met a young woman seismologist from Naples, who told me how thrilled she was to study a cognate landscape to her own in Italy...

Double Blind Study 2, 2012
Gelatin silver print on archival paper, 76.8 x 101.6 cm / 30 x 40 in

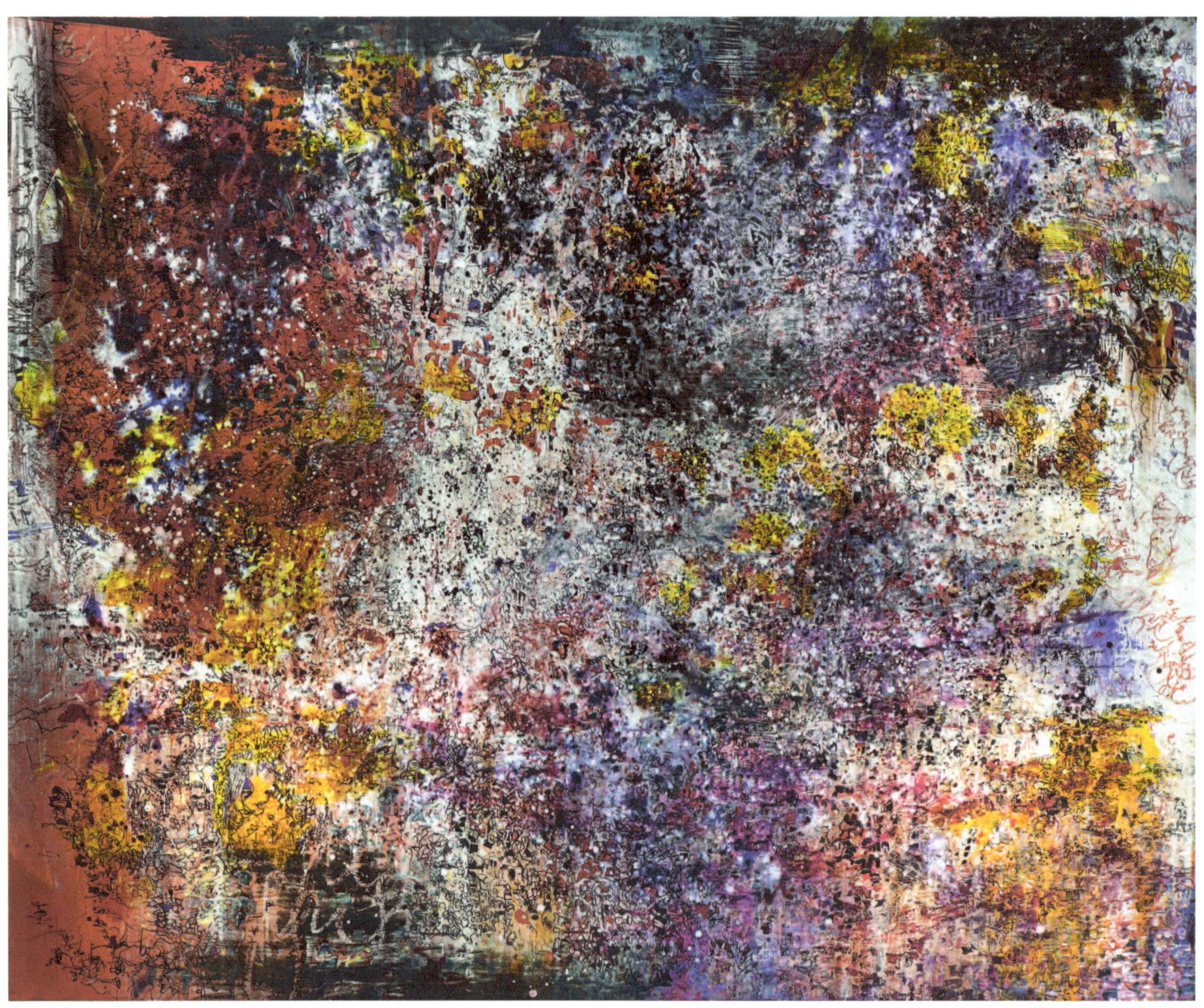

Prism Prison (After Angela Davis), 2016
Oil, ink, graphite, paper collage and gold leaf on canvas, 152.4 x 182.8 x 6.3 cm / 60 x 72 x 2.5 in; detail, overleaf

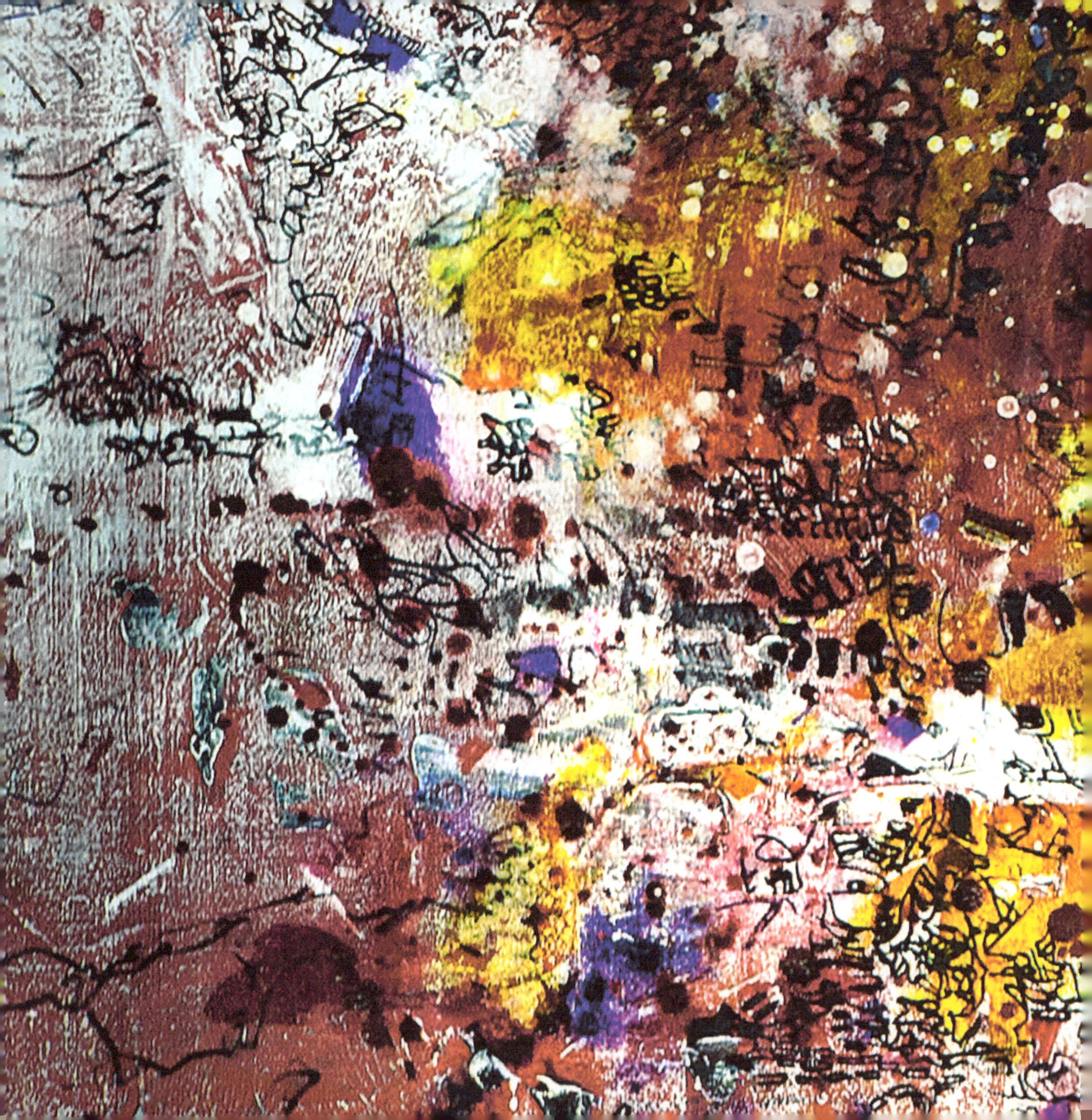

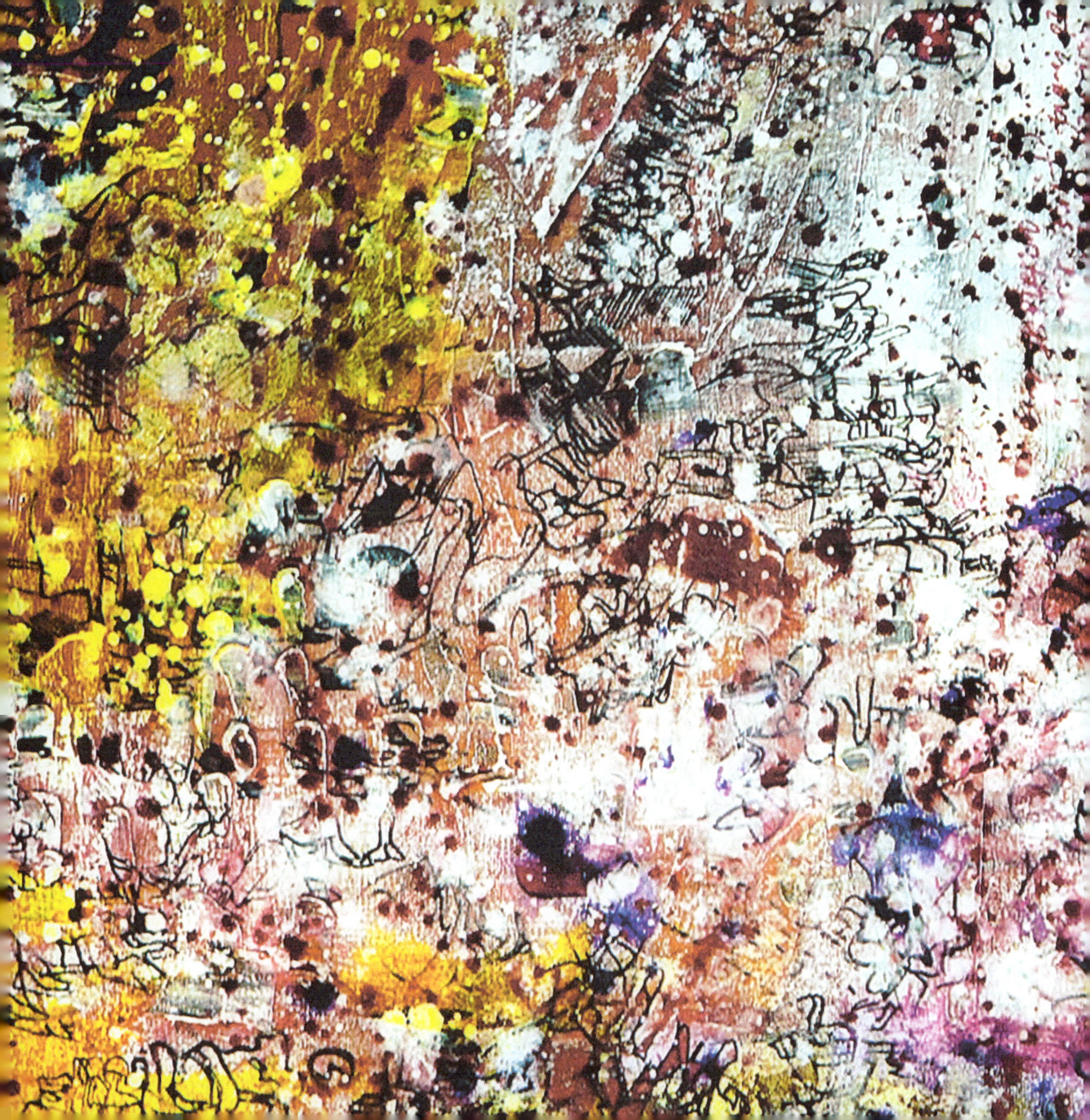

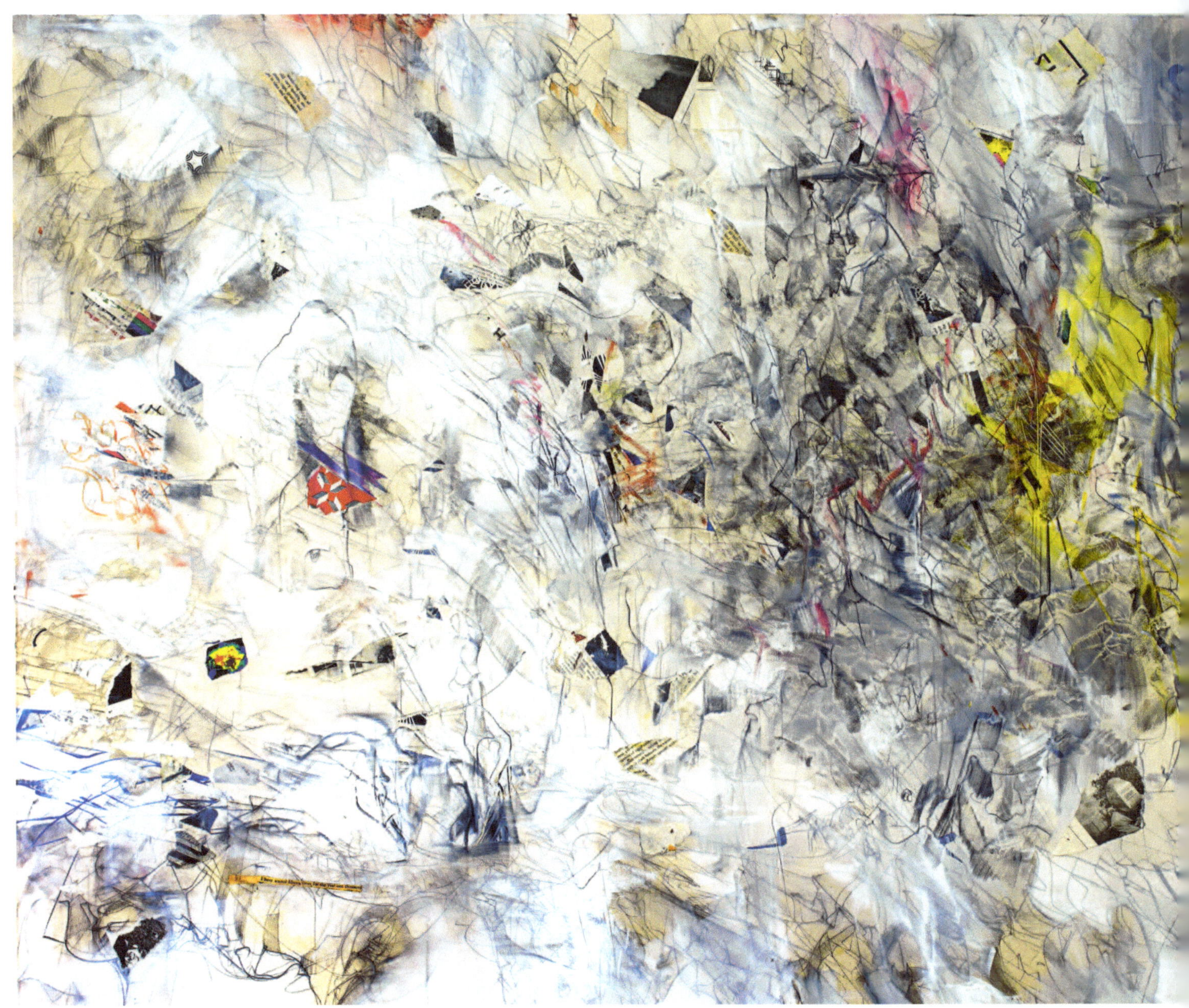

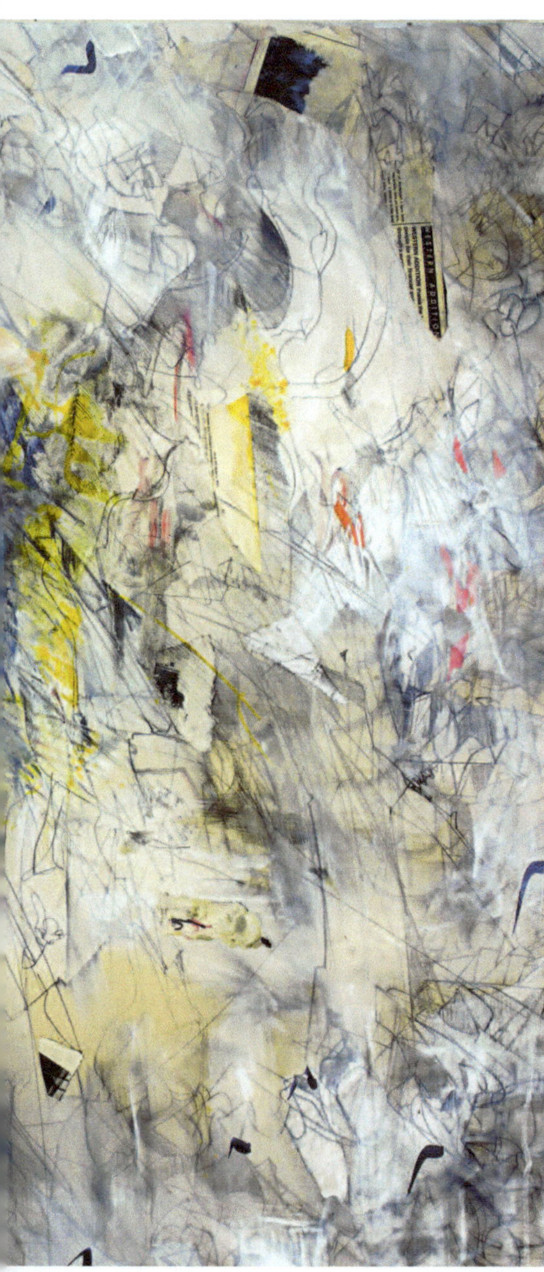

TESSERAE OF VENUS

MELISSA POTTER WITH CHRISTINA MCPHEE

[Excerpts, lightly edited: This interview was first published on *Bomb Daily* in October 2009. The *BOMB Digital Archive* is at http://www.bombmagazine.org.]

Birth of the Left Hand, 2017
Graphite, oil, ink, and paper collage from *Nature: Climate Change,* on muslin, 91.4 x 152.4 x 6.3 cm / 36 x 60 x 2.5 in|

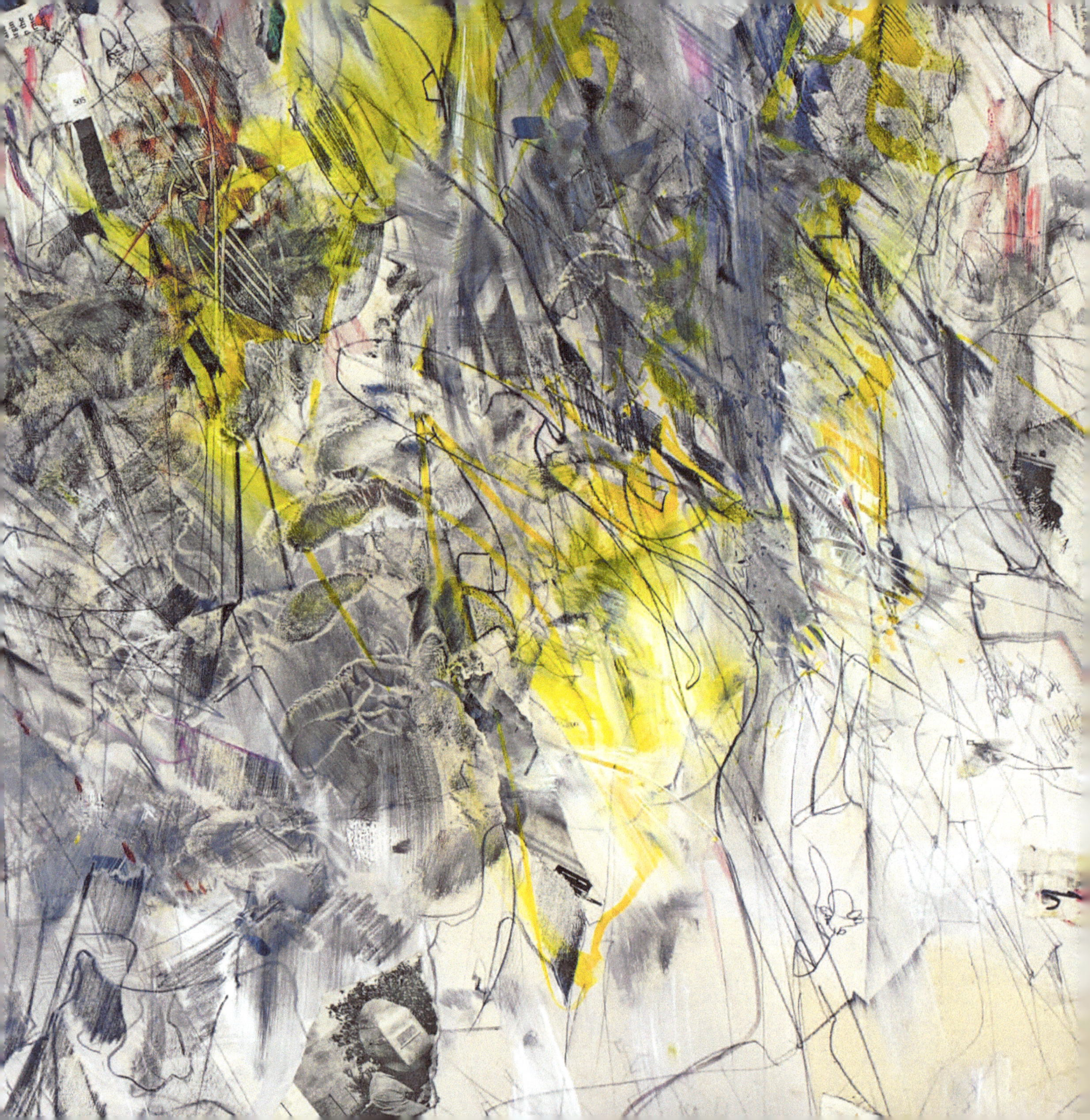

MP I'm fascinated with the contradictory implications of Venus' uninhabitable atmosphere as the inspiration for this body of work. It operates in these pieces both as a symbol for the earth after what you suggest is the inevitable moment of carbon saturation and as a fantastical shelter from this storm, something you've coined, "tesserae tents."

CM I started thinking about using the tesserae—complex ridged folds—of the surface of Venus, as a simple visual analog for carbon intensification in our atmosphere. It's thought that Venus may once have had water, even oceans, but that there is no carbon cycle on Venus, so there can't be any absorption; there are no oceans to take up the excess carbon. Most of us are wondering how much longer the carbon increases in our atmosphere can go on before there is massive loss of coastline, dramatic changes in ecosystems, and then what about us? So, imagine improvised shelters at, or inside, these neglected areas, often alluvial or littoral swamps, marshes, or riverbeds. I drew at intimate spaces on the scale of the waterfowl and the rushes; a mammal's-eye view in contrast, and immediate proximity, to alternative and traditional petroleum energy-producing plants on a huge scale. I felt that there was an invisible assemblage going on, maybe Venus-like intensifications of carbon in the air. I started to imagine how, as we try to quickly build and go online with alternative energies, at the same time we might not be converting away from carbon emissions fast enough. How abstraction is a kind of tactical move to deflect attention from the literal reportage of a photograph. That lag between the image recognition (the documentary moment) and the sense of an overwhelming dynamic system, something that can't be described by direct reportage. Drawing abstract studies based on the nineties-era Magellan Mission to Venus—I made a topologic fantasy of these photographs, found online thanks to NASA and the Jet Propulsion Lab. With a sense of nihilistic humor, riffing off these old-school photos, as if they could hold some clue, like a secret trap door, I was doing a kind of reverse of the tensegrity forms of Bucky Fuller. The tesserated (tiling) surface of Venus is a model of dissipation, entropy, or slow flow, the opposite of a Bucky-like structure. Balancing structures of large sheets of paper, hang them, crush them and pile them in precarious masses, I pour day-glo airbrush paint over them, then hose them down, letting the paint dry in rivulets. Often they are peaked or hooded, like masses of semi-collapsed tents. The hot colors offered, deliberately, a pleasure, to scream out "tacky shiny bad taste!" as Venus and her fans might prefer. Since these paper structures were kind of anti-models, really, then the color can go wild and schlocky and excessive. Assembling the stacks of folded paper sheets in precarious balances, I work with one hand on the sculpture, the other with a still digital camera or with my video camera, pouring water from the hose into the pooled iridescent and probably toxic puddles of airbrush paint, as at the same time I shoot and edit inside the camera.

MP I'm equally compelled by your concept of the kairotic or "bastard spaces," such as the Sunset Midway oil fields near Taft, California, that exist on the edge of civilization where you have been shooting video. Unwanted and neglected spaces seem to have something different to say to us, or even inspire solutions to this ecological conundrum.

CM I film on the fly at high-tech energy installations, shoot at dawn, dusk, or after-hours on weekends, a few minutes at a time. I shoot the video as a kind of drawing. I work within a sense of the rhythm of the site, for example, in response to the rich sound rhythms from turbines. The shoots—guerrilla-style as they are—involve a poignant gesture or kairotic moment, which in urban slang may mean, not only the "perfect time or apt moment of luck," but in a strange reversal also "is used to express gayness or queerness or just to make fun of people who you don't like, as in "go away you kairotic bastard." I've never actually heard anyone say this, but the *Urbandictionary.com* gloss on 'kairotic' as opportunistic, fortunate, and non-standard is so trippy. You can't really visualize what the world is going to be like if the Arctic sea ice melts. You can imagine drowning cities and things like that on a grand scale, but what about the intimate detail, the less obvious byways? In a sense, the future is a kind of forbidden landscape. It's possibly so alien to the familiar and the everyday that no speculative images exist yet of it. One is left like Blake to imagine dynamic worlds of elaborate strangeness. Or to create launch pads like installations for time travel to a future after oil, as Isa Genzken has done. So the thing to do is to shoot at difficult-to-photograph sites. At Sunset Midway, I get stopped by security even when I am shooting from the public road. I am told that the airspace, the view itself, is a property of the petroleum companies!

Detail, *Birth of the Left Hand*

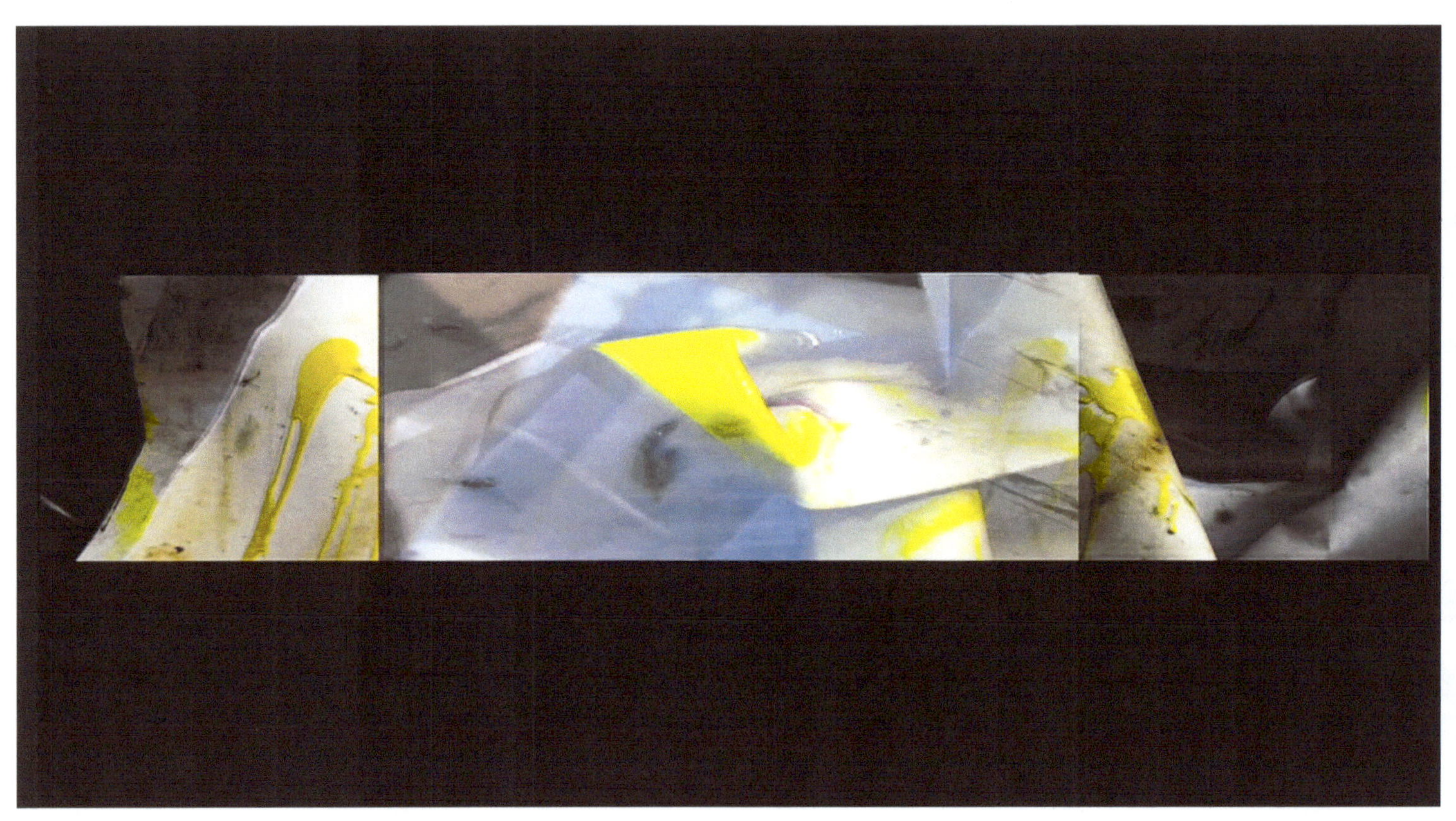

Energy extraction is going on in neglected natural areas, especially littoral or marginal streambeds, riverbeds, and swamps or sloughs, in estuaries near the ocean, because of the need for large amounts of water for cooling. An assemblage of disconnected elements are thrown together. The point of contact is a kairotic moment—that's where the videomontage attempts to condense these points and extract their sweetness, like squeezing fruit for a stream of luscious juice.

MP Your method of translation from video to layered and sequenced stills provides a 2-D foundation for these investigations. You mention that you seek traces of something not found in the video footage. What are you looking for? What have you found?

CM Printing these photomontages as physical objects is, in miniature, accelerating the accumulation (of carbon) climate change. I think of the magical geomorphologie of Constant. His *New Babylon*, as if suspended like night-necklaces over the plains of Northern Europe, prefigure networks. So if that's where we live now, what happens to the agency of the artist? I think there's still nature beyond our control even though we are inside it and complicit. There's still that absolute process. The tesserated image comes into the physical but moves back into and through the network, as the images are doing in this interview. In the photomontage process, I sense that the image sequence becomes a solid like a wall or a ship's hull, patched or soldered together in tiles. The future, far from immaterial, feels like a mass we can almost touch. Maybe we could see it if we could just get inside the doorways, beyond the portals of the tesserae.

MP And yet, one of the elements of these works that is so startlingly beautiful is the use of drawing and painting as a way to explore the layering methodologies used to find traces of something not found in the video.

CM I wish to ask what it feels like to be alive now, as the climate is going crazy. One way to do that was to start from the extreme opposite position of fantasy—by drawing very loosely from the Magellan mission to Venus from small jpegs online. The drawings started to go feral, started to move farther away from the conceit of Magellan and into rushes of lyric, even cheesy iridescent paint. I began to use loud colors and "bad" paint and make the forms alternate between subtle topographic shifts in graphite and streaks of paint movement. At length, some of the drawings grew too large and moved outdoors. I would shoot video as I was also pouring paint or water on big swaths of paper stock hung like sheets to dry in the cool morning air. I worked in color sets—tesserae-yellow, tesserae-vermillion—as if to work up and down a chromatic scale, like "scoring" the models in a performance sequence. As soon as I could finish a sequence of video, I would arrange the raw footage of the tesserae models into sequences surrounding shots of the energy-producing landscapes, so that the tesserae would seem to be clashing or merging with the turbines and the steam vents. It was as if the video had become a middle term between drawing and painting on one hand and photomontage on the other. The videomontage cancelled intimacy in the impromptu tesserae models by setting them into the huge scale of energy production. As a countervalent move, I returned to photographing the models at the site of their conception, my studio yard and montaging the shots into my field photographs of places of abandoned technology overgrown with new growth forest and debris (rotting ocean piers, abandoned kilns).

Detail, *Tesserae of Venus (Ghostdance)*, single channel video, with sound by Pauline Oliveros, 2009

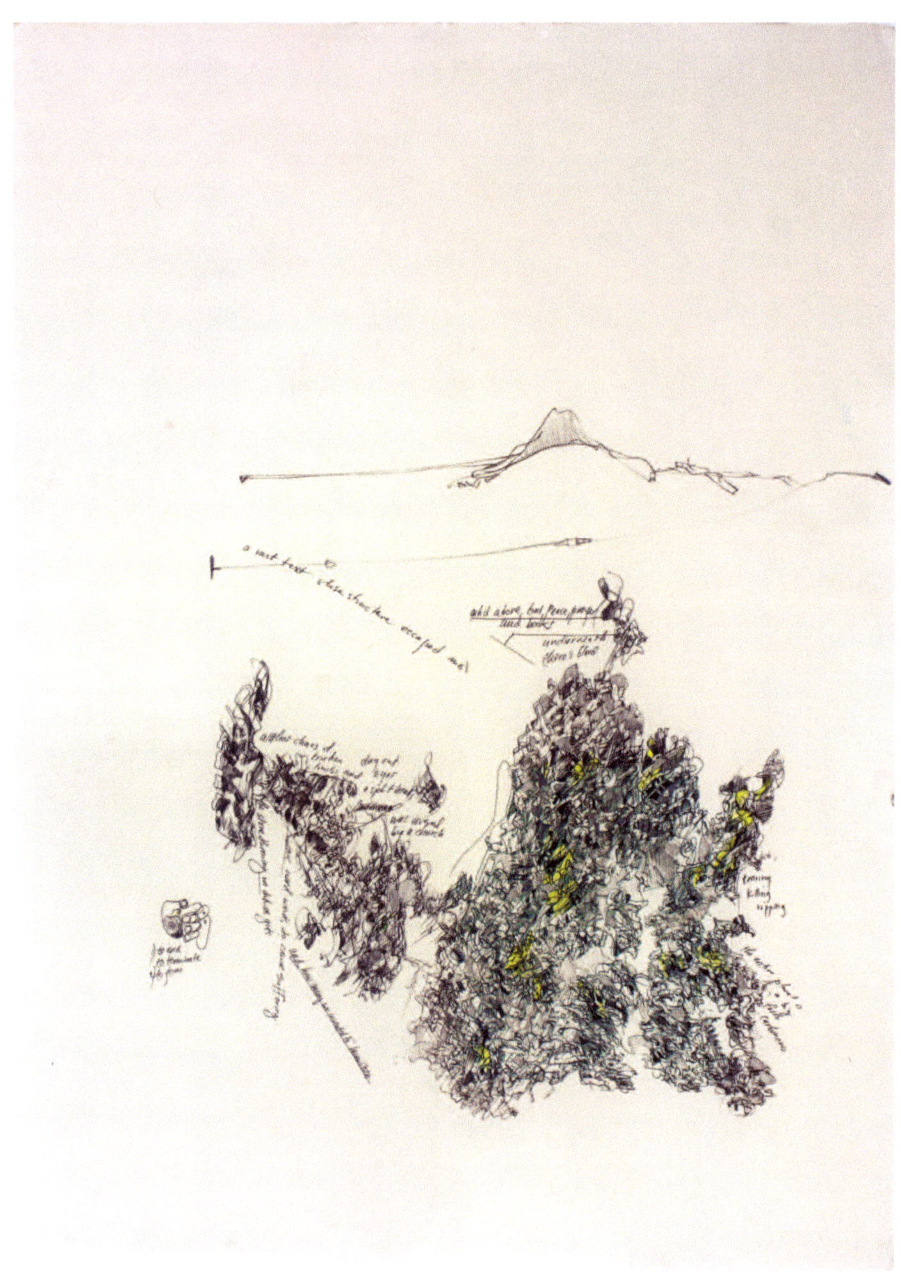

We Used Words To Cause Suffering (After Classical Maya Hieroglyphs and Elena Ferrante), 2016
Ink and graphite on Fabriano Rosaspina paper, 50.1 x 71.1 cm / 19.75 x 28 in

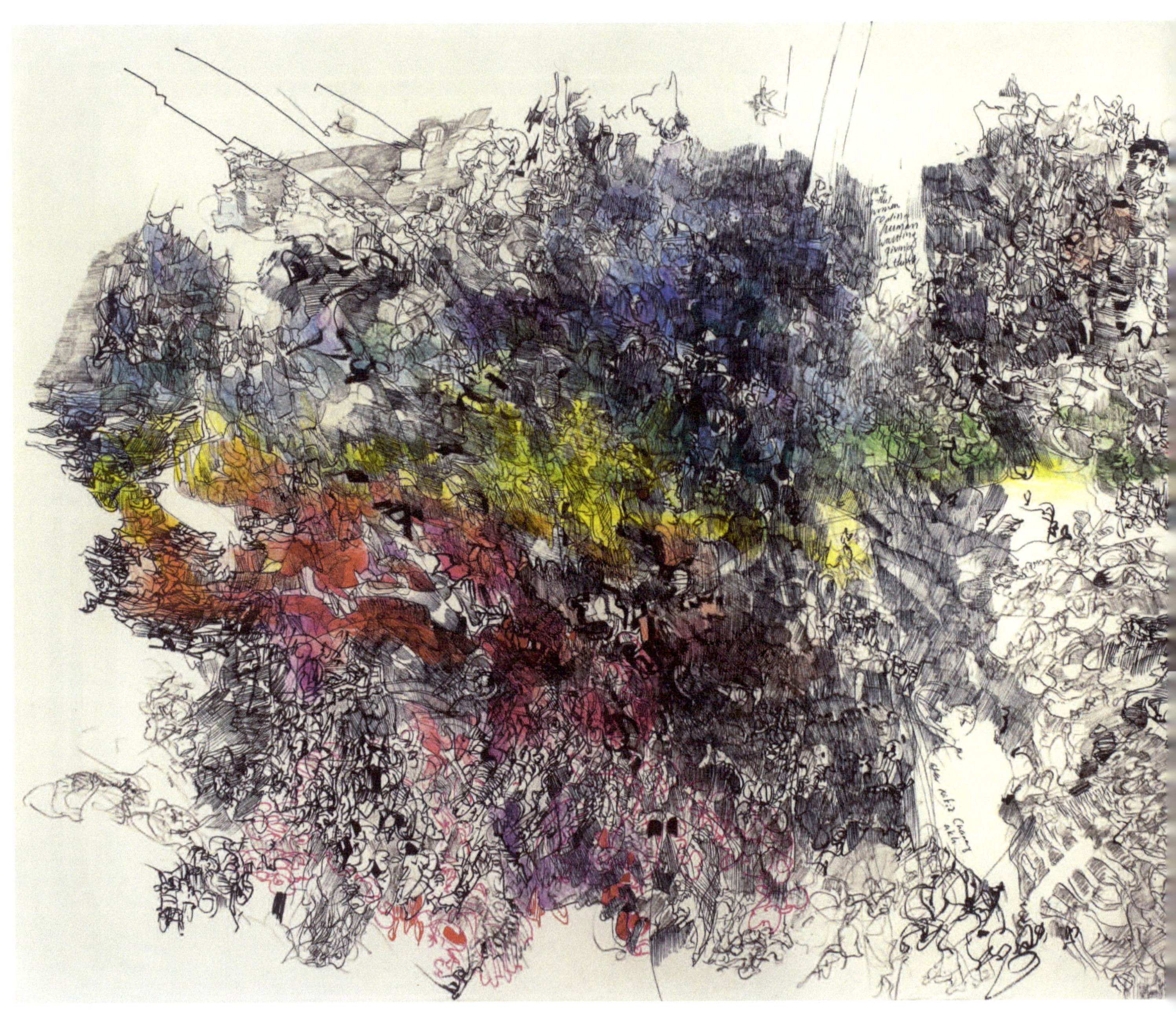

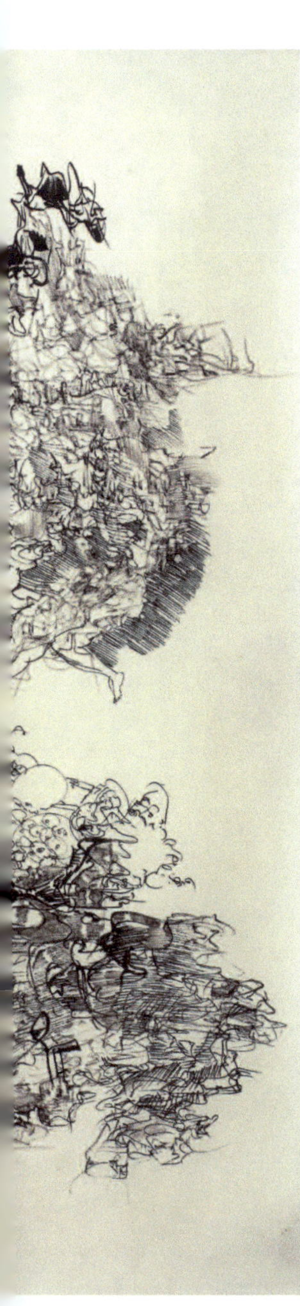

Woman Ceding Human (After Nikia Chaney), 2017
Ink, color pencil, and graphite on Takefu washi, 63.4 x 96.5 cm / 25 x 38 in

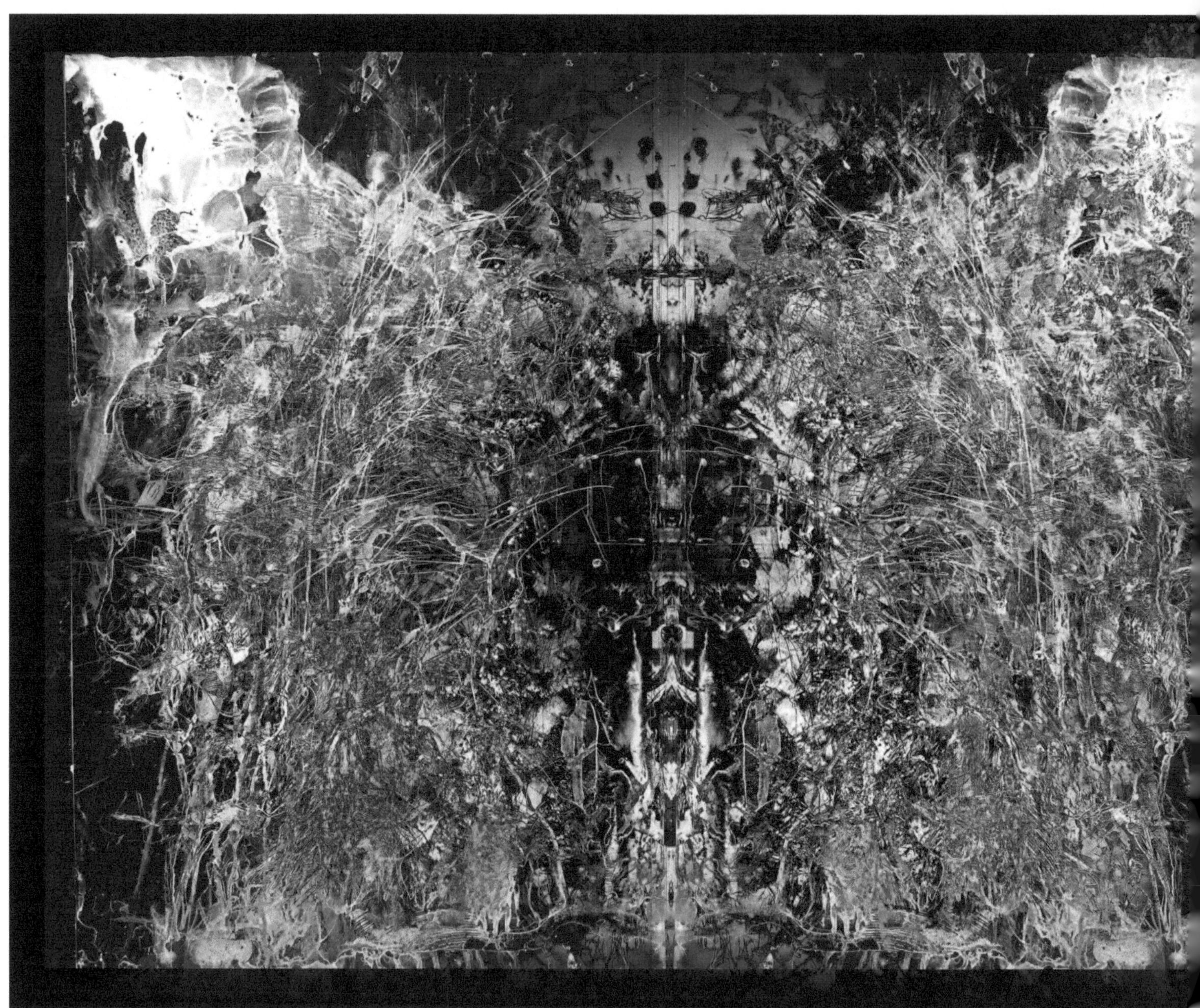

Double Blind Study 32, 2012
Gelatin silver print on archival paper, 76.8 x 101.6 cm / 30 x 40 in

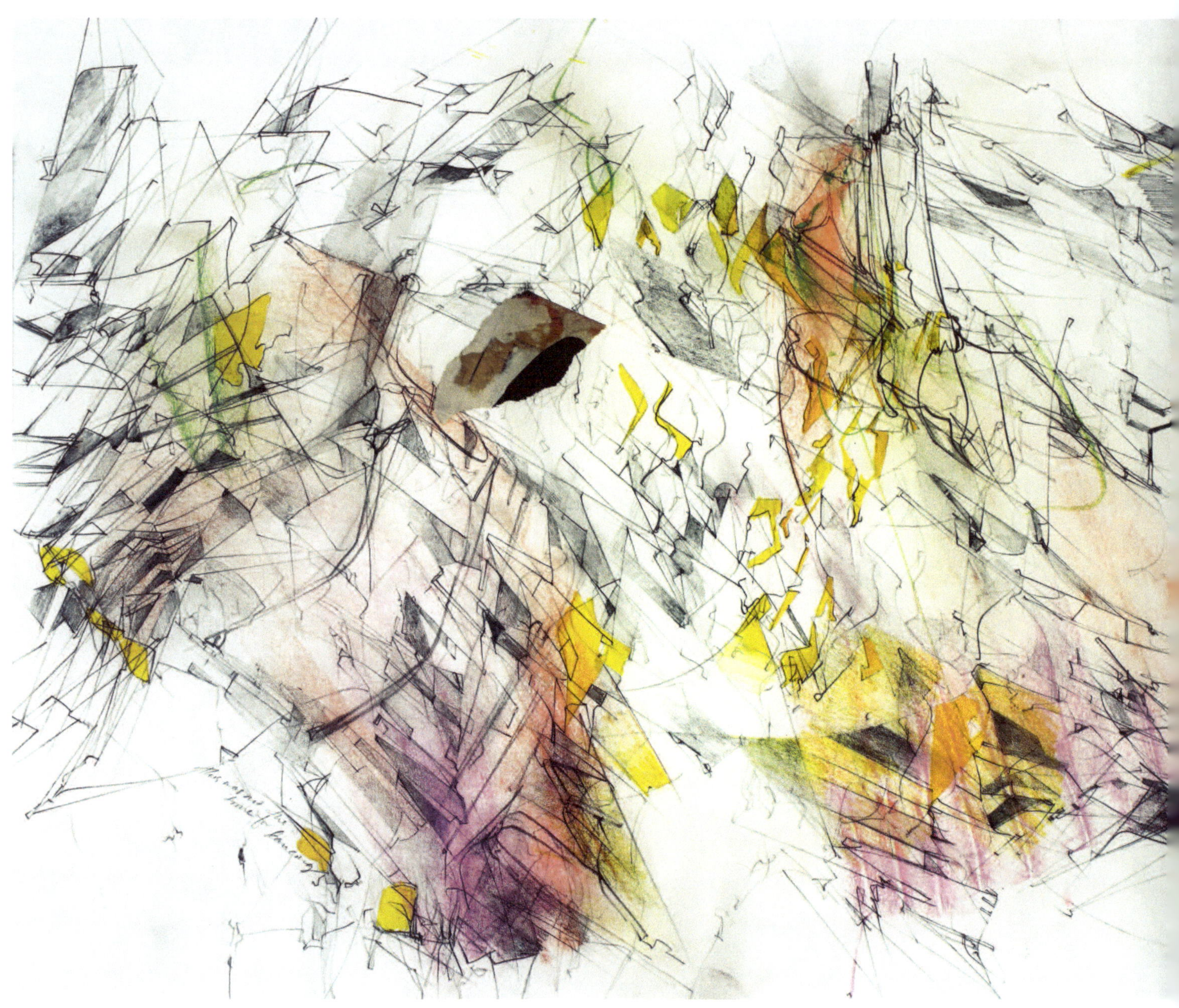

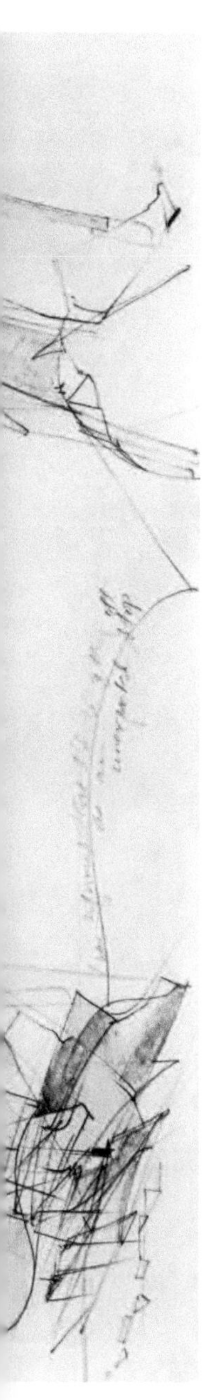

MURMURATIONS: ON GLYPHS, SHARDS AND TEOREMAS

ESZTER TIMÁR

'Murmuration' is the term by which we refer to a group of starlings flying in haphazard concert in the sky. Longish sessions at dusk, intensified during colder months, prepare their tiny bodies for the cold night by warming them up, and allows individual birds to compete for advantageous companionship. Each tries to get as close as possible to another, to later roost in warmth, and fly out together next morning.'Murmurations' in plural indexes the whirring of a thousand tiny wings. A choreography of calculated attachment,[1,2] this liquid dance assures no birds collide, as if volatile textures expand from corpus to pellicle. The ensemble moves like fluid in another fluid: it is singular (a position-sensing aviator body) and morphing, stretching, condensing, twisting, speeding ,and slowing. Black masses thicken, then loosen into grays.

Murmurations whisper and spurt birth semantics, chora, the experience of language as touch.[3] The inscriptions flow out not as law but as antinomies in concert, as "a system of movements, a coordination of independent initiatives, an organized multiplicity of origins."[4] Rhythm that's built on a continuous fast pulsation…constant running sets of rhythmic units, different melodies of different rates of speed…"[5] There is no present text in general, and there is not even a past present text, a text which is past as having been present. Painting is a poetics of relation at a periphery which turns out to be central. "Originary writing, if there is any, must produce the space and the materiality of the sheet itself."[6] Music that's over the edge destroying itself: "a beyond and a beneath of that enclosure we might term 'Platonic.'"[7] Murmurations are "not thinkable in an originary or modified form of presence. The unconscious text is already woven of pure traces, differences in which meaning and force are united; a text nowhere present, consisting of archives which are always already transcription."[8]

[1]www.christinamcphee.net/christina-mcphee-drawings-and-paintings-a-manifesto/ and p. 129
[2]NPR Music, "In Practice: György Ligeti's Piano Etudes." www.youtube.com/watch?v=MThql-WwzL78

[3] Jacques Derrida, "Freud and the Scene of Writing" (trans. Jeffrey Mehlman), *Yale French Studies*, no. 48 (1972), 78-117, p. 117.

[4] Ibid., 113.

[5] Ibid., 112.

6 Ibid., 92.

7 Ibid., 116.

8 Ibid., 92.

Time for Dancing (After Zadie Smith), 2017
Graphite, crayon, ink, and found magazine collage, 55.8 x 76.2 cm / 22 x 30 in

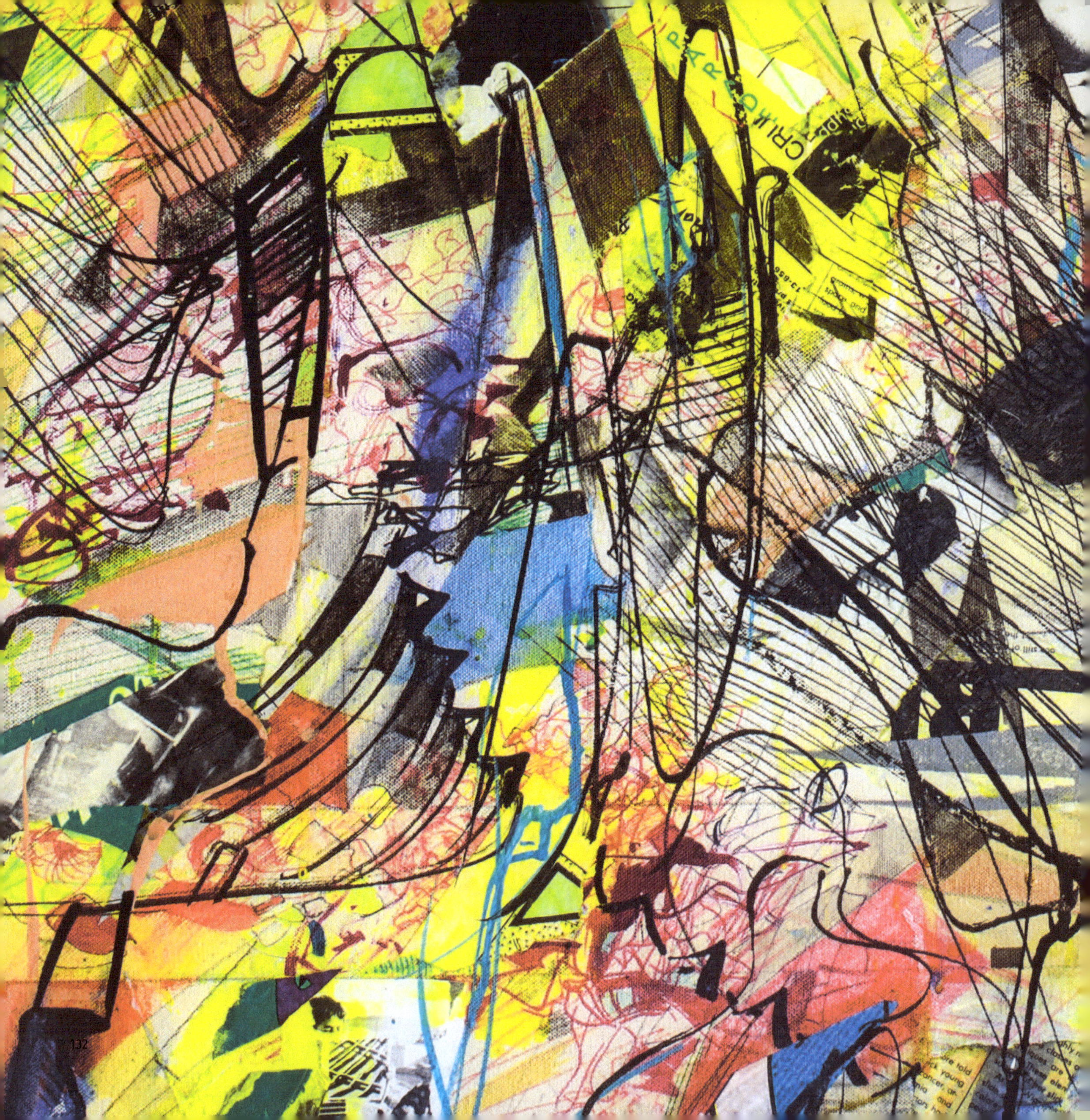

The paintings have their own half life.

The weird catch in the throat, that this is happening in fine grain
A clear linguistic fact and experiential fact of our existence as confronted with the 'alien' in the human
At the same time as we are always barreling inside the alien cognition
Recovering a distant geography from within the self, from the earliest days of life
Birth semantics, of the chora after Kristeva, the experience of language as touch
Alien-ness as a lived personal and collective experience—every body is elated, related, proverbial
Really hard to be with the paintings, who confront by hurling recognition-patterns from birth
Quanta reveal and prevent revelation–.a disturbing ground, an uncomfortable assimilation
The titles of the paintings might be proximate translations from a minor literature
Place-names in a legend on the lower left-hand corner of your map
The naming of paintings is a poetics of relation at a periphery which turns out to be central
Possibly the name will give a hook, a handhold while you plunge
Line is moving and coursing, a cursor flashes at various thresholds
At the point-shifts of planes and masses, shedding incidents and micro-events like droplets off the wet dog
Line scrawls through the wet prints, hunting uptakes, tracks in dark waters the shimmering letters
Paintings' images present mere patterned light from within ellipses....dot dash dot
An aphasia-ellipsis is an intimate and vast location, a very productive space in which to write a painting.
Agnes Martin says 'rest' is the most precious thing, while John Martin, Victorian, paints apocalypse
In the middle, Matta, whoozing shapes or
Detonation ripping out at you, as you. The canvas-crevasse spills out scores.
They reverse the sentences of the penal colony
The inscriptions flow out not as law but as antinomies in concert,
Lightness and heaviness play between support and mass.
The ground is no more stable than the delicate structure of support whose surface is as a drum
Silent but potentially sounding, storm of sounds might erupt at the touch
Like Ligeti etudes as played by Jeremy Denk
Scherzi and coda whip and pulse to locate points in a level of life at its strangest and most engulfing.

-CM, 2016

Detail, *Flores House*

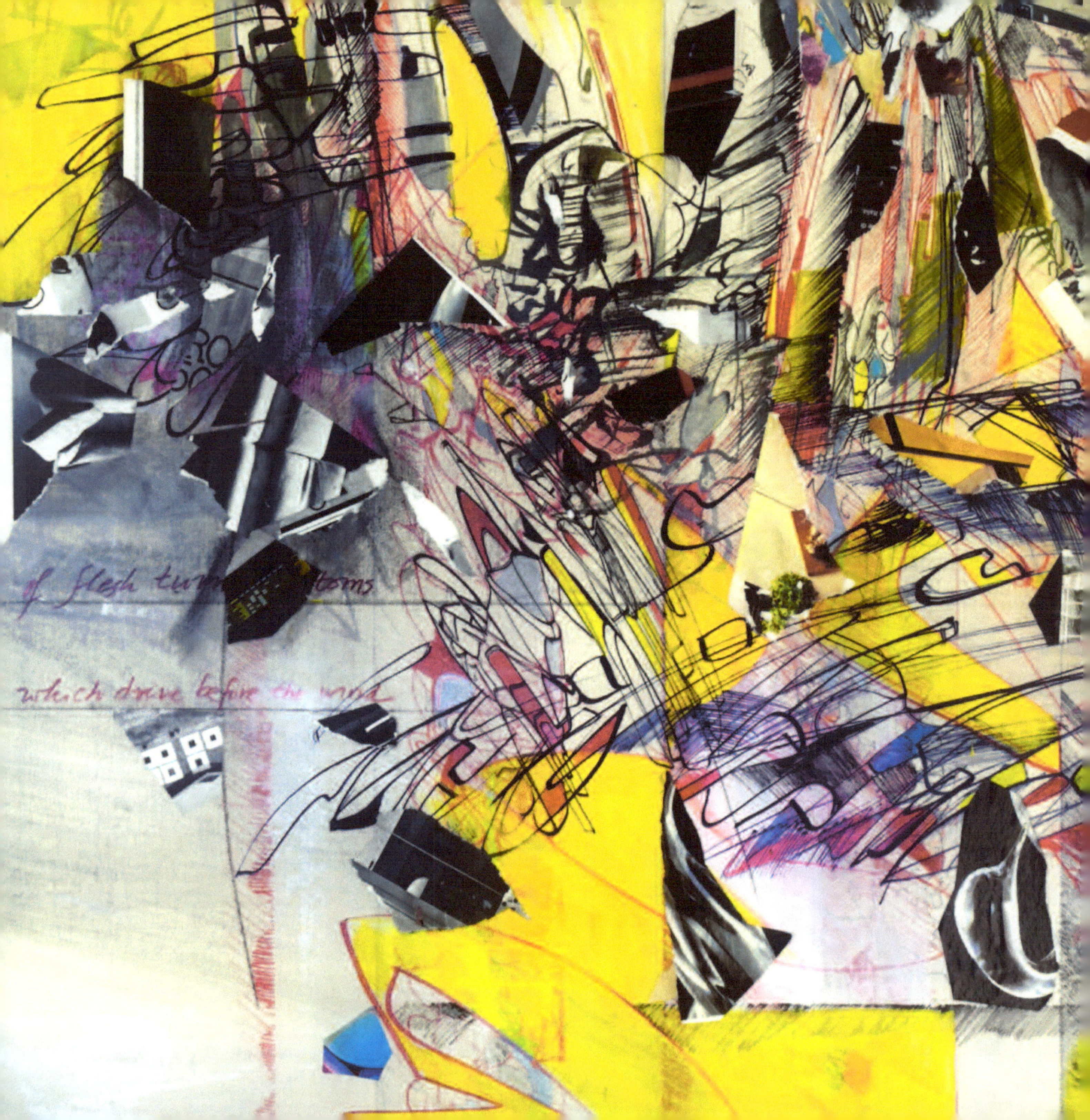
of flesh tur
toms
which drove before the wind

Detail, *Flesh Into Atoms*

Detail, *A Single Dose of Synthetic Estrogen May Prolong This Golden Hour*
Full image, overleaf

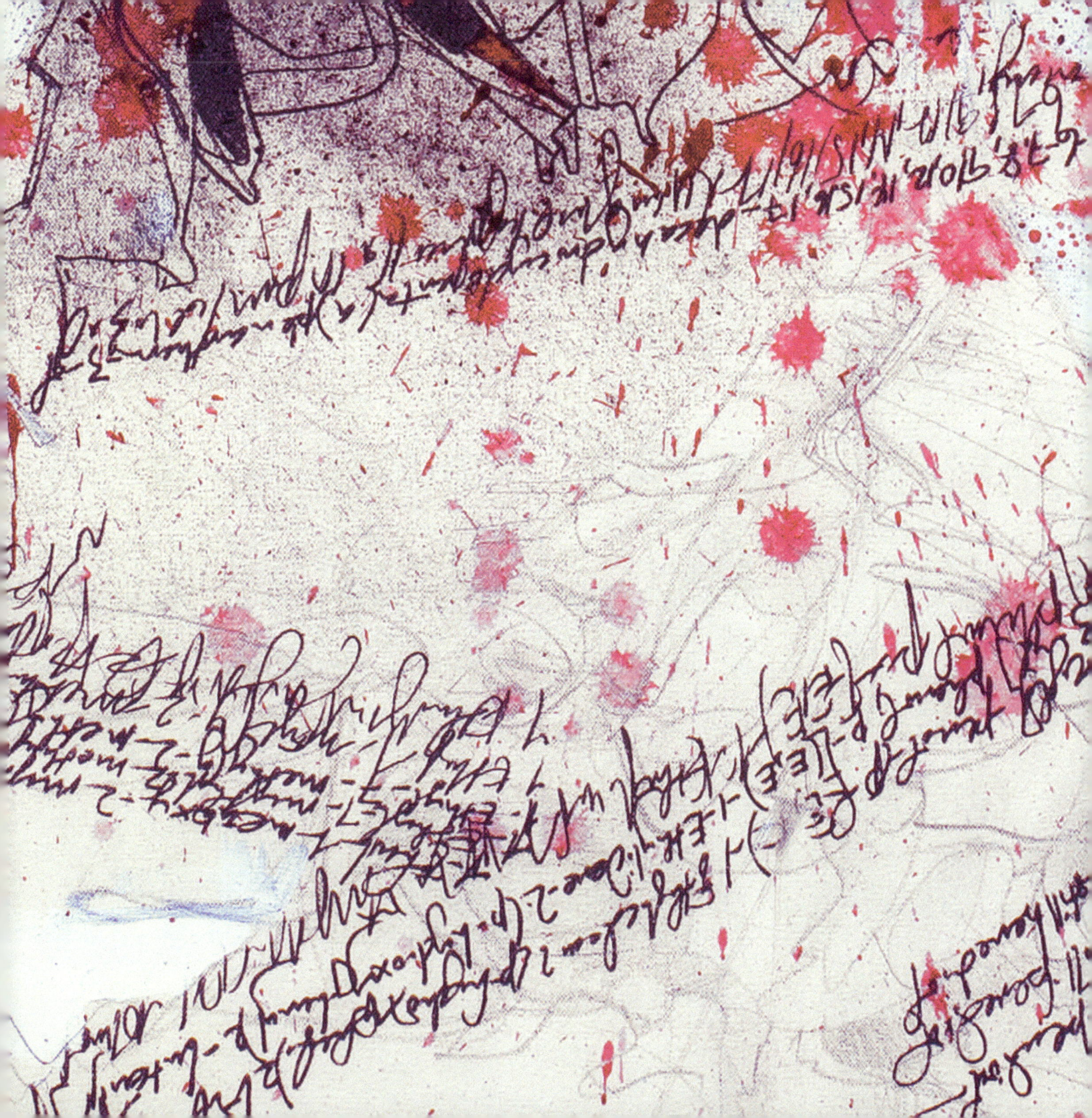

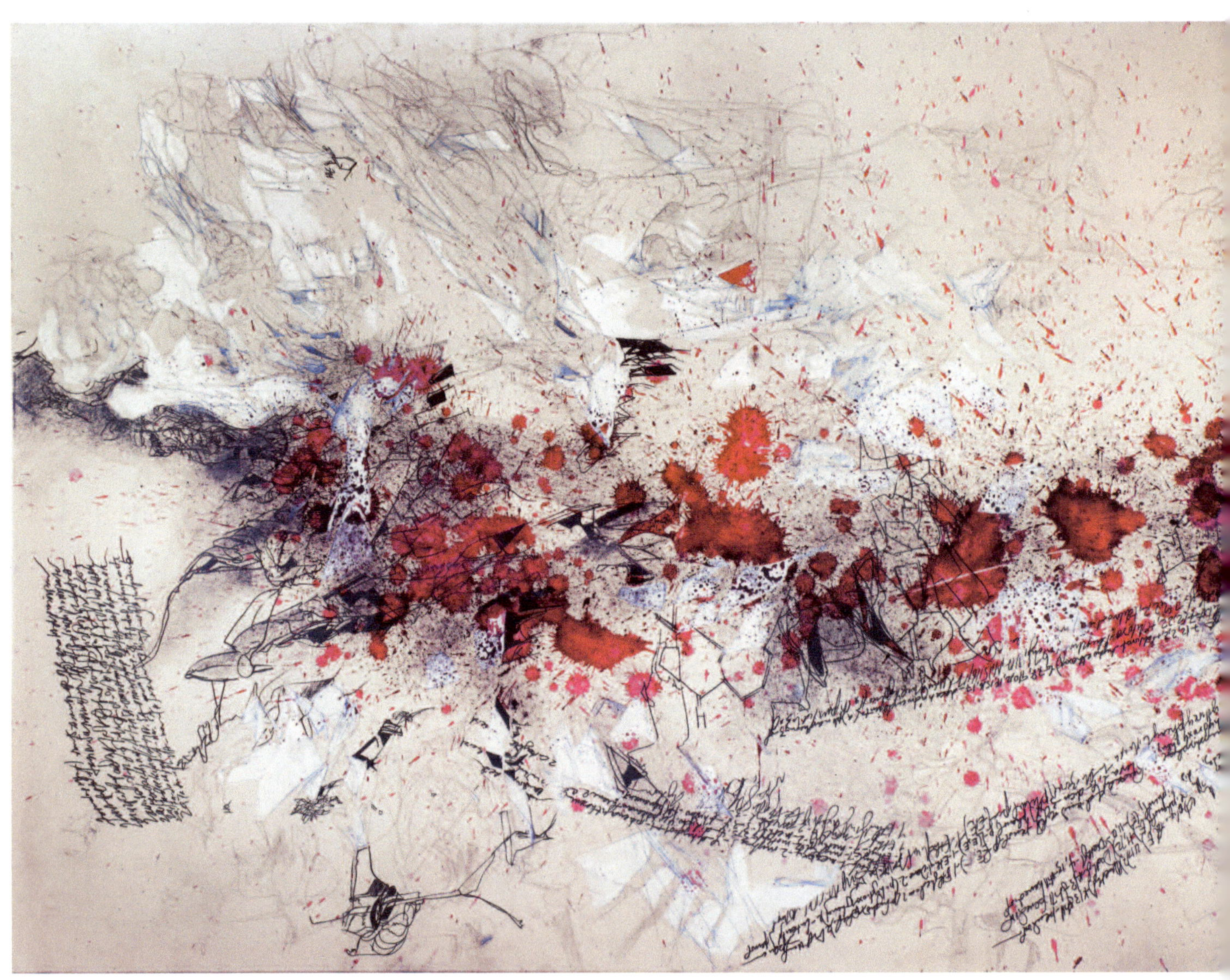

PATTERN DISCOGNITION

JAMES MACDEVITT

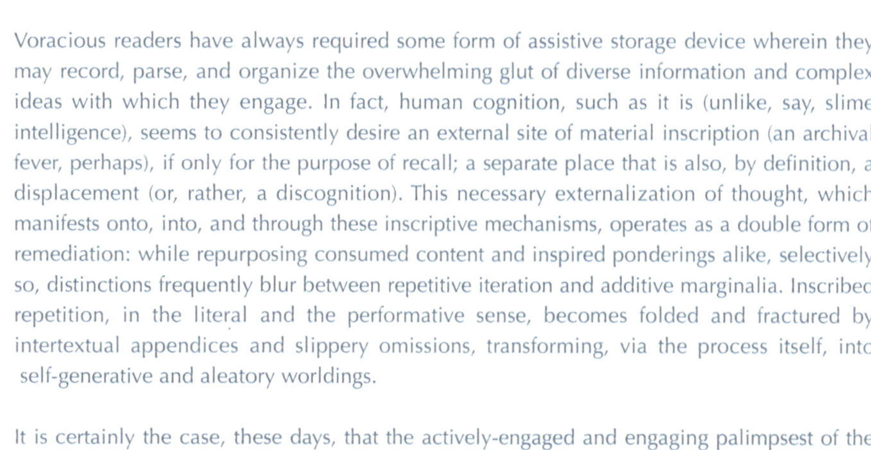

Voracious readers have always required some form of assistive storage device wherein they may record, parse, and organize the overwhelming glut of diverse information and complex ideas with which they engage. In fact, human cognition, such as it is (unlike, say, slime intelligence), seems to consistently desire an external site of material inscription (an archival fever, perhaps), if only for the purpose of recall; a separate place that is also, by definition, a displacement (or, rather, a discognition). This necessary externalization of thought, which manifests onto, into, and through these inscriptive mechanisms, operates as a double form of remediation: while repurposing consumed content and inspired ponderings alike, selectively so, distinctions frequently blur between repetitive iteration and additive marginalia. Inscribed repetition, in the literal and the performative sense, becomes folded and fractured by intertextual appendices and slippery omissions, transforming, via the process itself, into self-generative and aleatory worldings.

It is certainly the case, these days, that the actively-engaged and engaging palimpsest of the "commonplace book" has become less and less common, replaced instead by the passive associations produced through online platforms, from scrolling "newsfeeds" to clicking "likes," "hearts," and "pins". All these styles of readership have one thing in common: within diaristic recording, references may as serve as surrogate, or maybe as synecdoche, to biographical narration and, by extension, point to the individual user/archivist as a transcendent subject. By contrast, from note-taking to underlining, from marginal scribbles to the commonplace book, analog inscription problematizes a conception of the archivist as always outside of, and antecedent to, the archive. As numerous pedagogical studies have shown, writing itself, even doodling while listening to a lecture, is an essential component of effective memorization and a boost to cerebral processing.[1] Gestural marks, therefore, don't just point (or rather gesture) to external, or even self-reflexive, ideations; the actual physical act of making a mark, the spatial movement of the hand across the paper, also inscribes new neurological pathways within the brain, such derives from the Greek concept of *topos* (topics), a foundational aspect of rhetorical training, whereby authoritative arguments and prominent texts are absorbed by the student through repetition and prescriptive categorization. The more active and participatory the material externalization, the more permanent and profound the conceptual internalization. The archive quite literally produces the archivist, as much as the other way around. Around this embodied notion of the gesture and mark-making, the tradition of the commonplace book finds contemporary mutation in the creative practice of Christina McPhee.

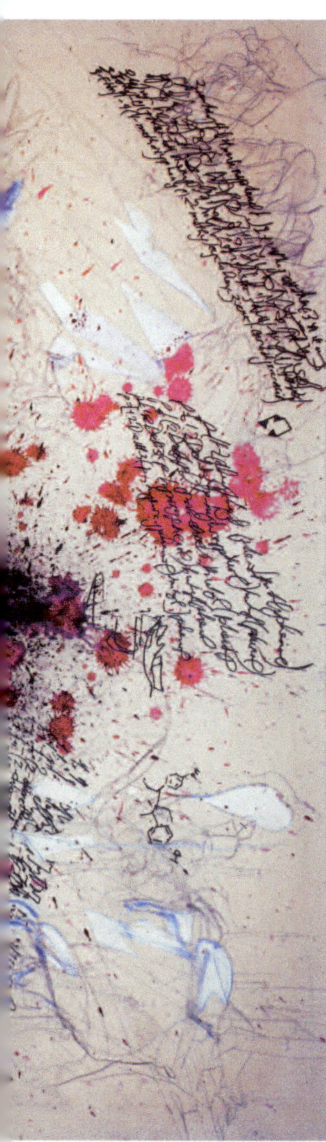

A Single Dose of Synthetic Estrogen May Prolong This Golden Hour, 2015
Ink, dye, oil, and graphite on canvas, 99 x 165.1 x 6.3 cm / 39 x 65 x 2.5 in

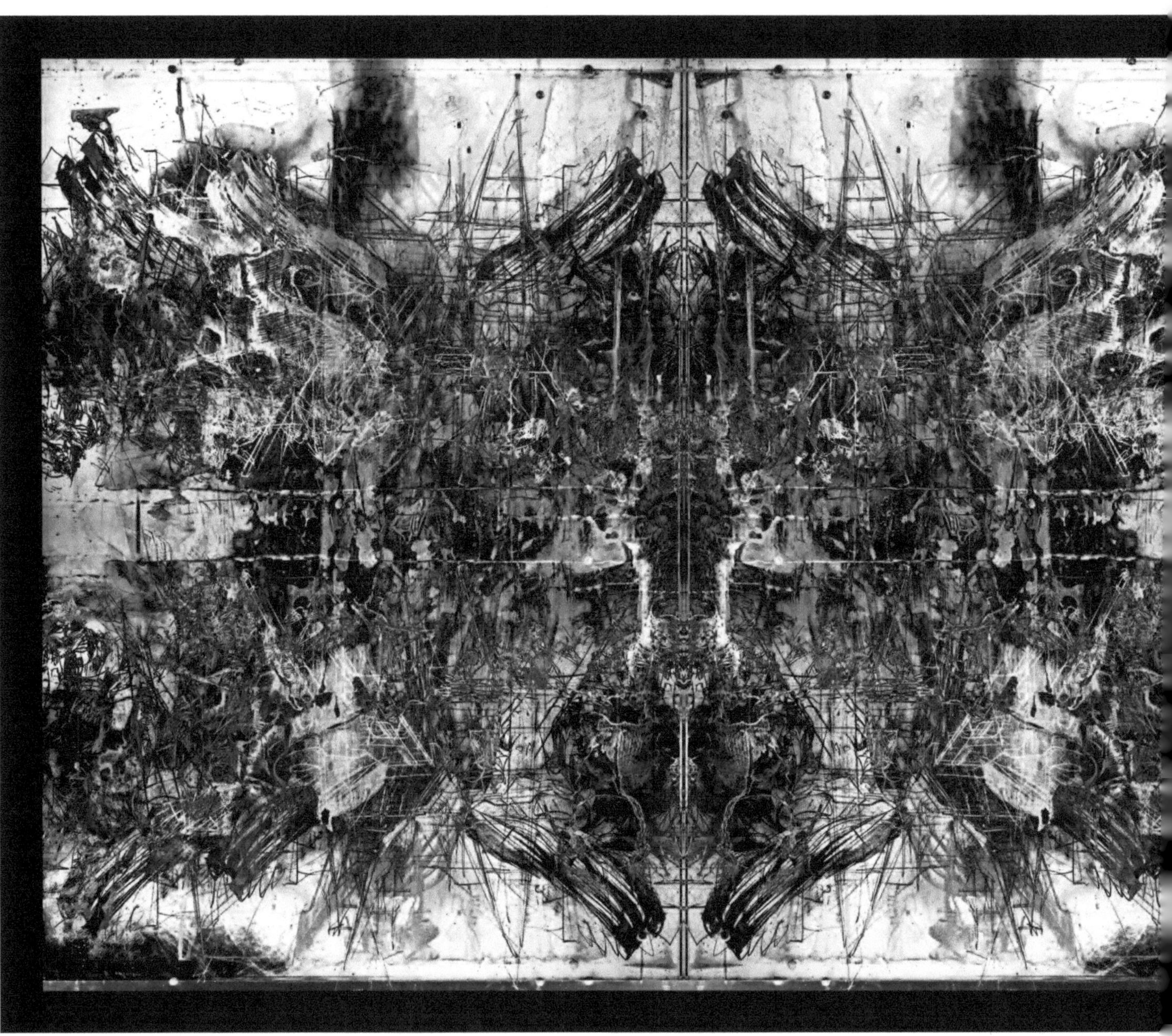

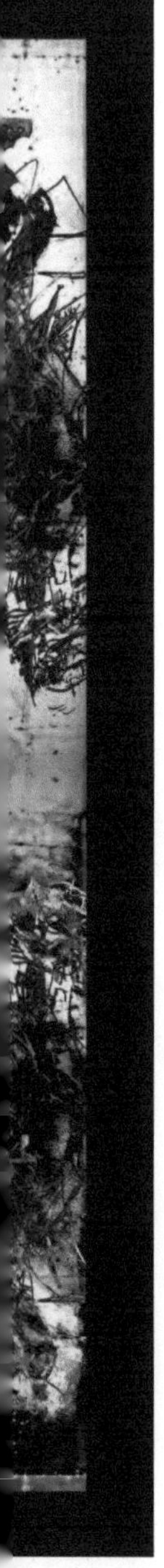

The term "commonplace," etymologically, is a fairly literal translation of the Latin *locus communis*, which itself derives from the Greek concept of *topos* (topics), a foundational aspect of rhetorical training, whereby authoritative arguments and prominent texts are absorbed by the student through repetition and prescriptive categorization. As Marko Juvan has pointed out:

> *Commonplaces supported the edifice of Western cultural memory: they were passed down with help of mnemonics in which images, ordered in spatial schemes, could be associated with pertinent categories of certain discipline or knowledge..speakers or writers were thus able to invoke a particular topos, not only with spontaneous associations, but also by their mnemonic skill...*[2]

In traditional practice, students would assemble commonplaces by labeling pages of an empty notebook with thematic headings (known alternatively as topics or places), and then fill those pages with relevant quotations from institutionally-sanctioned authors. In this way, they could memorize a set of officially preordained phrases and concepts that might be easily recalled and invoked within academic debates whenever the need arose. A rather similar form of rigid pedagogy around repetition was in use within the fine art academies throughout Europe at around the same time. Art students would produce drawn copies from engravings and plaster casts of prescribed masterworks, before turning to their own creative projects. In this way, it was assumed, they might, through a combination of muscle memory and learned visual preference, internalize classically-normative proportions, compositions, and techniques. Jean-Auguste-Dominique Ingres once stated, in defense of this process, "our task is not to invent but to continue...following the examples of the masters."[3]

By the time Ingres would write these words, the practice of commonplacing within a general humanities education had already changed quite dramatically. In 1706, John Locke published his influential text, *A New Method of Making Common-Place-Books*, wherein he posited an alternative agenda and structure for organizing commonplace books. As Michael Stolberg points out, "by Locke's time, commonplacing had long ceased to be a tool merely for the collection and memorization of quotations from classical authors. It was widely used also by physicians and natural philosophers as an important means to collect and organize excerpts as well as personal observations and empirical knowledge acquired from others."[4] Locke not only advocated heterogeneity in source material, but also launched an elaborate indexing strategy: multiple and seemingly unrelated headings (topics, places, etc.) would appear adjacent on the same page, collapsing previously distinct themes together into unexpected conjunctions, logical leaps, and conceptual gestalts.[5] As the commonplace book shifted away from a site to parrot 'universal' knowledge, it found a new, independent locus for interdisciplinary discovery and intertextual innovation.

Double Blind Study 36, 2012
Gelatin silver print on archival paper, 76.8 x 101.6 cm / 30 x 40 in

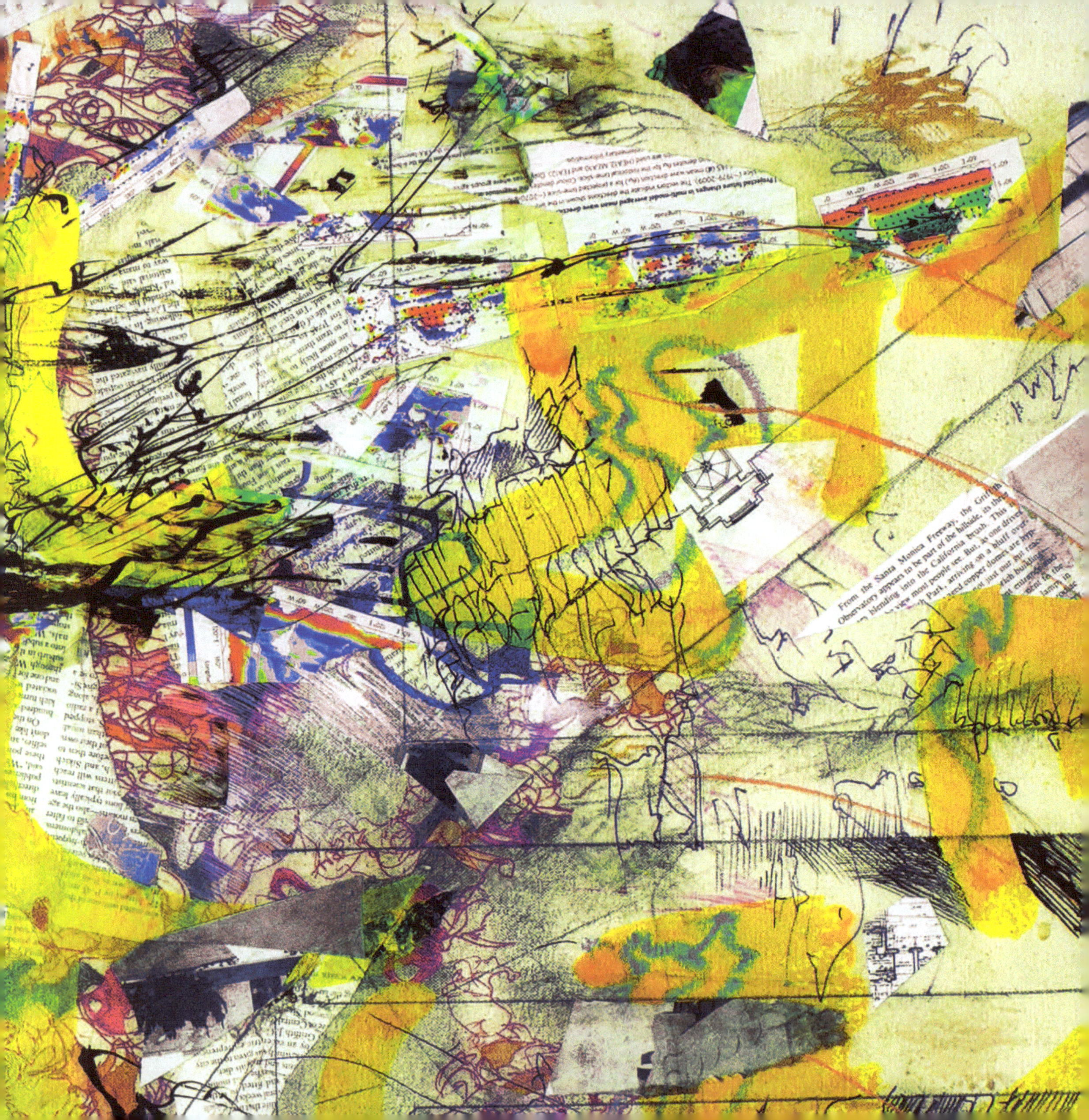

Christina McPhee works in a ludic and lucid meditative practice whose origins she traces to childhood. Her mother would prescribe drawing as a way to distract her daughter's imagination ("go draw it out," she would suggest): this was a free form complement to disclipine at parochial school, where children were set to task, to (apparently) endless copying of moral phrases on chalkboard, after class). Drawing, as such, became a *pharmakon*, both a poison to be expelled/expressed, as well as a cure to salve emotional states. In a mode of curative discognition, her drawings reiterate inscriptions, throw off aleatory lines of flight, and merge into adjacent, overlapping, gestural orbits. While it is easy to connect this practice to Surrealist automatic drawing, even to Bataille's concept of *l'informe*, for McPhee the catharsis seems to emerge from the act of creation itself, rather than revelation of unconscious trajectories. While certainly personal, little is explicitly biographical in the output. What surfaces is a lifetime of intellectual self-fashioning, developed through years of autodidactic study and the ongoing repetition of learned gestural patterns, culled from a plethora of distinct disciplines. Like a musician able to effortlessly improvise after years of playing repeated scales, McPhee enters this improvisational state of discognition in order to mine and combine the structural forms of different visual vocabularies, from geological and medical diagrams, to genres of cinematic display, to the conjugation of glyph-based languages.

In doing so, she presents a multifaceted ficto-criticism: she tells speculative stories within what anthropologist Michael Taussig, calls the "less conscious image realm…the dreamworld of the popular imagination."[6] Future-tripping into a schizo-ecology of molecular aggregates, she maps future behaviors of the carbon cycle, as if, through sustained accumulation of greenhouse gasses, a dense atmosphere might etch Earth's surfaces with the lines of Venus-like tesserations. Her images invite comparison to the ethico-aesthetics of what Donna Haraway calls the Cthulhucene—and, what a timely endeavor. As Haraway puts it:

> *It matters what stories tell stories, it matters what thoughts think thoughts, it matters what worlds world worlds. That we need to take seriously the acquisition of that kind of skill, emotional, intellectual, material skill, to destabilize our own stories, or retell them with other stories, and vice versa. A kind of serious denormalization of that which is normal is held still, in order to do that which one thinks one is doing. It matters to destabilize worlds of thinking with other worlds of thinking.*[7]

Detail, *P-22 in Griffith Park*

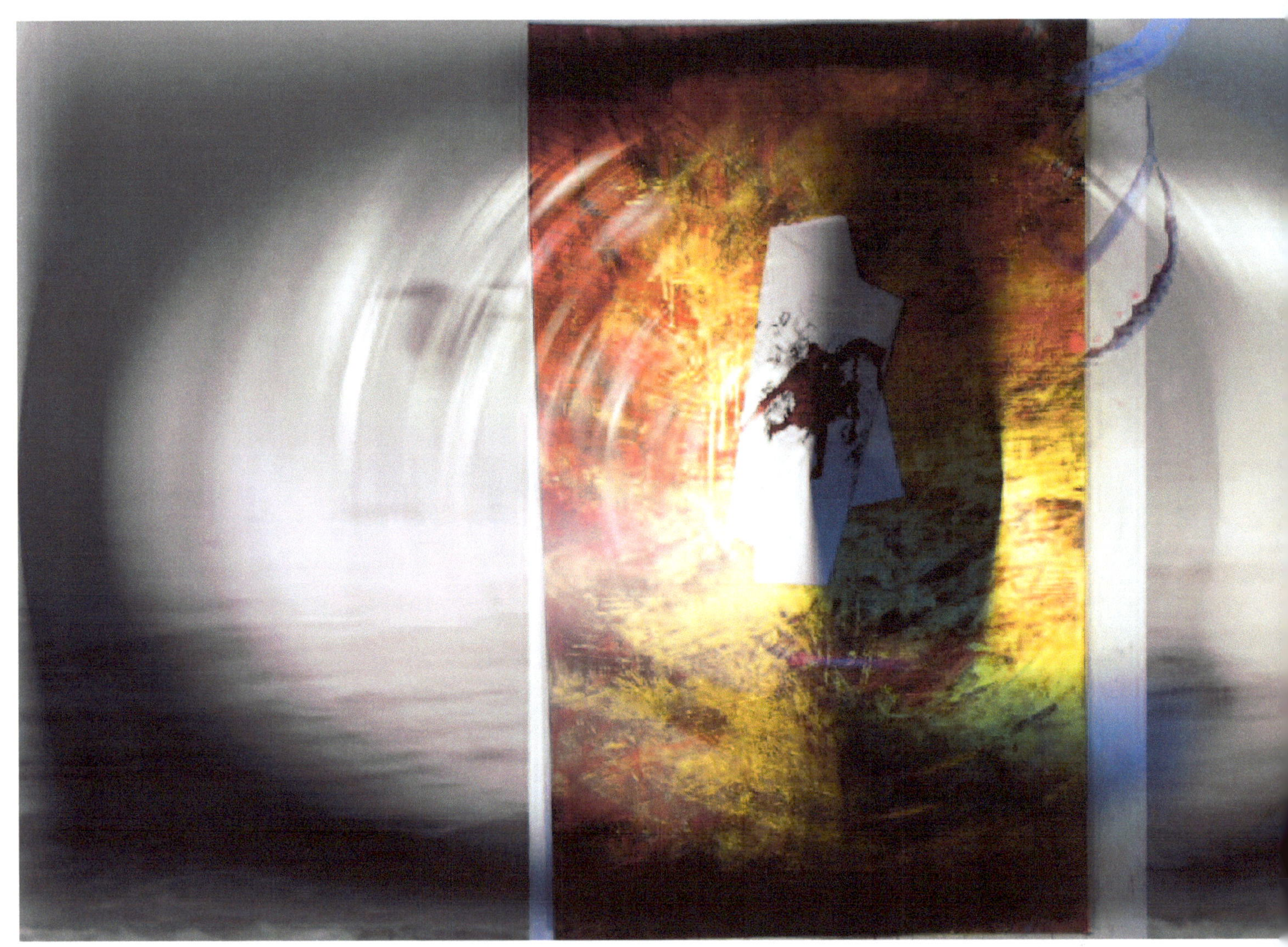

A dialogic, rather than dialectic, structure of McPhee's artistic practice corroborates Georges Didi-Huberman's assertion, in *Confronting Images*, that "to resemble no longer means, then, a settled state, but a process, an active figuration that, little by little, or all of a sudden, makes two elements touch that previously were separated (or separated according to the order of discourse)."[8] Even the media with which McPhee works refuse, under her direction, to sit still. By drawing on top of painting, she explicitly surfaces the linear scaffolding that more typically serves as the eradicated and inaccessible unconscious of the painted image. In her *Double Blind Studies* series (2012-), she photographs antecedent drawings, digitally butterflying and displaying them for forensic inspection via lush silver gelatin prints. Already existing at a remove from themselves, these Rorschach-like blots are glutted and gutted. In these dream-works, the box of representation is smashed open. As Didi-Huberman continues, "all contrasts and all differences will be crystallized in the substance of a single image, whereas the same substance will ruin all philosophical quiddity in the splitting up of its subject. Such are the disconcerting poetics of dreams: time is overthrown in them, rent, and logic along with it. Not only do consequences anticipate their causes, they are their causes—and their negation."

Nowhere is this more powerfully expressed than in McPhee's recent video, *Microswarm Patchwalk* (2016), which invokes a post-surgical walk down an empty beach, seen through the damaged, but recovering, eye of the artist herself, cut (interspersed and interlaced) by flashes of various coded systems, including previous drawings, remediated by the voracious hunger of the video camera. Instead of the Kantian eye of the connoisseur, for whom, as Kevin Hetherington points out, "aesthetic judgment is the product of a disinterested eye,"[10] here the viewer experiences the world through the artist's discognitive eye. Discognition does not here imply lack of thought—just the opposite, in fact—but it does link thought, as an ongoing exchange, directly to the flesh-of-the-world. Charlie Gere, in his essay "Slitting Open the Kantian Eye," discusses "the moment in Luis Buñuel and Salvador Dalí's film *Un Chien Andalou* when a young woman's eye appears to be slit open. This is the slitting of the Kantian eye, that allows all the heterogeneity to spill from within the subject into the material world of things."[11] McPhee has participated in her own curative cut, establishing reciprocal feedback around largesse, rather than lack. Hers is not a disinterested eye, but a distracted one, connected to a mind as generative as the world it regards. Such a mind inevitably finds solace and rejuvenation in a discognitive place of repetitive, but also creative, inscription; a (common-)place that is not so common, a place that can never be (just) one.

Detail, *Microswarm Patchwalk*, 2016
Single channel video with sound by Christina McPhee and Quinn Dougherty

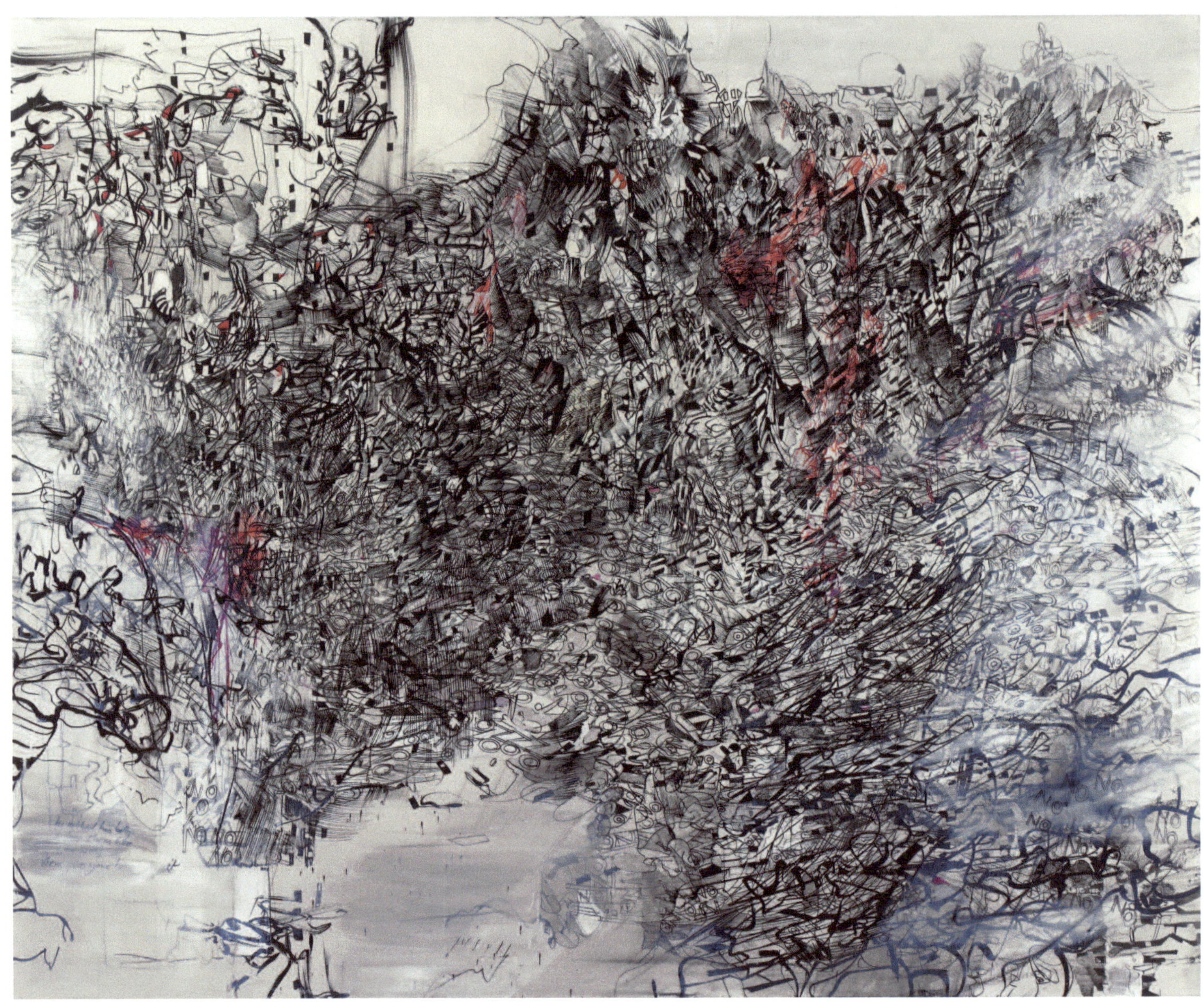

[1] Pam A. Mueller and Daniel M. Oppenheimer, "The Pen Is Mightier Than the Keyboard: Advantages of Longhand Over Laptop Note Taking," Psychological Science 25, 6 (2014),1.

[2] Marko Juvan, History and Poetics of Intertextuality (West Lafayette, IN: Purdue University Press, 2009), 20.

[3] J.A.D. Ingres, "On Art and the Beautiful," *Nineteenth-century Theories of Art*, ed. Joshua Charles Taylor (Berkeley: University of California Press, 1989), 107.

[4] Michael Stolberg, "John Locke's New Method of Making Common-Place-Books," *Early Science and Medicine* 19(5), 2014: 448-70.

[5] Ibid.

[6] Michael Taussig, *Shamanism, Colonialism, and the Wild Man: A Study in Terror and Healing* (Chicago: University of Chicago Press, 1987), 363.

[7] Donna Haraway, "Anthropocene, Capitalocene, Chthulucene: Staying with the Trouble," *Open Transcripts* (May 9, 2014), www.opentranscripts.org/transcript/anthropocene-capitalocene-chthulucene.

[8] Georges Didi-Huberman, *Confronting Images: Questioning the Ends of a Certain History of Art*, trans. John Goodman (University Park: Pennsylvania University Press, 2005), 150.

[9] Ibid., 148-49.

[10] Kevin Hetherington, "From Blindness to Blindness: Museums, Heterogeneity and the Subject," The Sociological Review 47, No. S1 (1999): 51-73 (66).

[11] Charlie Gere, "Slitting Open the Kantian Eye," in *Revisualizing Visual Culture*, eds. Hazel Gardiner and Chris Bailey (London: Routledge, 2010), 157.

Zebra Crossing, 2016
Shellac-based, sumi and acrylic inks; flashe, watercolor, and graphite on canvas 137.1 x 167.5 x 6.3 cm / 54 x 65.75 x 2.5 in; detail, overleaf

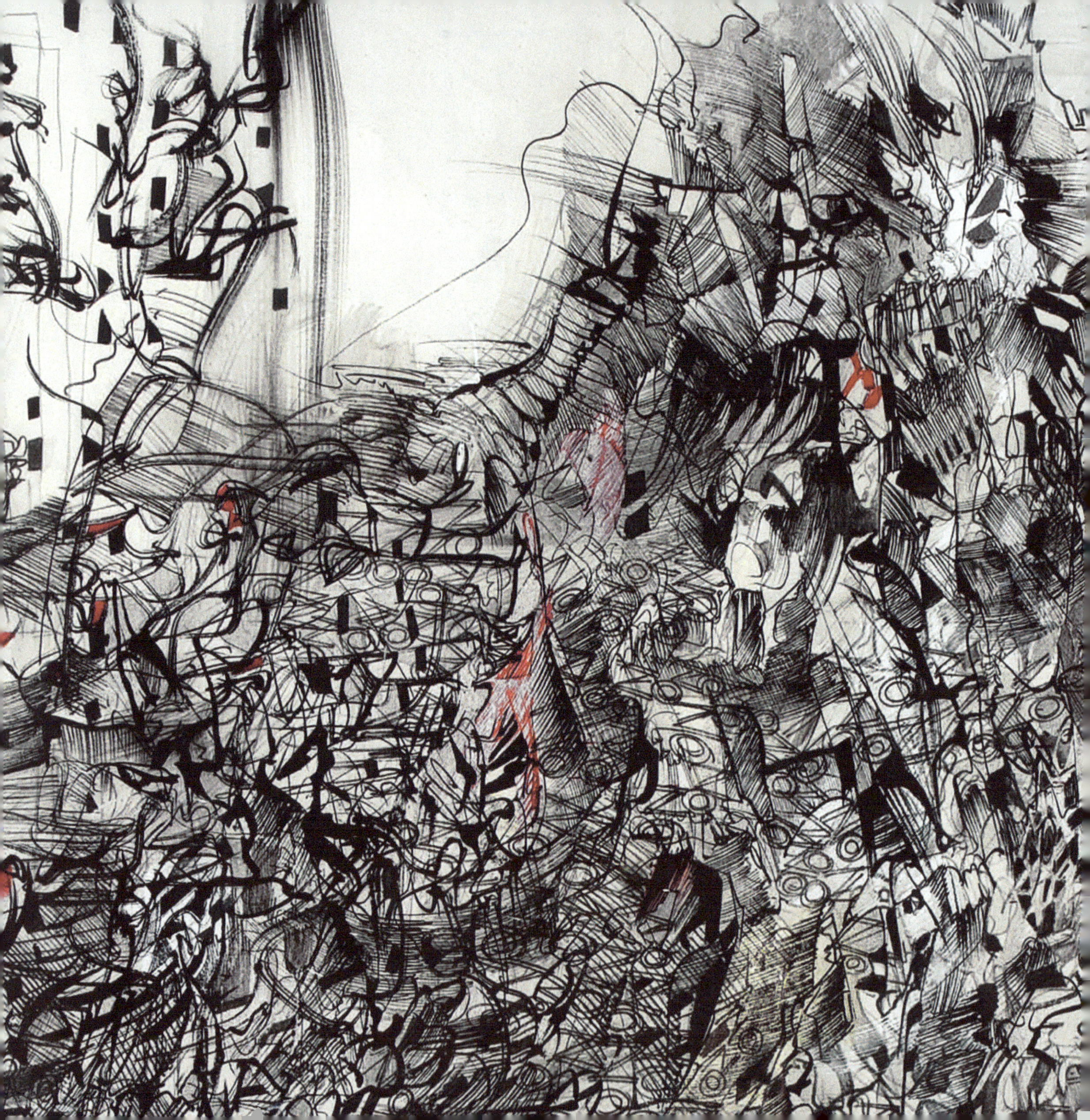

CONTRIBUTORS

Ina Blom writes on modernism/avant-garde studies and contemporary art with a particular focus on media aesthetics and the relationship between art, technology, media and politics. Her recent book, *The Autobiography of Video: The Life and Times of A Memory Technology*, is published by Sternberg Press, New York (2016). She contributes to *Artforum, Afterall, Parkett*, and *Texte sur Kunst*. She is a visiting professor in art history at the University of Chicago, and professor at the University of Oslo.

Phil King is a painter and writer who lives and works in London and the south of France. *The Studio of Giacometti,* by Jean Genet, is his most recent translation (London: Grey Tiger Books, 2013). He is an editor for *Turps Banana*, the London-based magazine on painting. He recently installed paintings in a 'ruin ripe for redevelopment' in Hastings, England, in a collaborative show with Nick Fudge, "Obscured by Clouds", a title "nicked from a really entropic 1972 Pink Floyd album."

James MacDevitt is a Los Angeles-based curator, with projects for California Museum of Photography, Sweeney Art Gallery at University of California-Riverside, as well as the multi-year *Los Angeles SUR Biennial*. At Cerritos College Art Gallery, he curated *Second Sight: New Work by Christina McPhee* (2016). He is a professor at Cerritos in visual culture and the history of art.

Donata Marletta is a writer, critic, and academic, based in Sicily. In 2012 she completed a PhD in Cultural Studies at the Faculty of Arts, Environment and Technology, Leeds Metropolitan University (UK). Her thesis, 'Sharing Bits': Creating Sociability in the Age of the Digital Agora" is an ethnographic study on new media and digital art festivals as the actual places where information, people, and ideas converge. She writes for *Digicult*.

Melissa Potter is an artist, curator, and writer, who engages in work with women through craft, gender rituals, and storytelling, in southeastern Europe, Venezuela, and the UK. In collaboration with Neysa Page Lieberman), she is curating *The Longest Revolution: Feminist Social Practice* (2017-). She writes for *Metropolis M, Flash Art, BOMB*, and *Art Papers*, and is professor in interdisciplinary arts at Columbia College, Chicago.

Judith Rodenbeck is an art historian of intermedia and generative arts practices in media ecologies of post-war and contemporary art. Since the release of her *Radical Prototypes: Allan Kaprow and the Invention of Happening* (Cambridge: MIT Press (2011), one of her lines of research concerns 'bipedal modernity', and draws on film, material culture and performance. She writes for *Grey Room, October, X-tra, Modern Painters, Artforum, Camera Austria, Women's Art Journal*, and CAA's *Art Journal*, the latter as a recent editor-in-chief. She is a professor in media and cultural studies at University of California-Riverside.

Eszter Timár specializes in courses and research on queer theory, sexuality and poetics; academic writing; performativity, and discourses on friendship, as a professor in gender studies at Central European University, Budapest.

Frazer Ward is the author of *No Innocent Bystanders: Performance Art and Audience* (Dartmouth: University Press of New England, 2012), wherein he argues for a complex understanding of audience and community as challenged, and formed, by foundational performance works by seventies-era performance artists. Professor Ward teaches courses on the history and theory of modern and contemporary art and architecture at Smith College, Northampton, Massachusetts.

Detail, *Zebra Crossing*

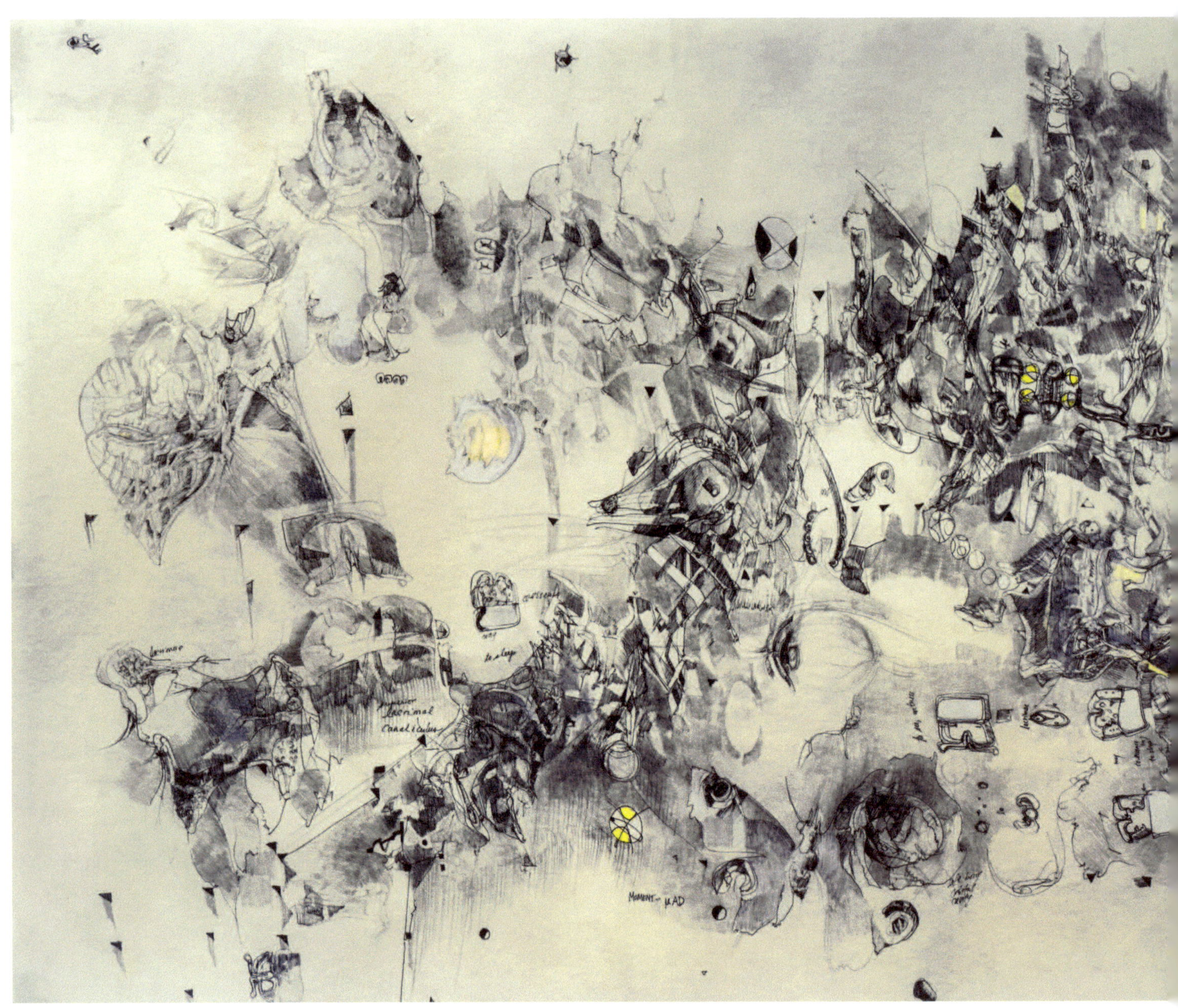
lacrimal
canaliculus

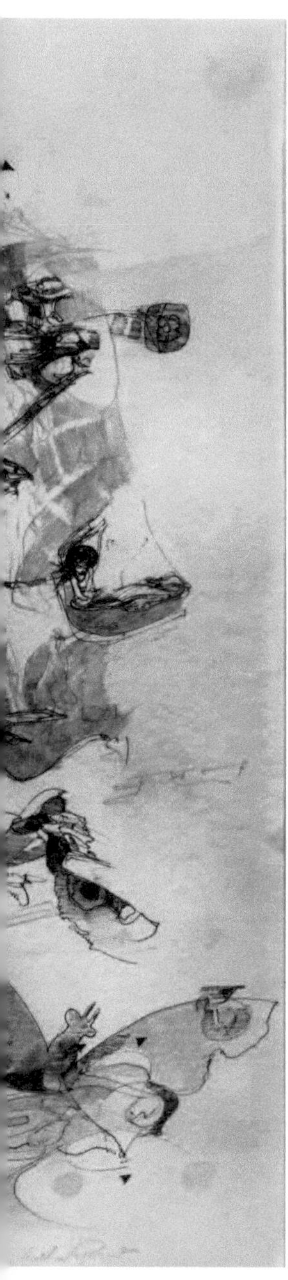

ACKNOWLEDGEMENTS

Christina and Eileen wish to thank the many friends and colleagues who have contributed to this commonplace book. Imagining a dossier of writings on the practice began with an idea from Michael O'Rourke. Terry Hargrave and Nava Hagighi set up design templates and advised on graphics. Ceri Hand critiqued visual content and design. Kristen McCants edited texts. Cara Megan Lewis, Linnea Spransey, Naveed Mansoori, Miranda Sklaroff, Karl Bob Johnson, Meghan Dorrian, Tenesh Webber,Tom McGlynn, Ian McPhee, Amy Wiley, Laura Krifka, Mary Allison Taft-McPhee, Whitney Moon, and Filip Tejchman stopped by the Shed in the first half of 2017. Molly McPhee and Rebecca Prichard sent energy-zaps from Oz. Bruce Tomb's recollections of the early days of *Archetype* in San Francisco were invaluable. The sudden passing of a beloved friend and mentor, Leigh Markopoulos, inspired the push to make this commonplace book something she'll have found in her after-life library. Love to Terry, for whom this commonplace is a farthest and nearest site.

Data Points Spring, 2016
Ink, color pencil, and graphite on Takefu washi, 63.4 x 96.5 cm / 25 x 38 in

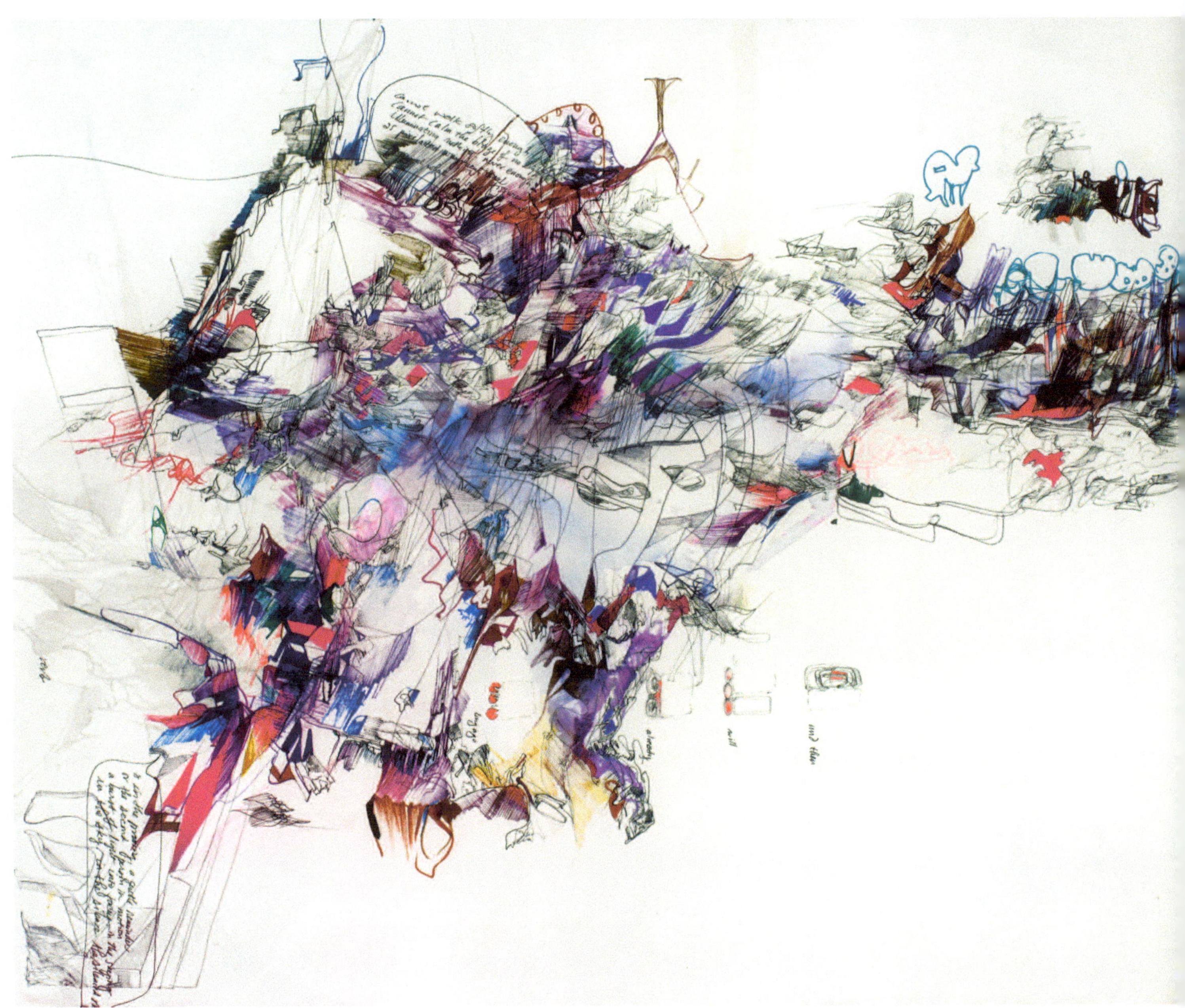

BIOGRAPHY

Christina McPhee's images move from within a matrix of abstraction, shadowing figures and contingent effects. Her work emulates potential forms of life, in various systems and territories, and in real and imagined ecologies. Her dynamic, performative, physical engagement with drawing is a seduction into surface-skidding calligraphic gestures and mark-making. The tactics of living are in subterfuge, like dazzle ships of camouflage in war. Lines throw down rope-like bridges, cat's-cradling figures, or a search for grounding and commons. Her work takes on violence, exuberance, and vitality from within a 'post-natural' experience of community.

Museum and public collections of her work include: Whitney Museum of American Art, International Center for Photography, Rhizome Artbase at the New Museum, and Storefront for Art and Architecture, in New York City; Kemper Museum of Contemporary Art, Kansas City; Thresholds New Media Collection, Perth, Scotland; Sheldon Art Museum, Lincoln, Nebraska; Cerritos College Fine Art Collection, California; Beach Museum of Art, Kansas; and Colorado Springs Fine Arts Center, Colorado. Solo museum exhibitions include the American University Museum/Katzen Art Center, Washington, D.C., and Bildmuseet, Umeå, Sweden. She has participated in group exhibitions, notably documenta 12 and Bucharest Biennial 3; as well as with the Museum of Modern Art, Medellín, Colombia; Bildmuseet, Umeå, Sweden; Berkeley Art Museum/Pacific Film Archive and California Museum of Photography, California; and the Institute of Contemporary Art, London. Together with Pamela Z, she was honored with the MAP Fund Performance grant and the New Music USA / Commissioning Grant Music USA award in 2012, for their collaborative work, *Carbon Song Cycle*.

Born in Los Angeles County, Christina McPhee was a student of Philip Guston (MFA, painting, Boston University, 1979). She studied at Kansas City Art Institute (BFA, painting and printmaking, valedictorian, 1976), and Scripps College, Claremont, California, where she was a Lois Langland Alumna-in-Residence in 2000.

Second Person In Motion (After Jen Hofer), 2016
Ink, watercolor, and graphite on Rives BFK paper, 57.7 x 76.2 cm / 22.75 x 30 in

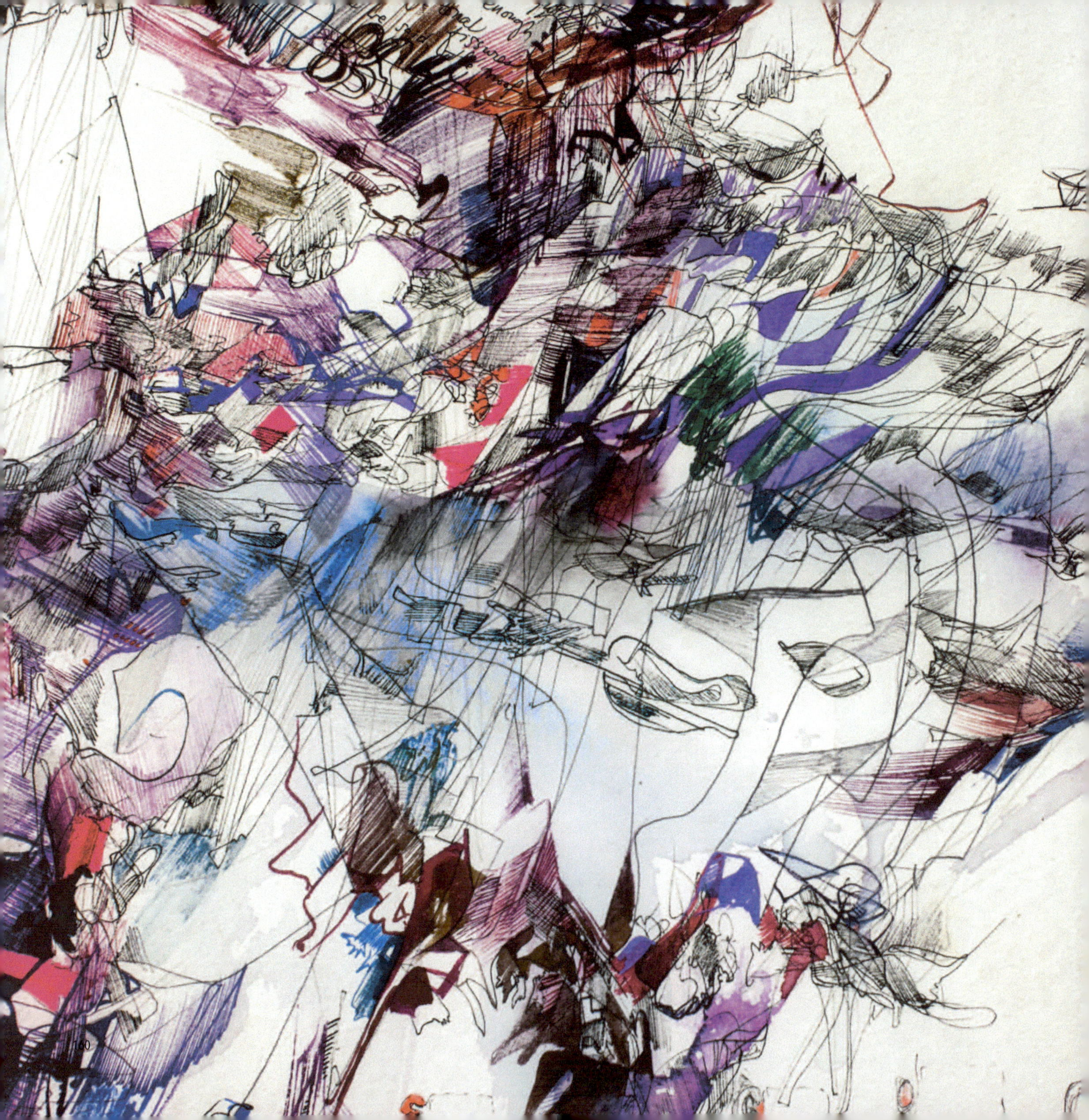

COLOPHON

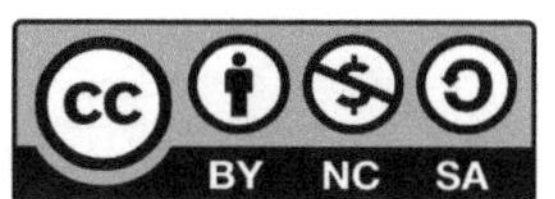

First published in 2017 by
punctum books
Earth, Milky Way
http://punctumbooks.com
ISBN-13: 978-1-947447-08-0 print
ISBN-13: 978-1-947447-09-7 ePDF
Library of Congress Control Number: 2017949734

Cover image: Christina McPhee: Detail, *P-22 in Griffith Park*, 2017

My Paralysis in the Face of Violence (After Classical Maya Hieroglyphs and Elena Ferrante), 2016
Ink, watercolor and graphite on paper, 50.8 cm x 70.48 cm / 20 x 27.75 in
Overleaf: detail, *Zebra Crossing*

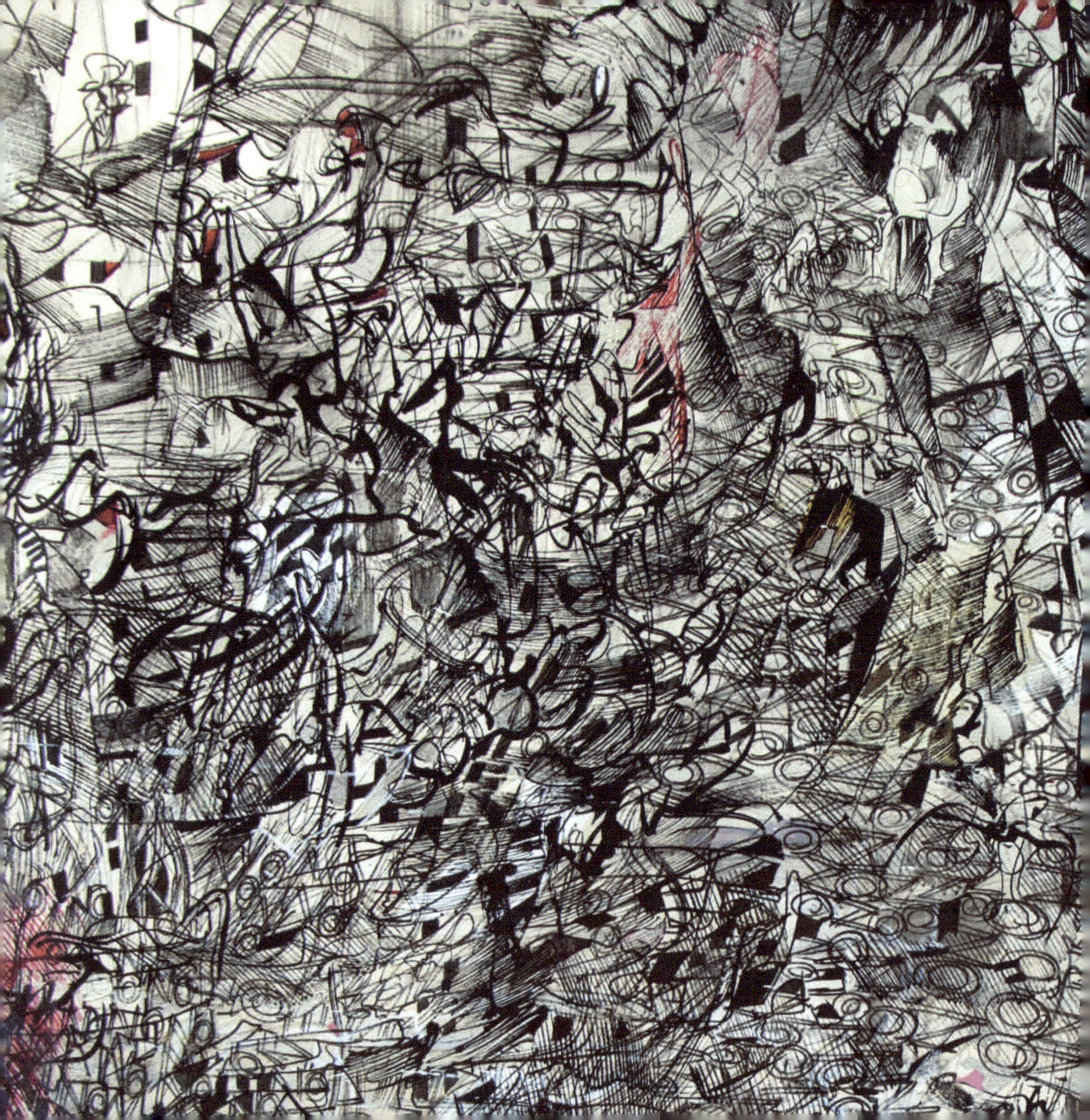

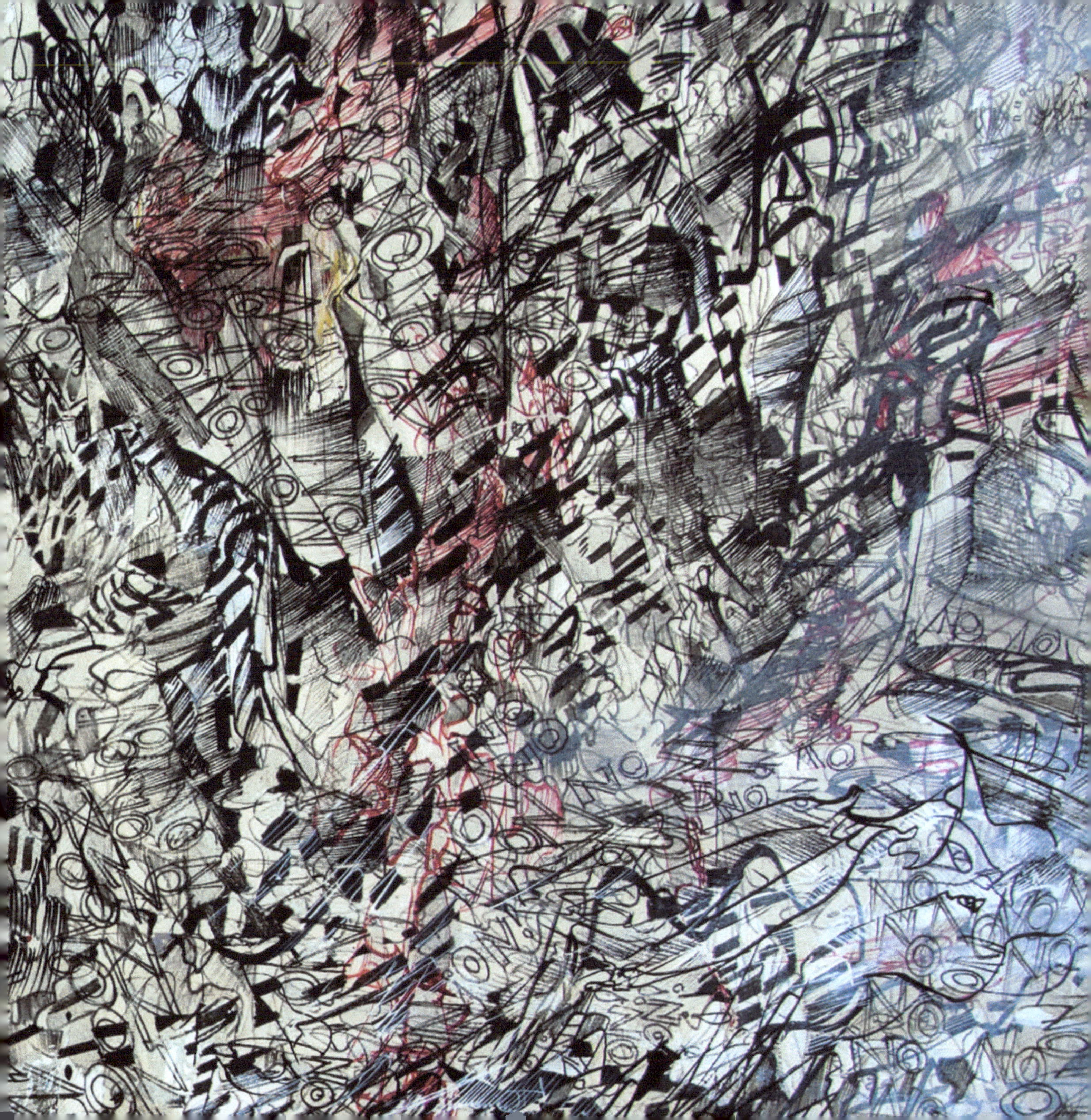

www.ingramcontent.com/pod-product-compliance
Lightning Source LLC
LaVergne TN
LVHW070213110826
845147LV00003B/565

9781947447080